Evidence in the Psychological Therapies

Research evidence is increasingly used as *the* benchmark of clinical quality. Using straightforward language and practical illustrations, *Evidence in the Psychological Therapies* explores why evidence is important, the forms it can take, and how evidence can be gathered and used across a range of practice from behavioural therapies to psychoanalysis.

Experts in law, sociology and philosophy look at the nature of evidence from first principles before commenting on its role in the psychotherapies. The merits of taking randomised trials to be the ideal source of evidence concerning psychological treatments are critically assessed. The uses of evidence in different therapeutic contexts are illustrated through discussions of: the place of hypotheses in the consulting room (and how these are likely to differ in different treatment models); the relationships between qualitative and quantitative research and treatment; and the contributions evidence from audit makes to the improvement of clinical services. Appraisal of evidence emerges as a longstanding if under-acknowledged element of good practice everywhere, whose potential is still far from being realised.

Evidence in the Psychological Therapies will help psychotherapists, psychologists, psychiatrists, counsellors, clients and service providers to be better informed about the place of evidence-based approaches in this complex and personal arena. In asking how far it is appropriate to apply the same standards of evidence to biochemistry and to emotional wellbeing, *Evidence in the Psychological Therapies* will also assist therapists of all persuasions in evaluating the promise and the limitations of evidence-based practice for themselves.

Chris Mace is Senior Lecturer in Psychotherapy at the University of Warwick and Consultant Psychotherapist to South Warwickshire Combined Care NHS Trust. **Stirling Moorey** is Consultant Psychiatrist in Cognitive Behaviour Therapy to the South London and The Maudsley NHS Trust and Honorary Senior Lecturer at the Institute of Psychiatry. **Bernard Roberts** is Consultant Psychiatrist in Psychotherapy to the Parkside Clinic.

Evidence in the Psychological Therapies

A Critical Guide for Practitioners

Edited by Chris Mace, Stirling Moorey and Bernard Roberts

First published 2001 by Brunner-Routledge
27 Church Road, Hove, East Sussex BN3 2FA

Simultaneously published in the USA and Canada
by Taylor & Francis Inc
325 Chestnut Street, 8th Floor, Philadelphia PA 19106

Brunner-Routledge is an imprint of the Taylor & Francis Group

Typeset in Times by Keystroke, Jacaranda Lodge, Wolverhampton
Printed and bound in Great Britain by TJ International Ltd, Padstow, Cornwall

British Library Cataloguing in Publication Data
A catalogue record for this book is available from the British Library

Library of Congress Cataloging in Publication Data
Evidence in the psychological therapies : a critical guide for practitioners /
edited by Chris Mace, Stirling Moorey, and Bernard Roberts.
      p. cm.
    Includes bibliographical references.
    ISBN 0-415-21247-2 (hbk. : alk. paper) — ISBN 0-415-21248-0 (pbk. :
    alk. paper)
      1. Psychotherapy. 2. Psychotherapy—Outcome assessment. 3. Evidence-
based medicine. 4. Evidence. I. Mace, Chris, 1956– II. Moorey, Stirling.
III. Roberts, Bernard, 1949–

  RC480.5 .E875 2000
    616.89′14—dc21   00--44647
ISBN 0–415–21247–2 (hbk)
      0–415–21248–0 (pbk)

Contents

Figures and tables

Figures

Tables

Contributors

David Allison, RMN, is a cognitive therapist at Addenbrooke's Hospital, Cambridge.

Mark Aveline, MD, FRCPsych, DPM, has been a consultant psychotherapist in Nottingham for 25 years. With interests in training, group and focal therapy he has held many administrative roles including the UK Presidency of the Society for Psychotherapy Research. His publications include *Group Therapy in Britain* (1988), *From Medicine to Psychotherapy* (1992) and *Research Foundations for Psychotherapy Practice* (1995).

Chess Denman, MB, BS, MRCPsych, is Consultant Psychiatrist in Psychotherapy at Addenbrooke's Hospital Cambridge and an associate clinical lecturer at Cambridge and East Anglia Universities. Trained in cognitive analytic therapy and Jungian analysis, she has written papers on sexuality and the evidence base in psychotherapy.

Kevin Healy, MB, BCh, BAO, DCH, DObs, DPM, MRCPsych, is Consultant Psychotherapist and Director at the Cassell Hospital, Richmond. Treasurer to the Association for Psychoanalytic Psychotherapy in the NHS, his publications cover clinical audit, psychotherapy purchasing and outcome research.

John Jackson, BA, LLM, barrister-at-law, is Professor of Public Law at Queen's University, Belfast. Formerly deputy director of the Institute of the Study of the Legal Profession at Sheffield University, he is co-author (with San Board) of *Judge without Jury: Diplock Trials in the Adversary System* (1995).

Simon Jakes, MA(Oxon), M.Phil., AFBPS, is a clinical psychologist with the Thames Gateway NHS Trust. A registered cognitive behaviour therapist he has written on the clinical application of CBT to hearing loss, tinnitus and psychotic illnesses.

Chris Mace, BSc, MD, MRCPsych, is Senior Lecturer in Psychotherapy at the University of Warwick and Consultant Psychotherapist to South Warwickshire Combined Care NHS Trust. Previous books include *The Art and Science of Assessment in Psychotherapy* (1996) and *Heart and Soul: The Therapeutic Face of Philosophy* (1999).

Frank Margison, MSc, FRCPsych, MD, is Consultant Psychiatrist in Psychotherapy at the Gaskell Psychotherapy Centre, Manchester Royal Infirmary. He is past editor of the *British Journal of Medical Psychology* and UK Vice-President of the Society for Psychotherapy Research. He has published extensively on the impact of illness on parenting, psychotherapy training, and research into psychotherapy outcome.

Stirling Moorey, BSc, MB, BS, FRCPsych, is Consultant Psychiatrist in Cognitive Behaviour Therapy to the South London and The Maudsley NHS Trust and Honorary Senior Lecturer at the Institute of Psychiatry. With Stephen Greer he wrote *Psychological Therapy for Patients with Cancer* (1989) and was co-editor of *Psychological Treatment in Disease and Illness* (1993).

Phil Richardson, PhD, is Head of Psychology to the Tavistock Clinic, London and Visiting Professor to the University of Essex. He is a past Chair of the Research Committee of the British Psychoanalytical Society and is currently editor of the *British Journal of Medical Psychology*. He has a special interest in the evaluation of psychological treatments across many areas of medical psychology.

Bernard Roberts, FRCPsych, is Consultant Psychiatrist in Psychotherapy to the Parkside Clinic. A member of the British Psychoanalytical Society, he has worked as a clinical manager within the NHS, having a particular interest in institutional health. He was convenor of the conference on which the present book is based.

Michael Rustin, MA, is Professor of Sociology and Dean of the Faculty of Social Sciences at the University of East London and Visiting Professor at the Tavistock Clinic. A co-editor of *Soundings*, his publications include *The Good Society and the Inner World* (1991) and (with Margaret Rustin) *Narratives of Love and Loss: Studies in Modern Children's Fiction* (1987).

Paul Sturdee, BA(Hons), MA, is a lecturer in the Philosophy and Ethics of Mental Health at the University of Warwick. An experienced postgraduate teacher, he is reviews editor of *Philosophy, Psychiatry and Psychology*, and has contributed papers on irrationality and psychoanalysis.

Digby Tantam, MA, MPH, PhD, FRCPsych, is Clinical Professor of Psychotherapy in the Centre for Psychotherapeutic Studies and Associate Director of the School of Health and Related Research at the University of Sheffield. A former chair of the United Kingdom Council for Psychotherapy and the Universities Psychotherapy Association, he has published widely in clinical psychiatry, psychotherapy and applied philosophy. He is editor of *Clinical Topics in Psychotherapy* (1988).

Graham Turpin, BSc, M.Phil., PhD, FBPS, is Professor of Clinical Psychology at the University of Sheffield. His extensive publications on the application of psychophysiology to psychopathology and clinical psychology include the *Handbook of Clinical Psychophysiology* (1989), and a co-authored guide to single case methodology for practitioners is forthcoming.

James Watson, MD, FRCP, FRCPsych, is Professor of Psychiatry to Guy's, King's College and St Thomas' School of Medicine. His publications cover cognitive behavioural therapy, cognitive analytic therapy, group therapy and service provision.

Simon Wessely, MA, MSc, MD, FRCP, FRCPsych, is Professor of Psychological Medicine at Guy's, King's and St Thomas' School of Medicine and the Institute of Psychiatry. An authority on chronic fatigue syndrome, his papers also cover pain, schizophrenia, treatment trials and epidemiology.

Figure acknowledgements

We would like to thank the following for permissions granted

Figure 4.1. From Jennings, C. Barraclough, B. and Moss, J.R. (1978) 'Have the Samaritans lowered the suicide rate?', *Psychological Medicine* 8: 413–422. Reprinted by kind permission of Cambridge University Press.

Figure 7.3. From Stephen Kellett and Nigel Beail: 'The treatment of chronic post-traumatic nightmares using psychodynamic-interpersonal psychotherapy: A single case study' *British Journal of Medical Psychology* (1997), 70, 35–49. Copyright © The British Psychological Society.

Figure 13.1 and 13.2. From Crombie, I.K., Davies, H.T.O. *et al.* (1993) *The Audit Handbook.* Chichester: Wiley. Copyright © 1993 John Wiley & Sons Limited. 'Reproduced by permission of John Wiley & Sons Limited'.

Every effort has been made to trace copyright holders and obtain permissions. Any omissions brought to our attention will be remedied in future editions.

Chapter 1

Evidence in psychotherapy
A delicate balance

Chris Mace and Stirling Moorey

'Evidence in the Balance' was the title of a conference organised by the Psychotherapy Faculty of the Royal College of Psychiatrists, the University Psychotherapy Association and the Association of University Teachers of Psychiatry. The discussions that took place of why and how psychotherapeutic services might be more 'evidence based' deserve a wider audience. Since the meeting, ways in which 'evidence' is likely to impinge on everyday practice have been clarified within the National Health Service's programme of 'clinical governance'. This strategy, and the wholesale reform of the service's institutions that it entails, has been a cornerstone of the drive to include quality assurance within the responsibilities of NHS providers (cf. Mace, 1999). Evidence-based practice is no longer a movement that any clinician can ignore.

The psychotherapies, given their respect for the uniqueness of the individual, the complexity of the questions with which they deal, and attitudes towards scientific method that range from willing borrowing to deep distrust, pose particular problems for this movement. The contents of this book should ensure that a psychotherapist, whatever his or her interests, is not only better informed about the clinical implications of evidence-based practice, but better able to recognise its strengths and weaknesses, and able to meet its requirements at the level of service organisation.

Science and psychotherapy

The relationship of systematic research to clinical practice has varied according to individual interests and the history of different psychotherapeutic schools. Cognitive-behavioural psychotherapies, with their past association with learning theories derived from animal experiment and laboratory studies of human cognition, have been seen as intrinsically more 'scientific' than psychoanalytic practices developed through engagement with patients in planned therapeutic environments. Hans Eysenck (1990) used to claim that a psychologist with no clinical experience, but properly versed in experimental method, required about six weeks to translate this scientific understanding into clinical practice. Despite the claims of both Freud and Jung to offer a scientific understanding of the unconscious mind, psychoanalysis has been regularly singled out by philosophers of science as a prime example of a 'pseudoscience' (e.g., Popper, 1962). These stereotypes may require some adjustment. While cognitive-behavioural approaches in clinical practice are increasingly based upon clinically rather than experimentally derived models, psychodynamic practice has been enriched by much closer reference to findings in developmental psychology (cf. Chapter 3 in this book).

In recent years, the efficacy rather than the validity of psychotherapy has been subjected to increasingly sophisticated scrutiny. Research into psychotherapy outcomes had been taken to support the view that psychotherapy was effective, but that there was little overall difference between different forms of psychotherapy. Following a suggestion of Lester Luborsky (Luborsky *et al.*, 1975) this is often called the 'Dodo bird verdict' after Lewis Carroll's *Alice's Adventures in Wonderland*. In Carroll's story, the Dodo proposes that a 'Caucus-race' is held and, after half an hour or so of running, announces that the race is over and 'Everybody has won, and all must have prizes.' One might question the rigour of the Dodo's methodology – the race course is a 'sort of circle', the participants all start at different points along the course, and they can begin running when they like and leave off when they like: a set of rules that seemed to have been used in some of the early psychotherapy trials! There is an increasing sophistication in outcome research, with attempts to specify the goals of treatment more clearly, to define the treatment delivered and to ask questions such as 'what therapy works for which condition' (cf. Roth and Fonagy, 1996). Techniques such as meta-analysis for aggregating research findings, which had supported the Dodo bird verdict, have been refined with more discriminating results. Some researchers are now reasserting that among the psychotherapies (in the words of another modern fable) 'some are more equal than others'.

Principles of evidence-based practice

While some psychotherapy practitioners have always been motivated to translate clinical questions into ones that can be answered through systematic research, the directional shift that turns research into an activity that should normally guide practice is new and decisive. It has been justified by the existence of findings in many clinical fields that appear sufficiently robust to provide a rational basis for selection between treatments in the care of individual patients. The underlying philosophy of evidence-based care can be summed up diagrammatically as a transition between two states of affairs (see Figure 1.1).

In the first situation (column 'A') ignorance about the relative efficacy of treatments prevails; the majority of available interventions are taken to be harmless, with small but significant minorities being either distinctly beneficial or clearly harmful. The task of evidence-based practice is to increase the use of the former and to eliminate the latter, this being the desired state of affairs represented by column 'B'. (Chapter 4 offers an

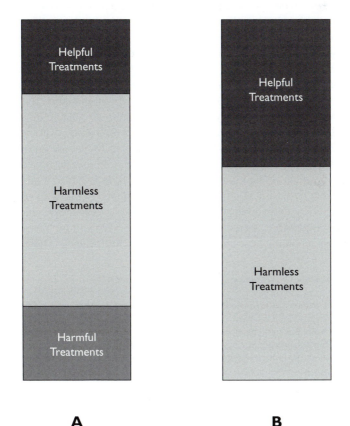

A   **B**

Figure 1.1 The aims of evidence-based practice.

exemplary discussion of the importance of both of these.) To do this, there not only need to be recognised standards of what kind of research findings will count as clinical evidence, but a mechanism for translating these into clear, widely disseminated recommendations that fulfil the needs of any clinicians and patients asking specific questions about 'best practice'. This is the role of clinical guidelines, statements that reflect the balance of research evidence and clinical consensus as to the action that is ordinarily appropriate to a given problem. This guidance will indicate the treatments that should be adopted and any that may be considered but which are no longer recommended, in accordance with the shift from 'A' to 'B' in Figure 1.1.

Decisions as to what counts as the most valid kind of evidence are unlikely to be universal across all kinds of clinical knowledge, nor to be immutable. However, it is fair to report that hierarchical judgements do prevail, and the grading given in Table 1.1, discriminating between the quality of evidence for an intervention's therapeutic effectiveness, is fairly typical.

The highest grade of evidence is identified with the Randomised Control Trial (RCT). Here, the impact of a treatment is studied following attempts to eliminate bias by randomly allocating alternative treatments to study patients according to a protocol over which an experimenter has no personal control. Assessments are conducted by people ignorant of ('blind' to) the nature of the treatment given, and ideally patients too remain ignorant of the kind of treatment they have received – an almost impossible requirement in psychological treatments. This ideal standard of objectivity can be diluted in a number of ways – whether evaluation was in fact comparative, the quality of matching between comparison groups, the extent to which those entering the study are followed up. These are all

Table 1.1 Levels of evidence of therapeutic effectiveness

Level 1   Either a systematic review of comparable randomised controlled trials, or an individual RCT with a narrow confidence interval, or introduction of the treatment has been associated with survival in a previously fatal condition

Level 2   Either a systematic review of comparable cohort studies, or an individual cohort study (which may be a RCT with a significant drop-out rate)

Level 3   A systematic review of comparable case-control studies, or an individual case-control study

Level 4   A reported case series (or poor quality cohort or case-control studies)

Level 5   Expert opinion based on consensus or inference from 'first principles' in the absence of formal critical appraisal

Source: After Ball et al. (1998)

reflected in the gradings described in Table 1.1. It does not and cannot take into consideration additional questions – vital to the validity of individual research reports as a means of addressing clinical decisions – such as how far treatments evaluated under experimental conditions resemble those provided in routine care, or how far outcome measures used by researchers are clinically meaningful.

At most levels, evidence can be in the form either of a report of validated research (e.g., a RCT), or a systematic review of several reports which fulfil clear criteria for their inclusion in the review. This has generated a need for information concerning individual research studies to be indexed and archived in formats which guarantee their accessibility to clinicians seeking evidence of the comparative merits of interventions they may provide. It has also meant that systematic reviews, collating all work meeting a given quality standard that allows a question to be answered, have assumed great significance. The trend for their compilation and dissemination to be sponsored is likely to grow. At the same time, recognition that the quality of systematic reviews is restricted by the availability (and completeness) of published reports of the work they examine is likely to fuel demands that the results of all funded research, whether these fulfilled a study's original objectives or not, are made publicly available for incorporation in systematic reviews (cf. Sturdee in Chapter 5).

Beyond the dissemination of evidence in pre-digested forms in these ways, evidence-based practice has been seen to depend upon the translation of evidence in practice guidelines. These distil the practical implications of research into clear advice concerning what kinds of action constitute 'best practice' in a given situation with the present state of knowledge. In this way, clinical guidelines, in defining objective standards of practice, provide a clear reference point by which actual practice might be audited and, in principle, improved. Whereas guidelines have been produced in the past by professional bodies, the introduction of such new structures as National Service Frameworks, and the National Institute for Clinical Excellence (NICE) within the National Health Service, provides a mechanism by which guidelines can not only be approved and disseminated but adopted as standard clinical practice throughout the public health system.

Evidence and psychotherapy

'Evidence' has several facets which are treated in turn through the remainder of this book. The first concerns the nature of evidence itself.

In an effort to dig behind the assumption that we all know what counts as evidence, the distinguished lawyer John Jackson was invited to explain the nature of evidence in law (Chapter 2). It is apparent that the legal concept of evidence – grounded in the need to resolve a case – differs significantly from the scientific one on which the evidence-based practice movement bases its proposals. In law, testimony is valued only for its contribution to resolution of a dispute – irrespective of how far it may also provide a truthful description.

The contrast with the view that equates evidence with that which is scientifically validated will be apparent from Chapter 4. In it, Simon Wessely justifies the importance that has been placed upon the randomised controlled trials among the kinds of research evidence that are available. As several other contributors highlight the special difficulties of conducting controlled trials for psychotherapeutic treatments (cf. Chapters 11 and 12) their necessity needs to be fully and widely accepted. The case Wessely presents is powerful, depending not only on the relative quality of RCTs as a form of evidence for the efficacy of a treatment, but also on their unique capacity to demonstrate in the face of received wisdom when treatments are positively harmful.

Wessely's polemical tone is reciprocated by Paul Sturdee's in Chapter 5 – a discussion of the dangers of allowing an evidence-centred approach to dominate clinical practice when the 'evidence' in question is only partial. Sturdee looks at the impact this attitude can have on the balance between physical and psychotherapeutic treatments for people with mental health problems – not only on how they are perceived, but on their potential availability. Indeed, Sturdee's objections to the selective use of evidence in the name of objectivity suggest that the courtroom model may not be such an inaccurate image of clinical debate. To correct things, Sturdee makes several suggestions. One, the idea that an approach is not properly evidence-based until all relevant evidence is actively sought and then taken into account, is slowly being accepted. However, some fundamental conflicts between the values of science and the individual that he also indicates seem more intractable.

A different evaluation of the evidential thinking in psychotherapy is offered by Michael Rustin (Chapter 3). While Wessely and Sturdee concentrate on the outcome or efficacy of psychotherapy, Rustin illustrates how research can be used to substantiate the theories which therapists use to guide their practice. Given that much therapeutic practice is founded on theories of human development and the impact of early experience on adult functioning, external evidence that supports these accounts of development will consolidate knowledge shared within the psychotherapeutic community. Evidence of this kind also exposes limitations of the drug metaphor. Psychotherapy sets out to explain as well as to treat, and gains a different kind of authority when its explanations are seen to have validity independent of their usefulness in treatment. However, this should not be confused with evidence that its treatments are effective, any more than evidence of a treatment's efficacy is a valid argument for the truth of its theoretical basis. (A definitive discussion of the difference between these arguments will be found in Grünbaum, 1984).

The heterogeneous nature of evidence in psychotherapy underpins Digby Tantam's essay on the relationship between reasons and causes (Chapter 6). Much confusion is attributed to assumptions either that the reasons people give for their actions are unrelated to their causes, or that they constitute the only causes for what people do. In a philosophically skilful argument, Tantam distinguishes between the two kinds of causes that these represent, illustrating the kind of evidence that is necessary to identify either kind with confidence.

If these opening chapters demonstrate that evidence takes many forms within such a psychologically complex field, they set the scene for the remaining chapters of the book. These deal with how evidence accrues, in research and in practice, and how it can be used by psychotherapists to enhance their practice.

The discussion of standards of evidence showed that, within scientific medicine at least, relatively little value was placed on the contribution that individual case studies could make (cf. Table 1.1). This view is likely to be reinforced as critical reviews of the evidence for the effectiveness of psychotherapy organise themselves around these standards when deciding whether a given therapy is 'empirically supported' (cf. Roth and Fonagy, 1996). Although the formative history of the psychotherapies was dominated by individual case studies, the tendency to minimise their significance seems to be increasingly common. Graham Turpin illustrates the contribution that individual case studies can still make to the evidence base, providing a survey of the strengths and drawbacks of qualitative methods in doing so (Chapter 7).

Whether or not individual treatments are reported, they can be evidence-sensitive in the way they are conducted in any clinical setting. Although interpretations of 'evidence-based practice' imply that formal consultation of an external evidence-base (to contextualise a treatment in the light of previous reports) is necessary for it to be 'evidence based', there are other means by which psychotherapy can be seen as rational and open to critical reflection. One of these recognises a psychotherapy as a series of opportunities to erect hypotheses concerning a patient which are then tested in the course of treatment (and its supervision). In the three chapters that follow, Kevin Healy, Simon Jakes, David Allison and Chess Denman illustrate with clinical examples how explicit formulation of a patient's problem identifies questions which inform the remainder of the therapy. The nature of these ideas and questions will differ according to the model of psychotherapy, with Healy providing examples of more psychoanalytic hypotheses and Jakes cognitive-behavioural ones. Allison and Denman jointly illustrate a subject of some confusion among clinicians – the difference in thinking and practice between cognitive analytic therapy (CAT) and cognitive therapy. Their chapter is a helpful illustration of how understanding of many practical disciplines is assisted by active comparison.

Beyond using opportunities for continuing critical appraisal within any psychotherapeutic treatment, there is a growing expectation that the best available evidence from external sources is taken into account in its planning and conduct. We have mentioned already how historically this interface has been most problematic for psychodynamic psychotherapies. In Chapter 11, Phil Richardson is concerned primarily with how the principles of evidence-based practice may be adapted to this group of treatments. He reviews how the standards of evidence discussed above (Table 1.1) are fulfilled within the research base of psychodynamic therapies.

Implementation of evidence-based practice (EBP) requires institutional as well as individual adaptations. These are a major concern in Frank Margison's discussion of how to make EBP work within a service (Chapter 12). Margison suggests ways in which issues raised by Richardson (e.g., limitations of drug metaphors and diagnosis) might be resolved in practice. However, when neither interventions nor the problems under treatment correspond with the clear lines of efficacy research in practice the format of the evidence base itself ultimately needs to adapt in the direction of 'practice-based evidence'.

The topic of clinical audit is a little older than EBP, but it is enjoying a renaissance as one of the key processes by which clinical governance will monitor and raise standards of care within public service providers. Standards of best practice are of little use if they do not have an impact on services, and audit is the method by which actual practice can be compared with these standards. An unashamedly practical review of the applications of audit in a modern psychotherapy service by Mark Aveline and Jim Watson therefore concludes the survey of evidence in practice.

The treatment of evidence here cannot claim to be exhaustive, nor hope to be, given the many sources from which evidence can emerge.

For instance, no contributor addresses the most objective measures of clinical change; that is, physical measures – although even this hard index is yielding. Short-term psychotherapy has recently been shown to have an ameliorative effect on the functional brain images of severely depressed patients that parallels their clinical improvement, yet is clearly distinguishable from the visible changes linked to antidepressant medication during recovery (Martin *et al.*, 1999).

Evidence in context

Within the scientific frame, the ideal types of efficacy research are likely to need to be considerably modified in order to be sufficiently sensitive to the specific needs of different populations and contexts of delivery. Unless there is a clear correspondence between the questions addressed in the studies that form the basis of 'best evidence' and those that the therapist is trying to answer in referring to them, its usefulness will be limited. Already the boundaries between local audit and research are being blurred as clinical effectiveness research attempts to study the impact of unmodified treatments in naturalistic settings through large but pragmatic national studies. Through initiatives like the Association for Psychoanalytic Psychotherapy's multi-centre study (Chiesa and Fonagy, 1999), detailed clinical data are being collected for the twin purposes of in-service audit and multi-centre collation for research at one and the same time. They promise to highlight any differences in the nature of demand, and its relevance to the impact of established treatments, faced by geographically distinct but apparently comparable services. Without this kind of information, fundamental questions of what would constitute equitable provision, as well as an effective one, cannot be addressed.

Alongside these developments, it has been an interesting and sometimes uncomfortable paradox of modern healthcare systems that, despite the growing formal emphasis on science, audit and evidence in clinical practice, the scope for irrationality within the system has been largely unchecked. This irrationality can operate at managerial, strategic and political levels. In the recent past a number of terminal threats have been made to psychotherapy services. These have sometimes been based on a limited and ill-informed view of the outcome evidence available for psychotherapy, but more often pay no attention to questions of effectiveness and efficiency at all. They seem to be more the result of destructive and essentially irrational dynamics. In the face of such attack, scientific evidence may be of only limited value to the case. Other kinds of evidence, as any politician knows, need to be summoned, and in a political context this often means demonstrating the value of the service to service users, potential users and those who represent them. This is a further illustration to those provided in Chapter 5 of how 'scientific evidence' does not exist in some isolated intellectual space but in a social and political environment where it can be used and misused for many purposes.

Evidence in evolution

This is a time of rapid change for most areas of clinical activity. The move to a more 'evidence-based' approach can seem to many to justify itself through its returns in terms of effectiveness and efficiency. The particular conclusions that comprise today's consensus regarding 'best practice' are likely to change more quickly than in the past. However, the process itself may be significant in other ways too. It harnesses the resources of information technology to put any individual in command of a set of recommendations for treatment that are more widely shared than ever before. As reviews and guidelines proliferate, evidence-based practice will depend less and less on individuals conducting their own 'research' into an issue. The whole balance within 'clinical opinion' between individual views and consensus is being fundamentally changed. Are there irreducible limits to such a development for psychotherapy, reflecting the impossibility of standardising any psychological treatment beyond a very basic level? The word 'psychotherapy' implies treatment by the mind, rather than treatment of the mind. Does it not inevitably have qualities inseparable from the personality of the practitioner, not all of which can be reduced to the impact of professional training and experience? If so, how is this impact expressed? These questions are also a reminder that the recent emphasis on evidence for the outcome and efficacy of treatments has tended to distract attention from an urgent need to bring an evidence-based approach to bear on the usefulness or otherwise of key components of training and supervision in the psychological therapies.

Undervalued questions like these need to be championed if a technology that is sufficiently sensitive to resolve them is to be developed. Once they are, the nature of the 'evidence' brought to bear on psychotherapeutic practice would inevitably change, very possibly in directions that will seem incompatible with today's interpretations of evidence-based practice.

References

Ball, C., Sackett, D., Phillips, B., Haynes, B. and Straus, S. (1998) *Levels of Evidence*. NHS R&D Centre for Evidence-based Medicine, at: http://cebm. jr2.ox.ac/docs/levels.html

Chiesa, M. and Fonagy, P. (1999) 'From the efficacy to the effectiveness model in psychotherapy research: The APP multi-centre project', *Psychoanalytic Psychotherapy* 13: 259–272.

Eysenck, H. (1990) *Rebel with a Cause – the Autobiography of H.J. Eysenck*. London: W.H. Allen.

Grünbaum, A. (1984) *The Foundations of Psychoanalysis: A Philosophical Critique*. Berkeley, CA: University of California Press.

Luborsky, L., Singer, B. and Luborksy, L. (1975) 'Comparative studies of psychotherapy', *Archives of General Psychiatry* 32: 995–1008.

Mace, C.J. (1999) 'Psychotherapy and the modernization of the UK health service', *European Journal of Psychotherapy, Counselling and Health* 2 (2): 217–227.

Martin, S., Richardson, M. *et al.* (1999) *Brain Function Normalisation on SPECT Scanning with Interpersonal Therapy versus Venlafaxine for Major Depression*. Proceedings of the annual meeting of Royal College of Psychiatrists, Birmingham, UK, p. 69.

Popper, K. (1962) *Conjectures and Refutations*. London: Routledge.

Roth, A. and Fonagy, P. (1996) *What Works for Whom?* New York: Guilford.

Chapter 2

A lawyer's view of evidence

John Jackson

Introduction

It is interesting to contrast the intense debate that has taken place within the medical profession about what constitutes best evidence practice with the almost complete absence of discussion of best evidence practice within the legal profession. It is commonly said, of course, that lawyers are not interested in evidence and the truth, yet the legal system seeks to reach truthful verdicts and is strongly criticised when it fails to do this. There is no shortage of suggestions for reform but these often fall on deaf ears within the legal profession, especially it would seem when the suggestions are made by scientists, psychologists and other professionals dedicated to seeking the truth. Indeed, one of the persistent themes of legal and psychological literature on legal processes is that there has existed a credibility gap between psychologists and lawyers whereby the claims of the former to be able to make positive contributions which have relevance for legal processes are disputed by the latter (Clifford, 1979).

Two particular claims have been made (Jackson, 1995). First, it has been said that psychologists can provide the basis for making specific changes to legal procedure and, second, it is said that psychologists can help decide questions of evidence in specific cases. Both these claims have tended to be treated with suspicion by lawyers although there has been a greater tendency for courts to accept psychological evidence in specific cases. From the early days of applied psychology, lawyers expressed hostility about accepting the findings of psychology. Much of this was directed at what were seen as unsophisticated and inappropriate techniques used by psychologists. Psychologists were quick to see the relevance of discoveries about perception and memory to the issue of witness reliability but the techniques recommended for testing the credibility of witnesses soon came under critical scrutiny by lawyers. One of the leading legal evidence scholars of the early twentieth century, J.H. Wigmore (1909), complained about the absence of exact and precise experimental methods of ascertaining and measuring the testimonial certitude of witnesses. Since these early days psychologists have refined their theories and methodology (Lloyd-Bostock and Clifford, 1979). Laboratory studies have been supplemented by field studies conducted within legal processes themselves and the focus has moved away from purely court processes to looking at the ways in which evidence is obtained before court. Yet there continues to be resistance.

Lawyers, judges and courts have been more willing to accept the evidence of forensic psychologists who have been able to assist in the evaluation of particular evidence, but even here the courts have been cautious about permitting psychological and psychiatric evidence to dominate legal evidence. This attitude was well captured in the comment made by Lawton LJ in a case over twenty years ago when he said that psychiatry has not yet become a satisfactory substitute for the common sense of juries.[1] In this case the accused was convicted of murder by battering a girl 15 times with a hammer. His defence was provocation: that he was deeply in love with a girl he thought was pregnant by him and he lost control when she told him she had been sleeping with other men while he was in prison. The defence wanted to call a psychiatrist to testify that the accused had a deep emotional relationship with the girl which was likely to cause an explosive release of rage when she confessed her infidelity, but the judge rejected this evidence and the Court of Appeal upheld this ruling on the ground that the jury needed no expert assistance in deciding on the credibility of the accused's defence.

This leads us to the question: why so much suspicion? One response is the rather cynical one that professionals have alway tried to keep other professionals out of their territory (Abbott, 1988). Professionals have continuously fought over jurisdictional areas of work and lawyers would appear to have been better than most at holding on to their traditional practices. At times there have been vigorous exchanges. A wide range of scientists have attacked the adversary system as a world of make-believe where evidence relevant to a case may not be presented, counter evidence may not be made known and contradictions are left unresolved (Marshall, 1966). Lawyers for their part have not only defended these practices as the best method of finding the truth but have also at times launched attacks on the so-called neutrality of experts. When the Court of Appeal quashed Judith Ward's conviction for the murder of 12 people who died after a bomb exploded on board a coach, the Court put a large part of the blame on the forensic scientists involved in the case.[2]

Aside from territorial rivalry and a natural tendency to blame others when things go wrong, however, it is important to be aware of the different contexts in which lawyers and scientists or doctors operate and the different methods of proof that operate in each context. These are the issues that I want to start looking at today. Then we can return to the question of how the courts ought to respond to psychological and psychiatric evidence. It will be argued that there are three possible approaches: first, continued suspicion; second, deference; third, education.

The context of litigation

Although many contentious issues in modern-day litigation involve issues of fact, the primary purpose of litigation is not to resolve issues of fact but to contribute to the peaceful resolution of disputes (Hart and McNaughton, 1959). Disputes do not have to be settled by litigation, and indeed there are a variety of other methods of dispute resolution that are increasingly being resorted to including negotiation, mediation and arbitration. The mediator helps the parties resolve their differences for themselves, while the arbitrator is chosen by the parties to reach a resolution for them. In either case the aim is not so much to look back at what has happened as to look forward to find a solution that will be acceptable to both sides. Even in litigation, where the parties take each other to court to have the dispute settled on the basis of existing rules or principles of law and it is important then to look back to examine the origins of the dispute, the main aim is not so much the enforcement of the rules as the resolution of the dispute. Most cases do not in fact go to trial but are settled through pre-trial negotiation. Even where enforcement of the rules is considered important as in criminal cases, most cases are resolved by guilty pleas which may be the result of negotiation between the parties.

The result of this is that fact-finding is not conducted in the spirit of scientific inquiry and may be compromised in the interests of reaching a settlement. Although legal procedures are often accused of being inordinately slow, there may be time limits which impose inevitable constraints on the fact-finding endeavour. Parties may, for example, be required to bring charges or claims before full inquiries have been made. Thereafter the focus will be on reaching a resolution as much as on further inquiries. Of course, there may be time constraints on scientific investigations as well but there is not the same pressure to reach a definitive conclusion one way or another to a particular question. The result is that decisions have to be made at times under fairly extreme conditions of uncertainty and various rules and presumptions are resorted to in order to aid this decision-making process. Rules are required to determine which party wins or loses and this is achieved by means of burdens of proof put on the parties. A failure to prove the material facts necessary to substantiate the charge or claim will mean that the defendant is not guilty or not liable. In addition, inferences or presumptions of fact may be made in order to expedite proceedings and judicial notice may be taken of certain facts which are difficult to prove.

Since it is impossible to achieve absolute certainty in this forensic process, there is also a need for rules to determine what standard of proof is necessary to enable the material facts to be proved. Of course, judgements are made in science under conditions of uncertainty as well, but since there is less need for final decisions to be reached, degrees of certainty at any stage can be defined by varying confidence levels. By contrast since legal judgements are final there is a clear need to set a definite standard as to what is to be considered proved. Moral and political judgements come into play in setting these standards as they essentially concern the extent to which the various parties should be exposed to risks of error (Zuckerman, 1989). So standards of proof are conventionally different in civil and criminal cases. In civil litigation involving a dispute between private parties the risks of error are allocated as evenly as possible, whereas in criminal cases the risks of error are allocated in favour of defendants as the risk of wrongful conviction is considered greater than wrongful acquittal. The result is that one particular allegation may be proved more easily in a civil case than a criminal case. Increasingly, victims of criminal offences, for example, are attempting to litigate criminal allegations in civil courts so as to get a determination in their favour which they may not be able to obtain in a criminal trial.

Another factor which marks out legal fact-finding from scientific inquiries is the need for public acceptability of verdicts. Of course, scientific methods must be accredited and results will be subjected to peer review and some scientists have likened this process of justification as conforming to the trial adversary model (Levine, 1974). However, legal verdicts must not only be acceptable to the parties involved but also they must command respect within the entire community. This need for public confidence may, however, constrain the search for truth as the public may not just be concerned with the accuracy of the outcome but with the fairness of the process which led to the outcome. Many, as we have said, have been critical of the adversary system; but such a system should be seen less as an ideal method of truth-finding and more as an ideal method of dispute resolution accepted by society at large. One of the advantages is that it gives the parties a voice in the proceedings, albeit through their lawyers, so that the parties can claim to have played a part in the eventual outcome. This is not a universally shared method of determining facts, but it is one which fits with societal conceptions of how disputes should be settled. Apart from procedural fairness, society also demands that there are limits on the extent to which parties may intrude on others in order to obtain information and there must be certain standards of propriety imposed on those conducting investigations. The rules regulating the way confessions are obtained and the privilege against self-incrimination arguably stem as much from concern about maintaining a proper balance of power between prosecution and defence as from a concern about confessions being true. Another factor that assists public confidence is the need to ensure that procedures are open and public, but this can also constrain truth-finding to the extent that it can inhibit persons from disclosing information relevant to the dispute.

All these factors – the need to prioritise settlement, finality of decision-making and public confidence – impose considerable constraints on legal fact-finding, quite apart from the constraints of time and resources that govern any fact-finding investigation. Any scientific criticism of legal procedure thereby runs the risk of failing to take account of the full context within which legal procedures have to operate. One example is the controversy surrounding the cross-examination of vulnerable witnesses in the courtroom. Psychologists have long pointed out the problematic nature of this process: witnesses respond badly to the pressure of open public cross-examination and it is especially difficult then to judge their credibility. The solution canvassed has been to use live video-links, and many psychologists have been satisfied that this is a more effective method of obtaining evidence from children (Spencer and Flin, 1993). This solution has been accepted for child witnesses but not, so far, for other vulnerable witnesses such as rape complainants. Critics of this procedure have argued that such changes have to be viewed in the overall context of the fairness of the procedures so far as the accused is concerned and the question of what is fair or not fair is not one that can be resolved by science.

Legal methods of proof

We have seen that the legal process must take acount of a whole range of considerations other than truth-finding if it is to achieve its aims of providing peaceful settlement of disputes and inspiring public confidence in its procedures. At the same time truth-finding plays an important role in litigation as confidence is undermined when judgements and settlement are seen to diverge too much from what is thought to have occurred. Within modern legal evidence scholarship, accuracy of decision-making is given a high priority (Twining, 1990). But this leads on to the question of whether there are certain specifically legal methods of proof which deviate from scientific or other rational inquiries.

We have seen that legal procedures can require findings of fact to be made under conditions of considerable uncertainty, whilst at the same time there is a need to ensure that any verdict arrived at has a certain seal of finality. If parties and indeed the public were able to question verdicts continually, this would significantly undermine the need to arrive at a final settlement. One way out of this difficulty is to privilege certain kinds of evidence which are accorded particular value by the society of the day, and when we turn to look at the history of legal proof we see that this is what has happened. In early centuries most of Europe was dominated by Germanic modes of proof which were based on the assumption that truth was revealed by an omniscient God. Germanic and Anglo-Saxon trials therefore prescribed certain authorised and widely accepted methods of proof through which God revealed the truth and the parties able to pass through the appropriate proof unscathed succeeded in their claims. Various methods were prescribed – battle, ordeal and compurgation (the use of oath-helpers). Through modern eyes such methods appear irrational, but it can be argued that if we place these methods in the context of early medieval life they appear perfectly rational. Damaska (1997a) has pointed out that most disputes were settled locally by persons who knew something about what had happened. When this failed to settle the matter, lawsuits were mainly determined by oath-helpers who risked divine wrath if they falsely swore to the justice of their party's cause. Trial by ordeal was a last resort, and although the ordeals chosen (for example, walking over red hot ploughshares without sustaining injury) appear totally irrational today they were an effective means of putting pressure on false claimants. Only those who were convinced of the rightness of their cause would be prepared to go through such ordeals.

Damaska's point is that these so-called magical or irrational forms of proof were really only used as a last resort and that the ordinary common sense of laypersons prevailed in many cases. When trial by ordeal was condemned by the Lateran Council in 1215, this signified the need to find alternative methods of proof by last resort, rooted more in secular than in ecclesiastical justice. The revelation of truth became a matter for Man, not God. In Roman-canon procedure, which succeeded the German system of proof in most of continental Europe, judges were appointed to hear the parties and they later appealed to a highly technical body of rules, a system of 'numerical proof' which required two credible witnesses for full proof. Circumstantial evidence, no matter how compelling, was not an adequate basis for conviction. Judicial torture, however, was permitted to extract a confession in cases where there was so-called half proof, one eyewitness or strong circumstantial evidence. This did not mean that judges were reduced to mere automatons; they were able to use much common-sense reasoning within the restrictions imposed by such a rigid system, but in the last resort numerical proofs provided a method of coming to decisions.

Instead of Roman-canon procedure, England put its faith in a new method of proof: trial by jury. Juries existed in medieval times as groups of people with local knowledge of disputes, and they came to accuse felons in the royal courts of justice. But in the thirteenth and fourteenth centuries they also came to actually try accused persons. At the same time witnesses were transformed from oath-helpers who vouched for a party's cause to persons who actually swore to the truth of events that were central to the dispute, and the testing of evidence became important. Over time the jury transformed from a group of people with prior knowledge about the case to a body which determined guilt on the basis of evidence presented to court. But it took some time before courts became confident in deferring the task of judging evidence to a group of lay juries. The Roman-canon rules of proof continued to cast something of a shadow over what has been called the principle of universal cognitive competence, or the idea that triers of fact should weigh the probative force of evidence on their own rather than by appeal to specific rules of proof (Cohen, 1982).

The two-witness rule emerged in various statutes in the sixteenth century, and the courts adopted a number of technical rules governing the competency of witnesses. Throughout the sixteenth and seventeenth centuries certain categories of witness – children, the insane, non-Christians and persons interested in the litigation – were considered incompetent and unable to testify. Moreover, even up until the late eighteenth century certain types of evidence were privileged over others (Landsman, 1990). In one of the first English treatises devoted exclusively to evidence and published in 1754, Geoffrey Gilbert, the Lord Chief Baron of Exchequer, organised various types of evidence in a hierarchical fashion, with the pre-eminent category belonging to written evidence. Official records under seal were classified at the top of the tree, followed by public records such as affidavits, depositions, etc., then private documents such as deeds. Unwritten evidence came a poor second in this hierarchy of evidence because witnesses who testified orally were subject to failures of memory and partiality while documents were 'the most sedate and deliberate acts of the mind'. In terms reminiscent of the old numerical Roman-canon system, Gilbert relied on the number of witnesses who gave evidence under oath rather than on the probative force of each witness's evidence. Finally, considerable weight was placed on the use of presumptions to make up for the absence of definitive written evidence.

All this meant that there was a limited role for testing evidence in court and consequently a limited role for lawyers and juries. Throughout the eighteenth century, however, the idea that evidence should be tested became much more pronounced and trial proceedings came to be viewed as a means of testing testimony rather than as a form for the presentation of a few carefully selected pieces of evidence. The best-evidence principle, under which pieces of evidence were categorised with varying degrees of weight in advance of the trial and only the best evidence would do, came to be replaced by the principle of universal cognitive competence under which it was left to juries to attach their own probative weight to evidence that was tested before them. As a result the preference for written evidence, the insistence on formalities like the oath and the competence rules excluding large categories of witness from giving evidence all declined. Gradually textbook writers came to recognise the importance of cross-examination, but it took a giant piece of evidence scholarship – Bentham's (1827) multi-volume *Rationale of Judicial Evidence* – to articulate fully this new approach and to reject the best-evidence principle. Bentham challenged all the old classifications and in their place advocated a system of free proof, by which he meant that all evidence relevant to a dispute should be admitted and evidence should be weighed solely on the merits of the individual case. Such a system of free proof was the natural consequence of the principle of universal cognitive competence. If it is the case that judge or juries can reason for themselves about evidence (without the need to rely on authoritative rules) there is no need for technical rules of evidence.

Common-sense reasoning applied by laypersons to evidence which is admitted into court but which is subjected to rigorous examination has thus become the modern method of proof. In many ways this conforms to a very rationalist model of adjudication (Twining, 1990). At the same time modern critics have pointed out that this system retains certain irrational or magical features (Jackson, 1992). Trials are still referred to in sporting terms, with judges high above the arena as umpires or referees in a contest between rival parties. Parties are still allowed to call character witnesses to vouch for the credibility of accused persons. Cross-examination of witnesses can become an occasion for partisan lawyers simply to rubbish the credit of witnesses. Judges and lawyers wear ceremonial garb, judges sit high above a gladiatorial contest between two sides and at the end deliver magisterial summings up to juries who then retire and emerge with a verdict which does not need to be justified.

Despite all this ritual the verdict does, nevertheless, come down at the end of the day, at least in criminal cases, to the common sense of ordinary jurors. But just when common sense would seem to have triumphed as the ultimate arbiter of legal disputes, a new method of proof has come to challenge the pre-eminence of common sense – the methods of modern science. More and more issues in modern litigation are now so susceptible to scientific analysis that there is a possibility that trials in the future will be dominated by scientists (Damaska, 1997b). An ever-increasing number of facts can be established by technical instruments, and scientific expertise has expanded into areas hitherto thought unimaginable. One only has to think of the growing importance of DNA evidence in many criminal and paternity cases. Even matters such as the credibility of witnesses, long considered the preserve of juries alone, are now increasingly the subject of social scientfic analysis.

The scientific challenge

At one level scientific methods should not be so alien to the common-sense methods of reasoning that have held sway in the nineteenth and twentieth centuries. The inductive methods of reasoning that are the standard fare of common-sense reasoning, starting with some basic data and moving by inductive generalisation towards a probable conclusion, were widely practised by seventeenth- and eighteenth-century scentists and were described by Hume as the 'scientific method'. The challenge kicks in at the level of the complexity of the subject matter. The danger is that juries and even judges will find it so difficult to understand the scientific evidence that they will end up judging cases on irrational grounds. Alternatively the courts may end up having to defer entirely to experts. Out-of-depth judges and juries will become dependent on court experts to dictate or strongly urge how cases should be decided.

There are various strategems that the courts can adopt towards the spiralling increase in the volume of scientific evidence. First of all the courts could, Canute-like, decide to ignore much of it by adopting stringent standards for the admissibility of such evidence. The courts have always adopted a rather grudging approach towards expert evidence. They have long recognised the need for assistance on certain matters of expertise and this has been facilitated by making an exception to the general rule that witnesses must state facts, not opinion, in order that they are properly informed about expert evidence. But they have then hedged such evidence in by a series of other rules which have had the effect of restricting the scope of such opinions (Jones, 1994). First of all, they restricted such evidence to matters beyond the competence of lay triers of fact. Then a number of rules such as the ultimate issue, the hearsay rule and the hypothetical question rule were applied and developed to prevent experts testifying on matters not presented to the court and on ultimate issues which were really for the jury to decide. This restrictive approach is still to be seen on the part of the courts, especially when experts appear to be blatantly usurping the role of the trier of fact. One recent example has been the courts' approach towards the admissibility of expert evidence on the question of whether a child is capable of giving intelligible testimony and is a truthful and reliable witness. In one case forensic psychologists had applied a special technique called THEMA to trace a process which led the child's evidence to become what was described as 'a comprehensive exercise in confabulation'.[3] The court's response to this evidence was to conclude that the time may come when this technique is recognised as a better means for evaluating truth and determining guilt or innocence than trial by judge and jury or magistrate, but that time had not yet come.

A second strategy, which has been increasingly resorted to in a wide range of issues, has been to defer to the opinions of experts. The courts have permitted experts to give opinions on numerous fields of expertise. The English courts have recently said that expert evidence is not limited to the old-established, academically based sciences such as medicine, geology or metallurgy and the established professions such as architecture, quantity surveying and engineering:

> Expert evidence of fingerprint, handwriting and accident reconstruction is regularly given. Opinions may be given of the market value of land, ships, pictures and rights. Expert opinions may be given of the quality of commodities, or on the literary, artistic or scientific or other merit of works alleged to be obscene . . . Some of these fields are far removed from anything which could be called a formal scientific discipline.[4]

The adversary system arguably acts as a check on undue deference being given to scientific evidence. But this assumes that parties hire lawyers who are well versed in the intricacies of such evidence or are able to find other experts who can put it to the test. The danger is that the courts – lawyers, judges and juries – may become bamboozled by spurious evidence which has no reliable foundation (see Huber, 1993). There have certainly been examples in a number of miscarriage of justice cases of exaggerated claims being made by forensic scientists for the strength of certain scientific evidence. The May Inquiry into the case of the Maguire Seven, for example, found that tests which were at the time of trial said to be foolproof methods for detecting nitroglycerine were later proved to be defective. More recently, there has been concern about the application of DNA profiling in certain cases, and there is a need for quality assurance to ensure that samples match and that the statistical probabilities for random matches are accurate. Another area of recent concern has been about the admission of pyschological and behavioural 'syndrome' evidence. Examples are battered wife syndrome, post-traumatic stress syndrome and child abuse syndrome, where experts have claimed that a person has suffered from child or sex abuse on the basis of various symptoms that an alleged victim possessed. The difficulty here is whether the alleged symptoms have been the subject of well-grounded, perhaps one might say, 'evidence-based' practice. The latest controversy surrounds the significance of recovered memory syndrome whereby it is claimed that victims who have made allegations of child or sex abuse have repressed their memory of the traumatic event for years after it allegedly occurred.

One solution to this problem is to insist that expert testimony is well grounded in the particular field of expertise. This approach was adopted for many years in the US where a test known as the *Frye* test insisted that expert testimony was grounded in scientific principle or discovery which was sufficiently established to have gained general acceptance in the particular field in which it belonged.[5] The difficulty with adopting an approach like *Frye*, however, is that it assumes that orthodox science is best and it prevents the use of scientific evidence based on emerging disciplines or cross-disciplinary studies. Another problem is that sometimes there are disputes as to what the accepted standards are. This comes to the fore in cases where scientific methods and medical practices themselves become the direct object of litigation, as in medical negligence claims. Here the legal standards become closely aligned to established scientific or medical practice. Negligence in this context amounts to a failure to measure up to the standard of the ordinary skilled professional and the court defers to the professionals to determine what that standard is. But this deferential approach has its limits when there are professional disputes about what the standards are. One classic example is the celebrated 1980s US case where a depressed physician sued a private hospital for malpractice on the ground that he should have been given state-of-the-art medication instead of psychotherapy treatment which left him to vegetate inside a hospital for seven months (Shorter, 1997). The issue was whether psychoanalysis met accepted standards of care, but the difficulty was over what were the accepted standards. In effect intensive psychotherapy was put on trial, with some psychiatrists arguing that its efficacy had never been properly established by controlled trials whereas the efficacy of medication had. The case was settled for an undisclosed sum and the impression left was that treating psychiatric illness with psychoanalysis alone constituted medical malpractice. The latest example of disputed medical practices concerns the litigation arising out of recovered memory therapy. The first court case in the UK involves a father and daughter suing a healthcare trust for the recovered memory therapy which led the daughter to make false childhood abuse allegations against her father. A recent survey commissioned by the Royal College of Psychiatrists has concluded that memories of childhood sexual or satanic abuse elicited by therapists are dangerous and not credible after finding that there was no evidence that some people repressed memories of abuse (*The Times*, 1 April 1998). But the survey has proved controversial. In these cases the courts have to focus on contentious treatment and ultimately reach a judgement themselves on it.

It has more recently been argued that the courts need to adopt a third approach towards expert evidence, neither one of outright suspicion, nor one of outright deference, but instead one based on understanding and education (Allen and Miller, 1993). The *Frye* test has since been replaced in the United States by a test which requires the judge to determine whether the expert's testimony relates to scientific knowledge that will assist the trier of fact to understand or determine a fact in issue. In *Daubert* v. *Merrell Dow Pharmaceutical, Inc.*, the US Supreme Court held that this means asking whether the reasoning or methodology underlying the testimony is scientifically valid, and it proceeded to lay down criteria which, arguably, did not differ much from the *Frye* test of general acceptance.[6] But the emphasis on the scientific evidence having to be of assistance to the trier of fact provides a basis for requiring that the evidence is sufficently explained so that jurors have a chance of understanding it, and some have argued that the decision in *Daubert* can be interpreted as rejecting the deference approach and pointing towards an educational model. As one commentator has put it, *Daubert* requires that the trial judge first of all learns about the scientific technique to determine whether it will assist the trier of fact and then ensures that the trier of fact is educated about the technique (Inwinkelried, 1997). 'Like Chaucer's Clerk, the judge must learn and then help teach.'

There is presently a debate going on about how precisely such a model could be made to work. The challenges are immense. First of all, there is the question whether it is even worth trying to educate lay persons or even judges in the intricacies of scientific evidence. Are there certain cases where jurors simply could not understand the evidence no matter what resources and procedures were employed to try to educate them? Second, there are large costs involved in education and questions then arise about who should bear these costs. Judges would have to be trained in scientific techniques and in jury trials jurors would also have to be trained. Third, changes would have to be made to legal procedures. Adversarial point-scoring is hardly an adequate method of education. Some have argued in favour of new didactic procedures to educate judges and juries (Inwinkelried, 1997). Judges would appoint scientific advisers in certain cases to help them understand the evidence. Then judges would make use of the education they had received to notice facts judicially and to lecture the jury on relatively indisputable propositions. Finally, court-appointed experts would serve as teaching assistants to ensure that jurors understood the propositions covered in the judge's lecture and there would be question and answer exchanges between jurors and experts. Parties would not be prevented from calling their own experts, but it has been argued that juries would be better equipped to resolve the battle between the experts. Others have argued against these ideas on the ground that they still privilege certain scientific propositions or methods (those of court experts) over others (those of the parties), with judges and jurors inevitably deferring in favour of the former (Edmond, 1998). As well as this, giving jurors a lecture on relatively indisputable propositions may not be that helpful because those cases which end in litigation are often the ones where the real issues in dispute are far from simple or indisputable. An example would be toxic tort litigation where the effects of a drug or chemical exposure and the different methods of calculating risk (e.g., what are the health risks of taking Benectin?) are so debatable.

Conclusion

The difficulty the legal system has in adopting educational approaches harks back to the question raised at the beginning: to what extent can the legal system institute rational fact-finding methods of inquiry when there are limited resources available and a pressing need to reach a resolution of a specific dispute? These pressures call into play certain specifically legal methods of fact-finding which may appear to go beyond rational discourse but which are often the best that can be achieved within the constraints of litigation. Ultimately, what is important is to reach verdicts which are considered legitimate and are consequently accepted by the parties and the community at large.

In the past, and still to some extent, magical or irrational elements accepted by the community were allowed to permeate the legal decision-making process. They have given verdicts the seal of certainty that is so important if the verdict is to be accepted. For some science may seem the new saviour, as there is an attraction in verdicts being based on the say-so of hard science rather than on the frailties of common-sense reasoning. The difficulty is that, as sociologists of science have been saying for some time, scientists as much as other witnesses adhere to different interpretations of reality and what is accepted as a scientific fact in one context is not necessarily accepted as such in another. And as the community becomes more and more exposed to the arguments of scientists, so the legal system must allow for these disagreements within its own procedures. The question remains whether the final decision should be made by scientists themselves or by lay or professional judges. The difficulty with the former approach is that the legal system would be abandoning its claim to provide autonomous judgements over question of fact and there would be questions over how acceptable this is to the community. But the difficulty with continuing to place the final judgement in the hands of lay or professional judges is whether there can be confidence in their verdicts without a massive attempt at education. Education may be the most rational approach, but short of this the system may need to settle for something less: continued use of dialectic party presentation of expert evidence but with greater intervention from judges – less to educate the jury as to correct any imbalance in the presentation of the evidence. It may be too much to educate the jury, but is it too much to try to educate judges and lawyers in some of the areas of expertise that are increasingly relied on as evidence in our courts?

Notes

1   R. v. *Turner* [1975] 1 All ER 70, 75.
2   R. v. *Ward* [1993] 2 All ER 577.
3   G. v. *DPP* [1997] 2 All ER 755.
4   R. v. *Robb* (1991) 93 Cr App R 161.
5   *Frye* v. *US* 293 F.1013 (1923).
6   509 US 579 (1993).

References

Abbott, A. (1998) *The System of Professions*. Oxford: Blackwell.
Allen, R.J. and Miller, J.S. (1993) 'The common law theory of experts: deference or education?' 87 *NWULR* 1131.

Bentham, J. (1827) *Rationale of Judicial Evidence*. New York: Garland.

Clifford, B. (1979) 'Eyewitness testimony: the bridging of a credibility gap', in D. Farrington, K. Hawkins and S. Lloyd-Bostock (eds) *Psychology in Legal Contexts*. London: Macmillan.

Cohen, L.J. (1983) Freedom of proof, in W. Twining (ed.) *Facts in law*. Wiesbaden: Verlag.

Damaska, M.R. (1997a) *Evidence Law Adrift*. New Haven: Yale.

Damaska, M.R. (1997b) 'Rational and irrational proof revisited', 5 *Cardozo Journal of International Company Law* 25.

Edmond, G. (1998) 'The next step or *moonwalking*? Expert evidence, the public understanding of science and the case against Inwinkelried's didactic trial procedures', 2 *E&P* 13.

Grünbaum, A. (1984). *The Foundation of Psychoanalysis: A Philosophical Critique*. Berkeley, CA: University of California Press.

Hart, H.M. and McNaughton, J.T. (1959) Some aspects of evidence and inference in the law, in D. Lerner (ed.) *Evidence and Inference*. New York: Free Press.

Huber, F.W. (1993) *Galileo's Revenge: Junk Science in the Courtroom*. New York: Basic Books.

Inwinkelried, E.J. (1997) 'The next step in conceptualising the presentation of expert evidence as education: the case for didactic trial procedures', 1 *E&P* 128.

Jackson, J.D. (1992) 'Law's truth, lay truth and lawyers' truth: the representation of evidence in adversary trials', 3 *Law and Critique* 29.

Jackson, J.D. (1995) 'Evidence: legal perspective', in R. Bull and D. Carson (eds) *Handbook of Psychology in Legal Contexts*. Chichester, UK: Wiley.

Jones, C.A.G. (1994) *Expert Witness: Science, Medicine and the Practice of Law*. Oxford: Clarendon.

Landsman, S. (1990) 'From Gilbert to Bentham: the reconceptualisation of evidence theory', 36 *Wayne LR* 1149.

Levine, T. (1974) 'Scientific method and the adversary model', 29 *American Psychologist* 661.

Lloyd-Bostock, S. and Clifford, B. (1979) *Evaluating Witness Evidence*. Chichester, UK: Wiley.

Marshall, J. (1969) *Law and Psychology in Conflict*. New York: Doubleday.

Shorter, E. (1997) *A History of Psychiatry from the Era of the Asylum to the Age of Prozac*. New York: Wiley.

Spencer, J.R. and Flin, R. (1993) *The Evidence of Children*. London: Blackstone.

Twining, W. (1990) *Rethinking Evidence*. Oxford: Blackwell.

Wigmore, J.H. (1909) 'Professor Munsterburg and the psychology of practice', 3 *Ill LR* 399.

Zuckerman, A.A.S. (1989) *The Principles of Criminal Evidence*. Oxford: Clarendon.

Chapter 3

Research, evidence and psychotherapy

Michael Rustin

Introduction

This chapter reviews the idea of research, and the evidence on which research is based, from the perspectives of psychoanalytic and systemic psychotherapy. It argues that the processes of knowledge generation in these clinical fields are not adequately captured by conventional concepts of research in psychology and psychiatry, which do not do justice to the methods on which sound clinical practice is based. The article argues for a clearer understanding of the distinctiveness of clinical research procedures, and for the recognition that knowledge is generated by different means in different contexts. Valuable convergences are now taking place between psychoanalytic research and some forms of empirical developmental psychology. These convergences demonstrate the fertility of a methodological pluralism in the mental health field.

'Research' and its terrors

My experience as a supervisor of research undertaken by psychotherapists, both systemic family therapists and psychoanalytic child and adolescent psychotherapists, is that 'research' is an idea which arouses a great deal of anxiety, inducing a highly persecuted state of mind in those about to engage in it. Somewhere, the word 'research' invokes a severe judge, minded to announce at any point, to an imaginary but ever-present court, not only that the wrong answer, or no answer at all, has been given, but also that the wrong methods, or no methods, have been used in coming to it. I find this state of mind in these research students highly resistant to treatment. We read and discuss in our seminars some of the large and interesting literature on existing varieties of scientific investigation. Students become interested in the debates on these questions, and appear to recognise that knowledge is obtained by different means in different fields. Yet their anxieties persist. They fear that whatever 'research' may be, *they* are going to be found not to be doing it, or not to be doing it properly.

It is not even that everyone has clearly in mind an example of what a sound piece of research is. It is, more often, a fantasy, the expression of the impossible aspiration that candidates have just unwisely allowed themselves to fall victim to by choosing to undertake a research degree, and which they fear is soon going to find them wanting.

In the hope of exorcising this spirit I have sometimes asked students of psychoanalytic psychotherapy, and of family therapy, to tell me about some of the most important scientific discoveries in their field. I expect these particular students to tell me about Sigmund Freud or Melanie Klein, for example, if they are psychoanalytic in approach, or about Gregory Bateson if they are systemic therapists; or to give examples of more specific recent studies in these two genres. But they do this very hesitantly. The idea is not far from their minds that whatever these giant founders of their fields may have done, it was not 'research'. They are half-convinced that there has so far been no 'research', or no 'real' research, in their fields at all, and it is the task of beginning the research that does not yet exist that they are supposed to be taking up. No wonder they are frightened!

But I ask them, as experienced family or child psychotherapists (many of these students are professionally quite experienced, and anyway their anxieties are often shared by their even more experienced clinical teachers), don't you feel that you already work from a basis of knowledge and understanding? Oh yes, they say, slightly brightening up, we do know quite a lot, of course. For example, how to recognise a change of perspective in a family dialogue, or a particular state of mind in the patient's transference-relation to the therapist. But it turns out that the concepts of double-binds or paradoxical injunctions, or the Oedipus complex or the paranoid-schizoid position, repeatedly illuminating as they may be in clinical work, are felt in some way to have nothing to do with what they imagine to be science. These clinical disciplines are half-believed, in other words, to rest on no 'researched' knowledge-base at all.

There may be some readers who will chuckle with agreement at this point – out of the mouths of babes and sucklings comes wisdom, etc. These students may be believed to have these misapprehensions for sound academic reasons. They certainly have them for sound practical reasons, since the ghosts they imagine looking over their shoulders are cousins of their colleagues in the hospitals and clinics where they work, who criticise the non-scientific basis of many psychotherapies. And they are ghostly relations also of the Health Service managers and purchasers who demand evidence to justify the expenditure of time and money that psychotherapy entails.

But I want to argue in this chapter that what underlies these anxieties is a view of the human sciences, which is both idealised and simplistic. We need, I will suggest, to think in more grounded and less abstractly prescriptive ways about scientific work if we are to make any progress in our understanding.

Some recent discoveries and their methodologies

I will proceed inductively, by looking at some examples of important recent work in human sciences that are close to the interests of psychotherapists.

The observational study of early infant–mother relationships

In the past twenty years or so, a combination of the theoretical perspective established by 'attachment theory' and observational techniques making use of video-cameras has thrown new light on the early development of infants (Holmes, 1993). It has been demonstrated that infants recognise and remember their mothers from the earliest days after birth. It has been shown that infants and mothers engage in an intricate and animated pattern of loving interaction, in which mother's voice and intonation, facial expressions, and response to her infant's first gestures and movement, engage the infant in a relationship from the beginnings of life. These processes, described by Daniel Stern as 'multi-modal attunement' (1985, 1994), Trevarthen (1979; Trevarthen et al., 1998), Brazelton (Brazelton and Cramer, 1990) and others have revealed that quite complex mental capacities exist from the start of the infant's life. (One is inclined to say, have revealed what mothers innately knew already, since how otherwise would they have performed according to these behaviour repertoires for millennia?) It is infants' engagement in relationship with a known and attentive parental figure which begins the processes of development that lead to the command of language and to a capacity to form relationships. The study of what happens when mothers are unable to respond to their infants in appropriate ways, through depression or other mental illness, has demonstrated the consequences of such deficits to infant development and is throwing some light on the onset of autistic defences and conditions.

The point here is not a substantive theoretical one, though the theoretical issues and their relevance for the psychotherapies are important. The issue here is rather one of method. These findings emerged from the recorded observation of infants and their mothers, both in specially framed 'laboratory' settings and also in neonatal wards set up to allow *in situ* observations. Discerning these patterns required the capacity to record, play back, and analyse sequences of interaction – 'slowing down', so to speak, our normal perceptions of these events, so that sequences of interaction (who does what, when, and in relation to what actions of the other partner) could be analysed.

No doubt many thousands of instances of such interactions have by now been studied, and these findings have been given additional credibility by numbers. But numbers were not, I think, the crucial issue. This discovery was more like the outcome of an experiment in a laboratory, or the discovery of a critical datum, such as a marine fossil half way up a mountain, or a cosmic event. Once a few evidently normal infants and mothers were shown to manifest these interactional patterns, at an age when these had been formerly thought not to be possible, the crucial discovery had been made. What remained was replication, or more productively the elaboration of findings to discover more elements of the interactional process, and more sources of variance.

In Rom Harré's terms (Harré 1993) these major findings emerged from investigations of an 'intensive' and not 'extensive' kind; that is, from isolating a 'pure kind' of phenomenon, and analysing some of the causal interactions involved in its construction. These are both at the micro-level (how mother's voice responds to, amplifies and begins to give meaning to the baby's), and at the macro-level (how mother's consistent failure to respond causes distress and perhaps developmental failures in baby).

Attachment research: the 'Strange Situation Test' and the 'Adult Attachment Interview'

Let us take another field of research within the attachment theory tradition (Parkes *et al.*, 1991). Mary Ainsworth, deeply influenced by John Bowlby, developed from 1969 onwards and through the 1970s the 'Strange Situation Test', in which infants of 12 months or 18 months are exposed, in a child study laboratory equipped with video recording facilities, to a limited experience of separation from and reunification with their mothers. It has proved an ingenious experiment, since the durations of the two separations (each of three minutes) is no longer than is likely to occur frequently in natural conditions, and since the infant is all the time in the company of a friendly and responsive researcher. Analysis of the recordings of these brief separations, however, proved highly illuminating. First, three distinct patterns of response of infants to this situation were discriminated and found to be reliable by independent rating of the recorded observations. Then a fourth 'type' was identified.[1] The theoretical 'lens' through which these infant responses were interpreted was provided by Bowlby's theory of attachment, separation and loss, but developed later by Mary Main and colleagues with a dimension of mental representation. Attachment to mother was conjectured to be adaptive to survival, in evolutionary terms. Separation caused anxiety and distress. But by the age of one, some measure of 'internal' attachment has normally already taken place, enabling the infant to hold his mother in mind, even in her absence, and to anticipate her return. This at any rate was deemed to be the 'normal' pattern of the securely attached infant. The other observed patterns were taken as evidence of a situation where for some reason this internalised attachment, the representation of mother in the infant's mind, had not fully taken place. The different kinds of adaptation that were observed were interpreted either as psychic defences against the anxiety of separation, or, in the most extreme case, as the manifestation of a state of extreme psychological fragility – existential panic – in the infant. These categories could be shown to map on to theories developed within child psycho-analysis – for example, in the case of avoidant attachment to Esther Bick's concept of the 'second skin' (Bick, 1968), and to Winnicott's and Bion's theories of containment. The concept of psychic 'resilience' developed by Peter Fonagy and his co-researchers (1994), and validated by the evidence of Adult Attachment and Strange Situation Test data, finds evidence in standardising and replicated procedures for phenomena of mental development earlier conjectured by Bion on the basis of his clinical investigations to depend on the earliest relationship of the infant and its parent figures.

Although the Strange Situation Test has now been replicated on many thousands of occasions, in many parts of the world, this instrument is also in essence an intensive, not an extensive one. That is to say, it isolates for investigation, under conditions of controlled observation, a particular aspect of the mother–infant relationship – what happens when a short-term separation occurs. The essential discoveries were made from quite a small number of these observations. (The Robertsons' films of young children staying in hospital unaccompanied by their parents, although in effect single case studies, had a similar effect in transforming our perceptions and understandings of what were then everyday practices, even though they involved inflicting pain and even emotional damage on young children.) Of course, it was important to replicate these studies,[2] but we need to distinguish between verification or proof, and the essential discovery which usually precedes this and indeed makes it possible. The main insights or discoveries which were made by means of the Strange Situation Test came not from its replication but from its original 'ideal typical' demonstrations. One might say that if an experiment is well-enough designed, repetition is not going to add a great deal of new understanding, though it may be only successful repetition which can confirm that the research design was indeed a good one.

However, still more remarkable findings were to follow from work in this genre. Mary Main, who had worked initially with Ainsworth, developed an additional research instrument – the Adult Attachment Interview. This involves inviting subjects to tell their life story, as a narrative structured by themselves, with minimal interruption and prompting from the researcher-interviewer. The life stories are tape recorded and transcribed. The ensuing transcript is then subjected to a form of analysis whose interest lies primarily not in the content of what is described (as defined for example in terms of trauma or emotional difficulty), but in the form the narrative is given. What is being 'read for' is the degree of coherence, and of correspondence with the self-reported facts which these biographical narratives manifest. Narratives will range from the coherent to the incoherent. They will also provide more or less factual detail, and this detail will be more or less consistent with the facts described and the attitudes expressed towards them. The narratives which give most cause for concern, from the point of view of psychological diagnosis, are those which are low on coherence, and/or where the attitudes and opinions expressed within a biographical narrative seem at greatest variance with, or give the least detailed account of, the facts described.

The theoretical framework deployed here is the idea of the mind as being more or less capable of registering and representing emotionally significant experiences. It is a deficit in the capacity to 'hold in mind' distressing experiences which is taken as a likely indicator of psychological difficulty. This model of mental representation also maps on to the psychoanalytic theory of containment, and of the developing mind, developed independently of this research by Bion in particular.

What has been extraordinary is the way in which the findings of these two independent measures – the Strange Situation Test and the Adult Attachment Interview – have been shown to correlate with one another, in blind trials, and across substantial intervals of time. Parents with adult attachment interview assessments which indicate that they have little capacity to reflect on their experiences are much more likely to have infants who manifest anxious–ambivalent behaviours in the Strange Situation Test. These correlations are unusually strong. Even if the Adult Attachment Interview and the Strange Situation Test are widely situated in time (if the AAI is undertaken before any children have been born to subjects, for example) they still 'predict' (also retrodict) accurately. The measures also discriminate between members of a parental couple. An infant's strange situation response is correlated with the 'attachment' attributes of a particular parent. That is to say, it is specific to relations with a particular person, and is not a function of parenting in general. The explanation of this correlation lies in the idea that the capacity to reflect on emotional experience is a key element in the development of relationships between a parent and his or her infant. Where they have this, infants can develop secure attachments. Where they have not, infants find attachment more difficult to achieve. This finding throws new light on the transmission of developmental difficulty through the generations, since parents subjected to a deficit of parenting, in the dimension of the capacity to process feelings, are more likely to pass on to children their own emotional deficits, whatever their conscious intentions may be. As Fonagy *et al.* (1991) have pointed out, the discovery of the importance of mind in the nurturing process throws theoretical light on the 'ghost in the nursery' phenomena first described by Selma Fraiberg (1975). This theory also identifies the need and an optimal site for preventive and/or therapeutic intervention, since it has described the preconditions of a crucial form of interaction between infants and their parents.

The methods used in this unusually successful research programme have been both 'intensive' and 'extensive'. They are intensive because the Adult Attachment Interview is a purpose-designed research instrument, requiring to be administered in conditions of 'purity'. It is the virtual equivalent, for discursive, narrative methods, of a laboratory experiment. And also because the hypothesised connection between the findings from the two instruments – the one reporting states of mind in infants, the other states of mind in their parents – depends on theoretical assumptions about the role of mental representations in making secure relationships possible, and on the 'work' that the mind needs to do to process and modulate painful feelings. The 'extensive' dimension of this research comes from the proof of empirical correlations between the findings of these two independent measures. No doubt the initial correlations, from the first small samples, must have held considerable conviction. It is unusual in the human sciences to obtain such a good fit between measures as independent of each other as these were (for example between measures identifying and predicting behaviours separated by many years), so its occurrence was an unusual event. But the research discipline of independent ratings and double-blind trials was important in establishing the reliability of these findings, not least because of the possibility that without such rigour the independence of the two measures would be compromised.

What is clear is that these discoveries depended on an original conjunction of a powerful and evolving body of ideas (the theory of attachment needs, extended and elaborated into a theory of mental representations and its prerequisites), with original and inventive quasi-experimental methods. One of these made use of the technology of video recording and the timed analysis of very short sequences of interaction. (Video technology has a role here similar to its use in the observation of mother–baby interactions.) The other method was a particular form of life-history interview, which as far as possible left respondents, not interviewers, to generate whatever narrative structure there was. And which, more particularly, made use of discriminations of sense and reference (internal coherence and correspondence to facts) in the analysis of transcripts. This procedure of analysis appears to be convergent with contemporaneous developments in the philosophy of language, with its models of different kinds of 'speech act', though it is not clear to me how far this has been an explicit methodological source for the attachment theorists.[3]

Recent developments in neuro-science

For a third example of a research methodology relevant to the concerns of psychotherapy, let us consider recent developments in neuro-science. A combination of behaviour observation, techniques for mapping and recording brain activity, and computer simulation has led to a revolution in the understanding of the brain and its functions. Gerald Edelman's 'neural Darwinism' (Edelman, 1992) outlines the hypothesis that an evolutionary process takes place in the development of each individual mind, as neural patterns are laid down as adaptive responses to experience. There is thus an organic basis for individual psychic differences. Understanding of the different organic sites and levels of brain function has enabled affectual or 'instinctual' dispositions to be identified as distinct from the less 'primitive' cognitive mental processes, but as nevertheless linked to them as ordering principles. In parallel work reported by Antonio Damasio (1994; 1999), clinical observation, directly or from a previous descriptive record, of patients known to have suffered from specific organic lesions has enabled 'natural experiments' to be conducted (analogous to those described by Oliver Sacks in many writings) in which various mental states can be correlated with their organic preconditions. The 'stratified', hierarchical model of the brain which is emerging from these studies begins to make sense of the idea of 'unconscious' fantasies and predispositions, as those mental attributes which may be laid down in the most primitive areas of the brain, in the earliest years, and which may or may not be capable of being processed through the more advanced and later-developing mental functions (Shuttleworth, 1998). Not only may there be organic correlates to basic perceptual and motor functions, as has long been known, but there may also be organic correlates to the capacity to feel, recognise and respond to others' feelings, basic requirements of becoming or remaining a social being. Damasio's reports of subjects who retained their full cognitive capacities, but had become gravely handicapped in terms of relational capacities as a result of injuries, indicate that there can be an empirical basis for understanding the relation of affectual and cognitive aspects of the mind, and for rescuing the affectual from its long years of relative neglect by psychologists.

As in the other three examples of methods given, this area of research is also largely intensive, not extensive, in its approach. Models of the neural system have gained in complexity from the earlier false starts of Artificial Intelligence, in part as a result of advances in information and computer science. Evolutionary approaches have focused on the instinctual and affective elements which human beings have in common with other species, and have called in question abstracted cognitivism. (The emotional blindness of certain kinds of rationalistic psychology aspiring to the status of a physical science was projected onto its human subject matter.) Attention to the moral and emotional repertoires of clinical subjects has enabled them to become a distinct field of study.

Many important issues are raised by this rapidly growing research field. For example, will its results lead to a recognition that the complexity of experience which the 'talking cures' have always sought to recognise has a neurological basis, and discourage scientistic reductionism and blindness to the phenomenology of experience which has characterised much psychological science? Will this work bring about an integration of psychoanalytic models of the mind (which attempts a stratified map of its development) with an understanding of the complexity of the neural system? Or will it produce a new kind of reductionism, in which each 'mental state' is inferred to be the outcome of a discrete piece of bio-chemistry, and the problem becomes not how better to understand mental states but how to target the biochemistry with smarter drugs?

Both developments seem possible, and both will no doubt be pursued as aspirations of scientific programmes. Psychotherapists will see improved neural maps as throwing light, by a kind of 'triangulation', on the capacities of mind they investigate through conversation and observation. The struggles of patients suffering from Asperger's Syndrome to make sense of the mental capacities they do not have, and to devise alternative ways of understanding intellectually what they do not understand emotionally, are illuminated by recognition that what they do not have available, or what exists only in a limited way, may correspond to a missing piece of software or hardware in the mind (Shuttleworth, 1998). At the other end of the psychiatric spectrum pharmacologists will seek to find ways of modifying mental states by 'direct' means, as in the drug therapies for attention deficit disorder or hyper-activity among children, which are now gaining ground in Britain after a long period in which drug therapies were only reluctantly employed in their psychiatric treatment. There are problems of value, as well as of verifiable effects, involved in these therapeutic choices, though there seems good reason to accept that both approaches have a legitimate place in mental healthcare.

Psychoanalysis and its research methods

I have argued elsewhere (Rustin, 1997) that psychoanalysis has always had its own distinctive research methods, and that these have been productive over a hundred years in enlarging the powers of the psychoanalytic paradigm to understand new areas of mental life. These have included new categories of patient (the development of the psychoanalysis of children, for example), and new categories of difficulty and disorder (psychosis, autism, 'borderline disorders', etc.). The methods used within psychoanalysis and psychoanalytic psychotherapy are of course distinctively 'intensive' – single cases, studied in the 'laboratory conditions' of the consulting room, in which, in the British School at least, the phenomena of the transference relationship are the main objects of investigation. Psychoanalytic 'technique' is as far as possible controlled and monitored by individual analysts, and by analysts working informally together as research groups. Clinical seminars or workshops may function in this way, the data consisting of reported case material, and comparisons between cases making it possible to recognise and explore variances between them. Holding constant as much as can be held constant is the standard rule of psychoanalytic clinical practice, not only for therapeutic reasons (patients benefit from a stable and reliable framework for psychotherapy) but also on heuristic grounds. The literature of scientific discovery in this field, that is to say the record of often-cited 'key papers' in which significant new findings or theoretical developments are reported, usually describes, using case material, the way in which an anomaly, within the terms of existing theoretical understanding, was first recognised and eventually accounted for. Thus Klein and her colleagues found, using psychoanalytic techniques based on play, evidence of unconscious fantasies among young children hitherto thought inaccessible to clinical study. It was previously thought that children did not experience such complex states of mind at this early stage of development (King and Steiner, 1991). Subsequently, within the same tradition, Paula Heimann (1950) described how she was able to gain new understanding of a patient through her reflection on the meaning of disturbing feelings in the 'countertransference' (feelings evoked in her by the patient) that she had hitherto thought of as an impediment to clinical understanding, not as a resource for it. What she had initially thought of as 'noise', a disturbance of perception emanating from her own lack of psychic equilibrium, she came to see, with the aid of the concept of projective identification, as an unconscious communication by the patient which could be recognised in the analyst's countertransference reaction. One could give innumerable other examples, both from the work of the founders of the psychoanalytic field themselves, and in more recent papers which enlarge its scope of explanation or application to a greater or lesser degree.

The evidence for the existence of such phenomena, previously unrecognised and thus not described in the literature, is normally conveyed by means of selected sequences of clinical narrative. The crucial data have been described recently in terms of 'clinical facts' (*IJP*, 1994), the nature of which has been the subject of a substantial debate. We might say, following Bruno Latour (1987), that whereas the main 'inscription device' of some physical scientists may be the report of a laboratory experiment, or the outputs of the instruments which measure this, the main 'inscription device' of psychoanalysis is the case-record, displaying variations from established types of condition or response. This method of presentation has recently been criticised, both by psychoanalysts (Spence, 1994) and by their critics, for being too abbreviated and for offering evidence in too theoretically pre-processed a form. The criticism is that in much of the psychoanalytical literature empirical observations and process material are insufficiently distinct from the theoretical inferences which are based on them.

It certainly would be illuminating to have clinical evidence more abundantly displayed, and procedures of inference demonstrated more transparently. But within the psychoanalytic research programme itself, as distinct from its dialogue with other research programmes, existing methods do seem to work effectively to generate new understanding. This is because the notation of clinical reports functions as a kind of shorthand, its brief fragments intelligible to those versed in the relevant tradition of clinical work. Its implicit references are to the work of other trained clinical practitioners, its court of appeal is to their judgements. It is of course normal in all sciences that only those qualified in a field of inquiry are expected to be competent judges of research undertaken in it (Collins and Pinch, 1993; Barnes *et al.*, 1996). As Wilfred Bion once wrote, 'I doubt if anyone but a practising psycho-analyst can understand this book although I have done my best to make it simple' (Bion, 1970).

What, one might ask, are the grounds for believing that this procedure for generating new knowledge 'works'? The evidence is the continuing evolution of ideas and clinical techniques which has taken place within the various psychoanalytic traditions, grounded almost invariably on the evidence of clinical cases. The representation of psychoanalysis, as unchanged in its essential theories and assumptions since Freud, could only be put forward by critics who have barely bothered to read anything written in this field since Freud's death.

Divergent and complementary goals in mental health practice

Here then are four genres of primary research in psychology. All of them are based on an 'intensive' method of research, their key findings often derived from studies, experiments or virtual experiments involving very small numbers of individuals. Our understanding of mother–infant relations, of the consequences of parental states of mind for their infants, of the role of emotions in the functioning of the mind and brain, and of unconscious structures of mind which give rise to mental pain and conflict, have all been, or are being, deeply affected by these researches. There is no one procedure common to all these fields of research. Research methods in each case were developed in a specific relation to a theoretical object of study. Assumptions about attachment, about the capacity mentally to process emotional experience, about the neurological origins of cognitive and emotional aspects of mind, and about aspects of mind and feeling not immediately accessible to self-understanding, in each case gave rise to an appropriate methodology. In the sciences, new conjectures and theories generally *do* lead to innovations of method, since new means are needed to 'see' or investigate hitherto unknown entities or structures. There is no one science, or scientific method, but many sciences and many scientific methods (Galison and Stump, 1996).

The division of labour between intensive and extensive methodologies is between discovery, achieved by the intensive methods of the laboratory or its consulting room equivalent, and testing and verification, achieved extensively by means of studies of large samples, such as randomised controlled trials. These latter can select good from bad theories, but do not generate the hypotheses which they test.

What are we to make, in this context, of the current demands for psychotherapeutic practice to be justified by 'scientific' evidence? There is a paradox in the origin of this demand so far as psychotherapy is concerned. Psychoanalytic and many other 'talking therapies' (that is, those which seek to work through modifying patients' or clients' self-understanding) have established themselves in Western society during the last century largely through choices made by individual patients, clients or consumers to seek out professional practitioners for themselves. It has been a treatment of choice for many individuals, partly because it has seemed less stigmatising, more private, and more respectful of individual choice and agency than many publicly provided psychiatric treatments. But of course only those who could afford to pay private practitioners could normally obtain services provided in this way.

It came to be believed that these forms of treatment would be of more general value, and that it was unreasonable to confine access to them to the upper and middle classes. And also that they could be of benefit to children, and that there would be social benefit in helping children with psychological difficulties at an early stage in their development. Thus a case was made for provision of such psychotherapies within public health systems, or in various forms of counselling within education or other services. Decisions about the availability of such treatment tended to be made by qualified professionals, who had the power to decide on treatments of choice in virtue of their authority and presumed expertise.

More recently, professionals in the health and other public services have been required to justify what they do by its empirically demonstrable results. When individuals were paying for a service, it was enough that they were willing to pay for it (though there is now a movement to register and regulate such services with institutions like the UKCP and the BCP emerging as the psychotherapy profession's representatives in these decisions). But when the taxpayer is paying, it is not enough that individuals find the services useful, or that professionals within the services do so. 'Evidence' of effectiveness is expected, although in the field of mental health there seem to be especial difficulties in collecting and assessing this.

It is something of a paradox that public services, whose object was originally to make available to wider publics forms of psychotherapy which only the privileged could pay for, are now imposing a new set of gatekeepers, acting in the name of cost-effectiveness, between the prospective consumers and the service providers. It is fortunate that these forms of psychological understanding and therapy were able to develop independently of these gatekeepers in the first place, or they might never have found space to develop.

The growth of understanding of the mind and its development and the availability of effective remedies and forms of treatment when mental health fails, are by no means the same thing. It may be true of all the fundamental discoveries described above (of infant–mother interactions, of the effects of separation and trauma over two generations, of the operations of different sites of the brain, and of the unconscious and its mechanisms) that whilst they illuminate our understanding of human nature and behaviour, they do not *ipso facto* generate means of intervention which can cure psychic ills. How can this be?

The reason is that the discoveries, made by 'intensive' means, by the study of 'pure types' of behaviour of mental functioning, are in essence theoretical or 'ideal typical' in character. They describe and explain how a 'pure type' of individual or relationship will behave in specified conditions. How one maps individuals asking for therapeutic help against such 'pure types', and what one can do to change their behaviour or mode of being in one way or another, is by no means the same as identifying these hypothetical structures or models of mind in the first place.

The fact is individuals requiring treatment are often not 'pure types' of anything, in the same way that the weather that comes across the Atlantic does not usually correspond to idealised climatic models. The practical problem in developing therapeutic interventions is to map what are discovered as 'pure' types in quasi-laboratory or experimental conditions, against the highly impure cases, shaped by many causal influences of different kinds, who walk through the door of a clinic. It is never going to be easy, in the psychological and social sciences, to find a perfect 'fit' between the ideal-typical constructions of 'science' and the actual constructions of everyday life. The primary discoveries of psychological science, in its different genres, are always liable to seem more profound and beautiful in their 'laboratory' settings than they are going to be when they are applied as therapeutic interventions in the outside world.

What clinicians have to do, not only in the mental health field but also in physical medicine, is to establish an adequate fit between the complex multi-symptom-bearing patients that come to them, and the 'pure' classifications of disorders and remedies that are established by research in their fields. Much of the 'normal science' in clinical fields consists in interpreting the variety and complexity of actual patients in terms of the repertoires of concepts, theories and techniques which may be relevant to their cases.

There is an additional reason for this discrepancy between pure models and their everyday application in the psychological sciences. In their physical biology, individuals are often happy enough to conform, or in illness to be brought back into conformity, with the norm of the heart or kidney function of an average individual of their age and physique. Why, unless one is an athlete, would one want to be exceptional or even different from this?

But in regard to their minds and social identities, persons in our culture usually have, where their powers permit, a different agenda. They are not psychologically satisfied merely to conform to a species norm. They are individuals, seeking meaning and fulfilment in relation to their specific biographies, and in the context of specific relationships (as children, parents, siblings, lovers, friends, fellow-believers) in which they are embedded and by which they have been formed.[4] Psychotherapies consist not merely of 'normalising' work, as we can say physical medicine mostly does, but also of 'identity work'.[5] Even individuals whose pain (from depression or anxiety) is so extreme that 'normalisation' (the reduction of this to tolerable levels) might seem for the present a sufficient aim, will often regain, once their pain is relieved to some degree, the aspirations of individuals with distinctive desires and goals. Reports of psychotherapeutic work with psychotic patients suggest that virtually all individuals, given the chance, will try to 'make sense' of their lives in a meaningful way, however great their distress or disintegration.

It is not just that individual 'patients' or 'prospective patients' are different from one another by virtue of the complexity of influences which shape them. (This is a normal problem in the application of all sciences, natural and human, once they step out from their laboratories into the real world of contingencies.) Persons also have an inbuilt and innate *will* to be different, to live and understand their lives in individual ways. Even if individuals may be shown to aspire to similar kinds of fulfilment within their life-cycles it is the nature of human beings in our culture, and to a degree in *every* culture, that they desire to do this in their own particular fashion. To this degree, no two psychotherapeutic interventions can be the same, and if they are there is probably something deficient in them. One of the main attractions of psychotherapy for its practitioners is that it allows them to become specialists in individuality, and in the particularity of relationships, both their own and other people's.

A major difference between the orientation of psychiatrists and psychotherapists is the priority that they are trained to give to these different goals – normalisation, by reference to standard diagnostic classifications of mental health and ill-health, for the psychiatric profession, and the elaboration of individual meanings, sense of self, and purposes, among psychotherapists. Each has its necessary function in the mental health field.

The more serious the mental illness, the stronger the grounds are likely to be for standardised procedures intended principally to reduce suffering and to restore a modicum of normal functioning. So painful are many forms of mental illness to its sufferers, and to those in contact with them, that interventions which achieve improvements are of course essential. Their cost, often recognised as such by patients themselves, is in the loss of personal autonomy that is involved in dependence on drugs, or on still more drastic physical interventions. Where mental ill-health is not entirely disabling, or where a measure of normal functioning is restored, a different agenda of self-reflection and self-control re-emerges. The appeal of the psychotherapies, to clients and professionals alike, rests on their consistency with cultural ideals of self-understanding and freedom of the will.

This is not an argument against the desirability or possibility of 'evidence-based psychotherapy', but only for the recognition that its scope is likely to be limited. Because the goals of psychotherapy are inevitably, or at least desirably, set by the patient as well as by the therapist, therapeutic outcomes and their appropriate measures are difficult to standardise. There is every reason to be as specific as one can be in monitoring forms of treatment, from initial diagnosis to long-term output, and there is no reason to be fearful about such procedures. But the difficulty of matching 'ideal typical' diagnoses with presenting cases, and of even deciding upon the value-added achieved by a treatment programme given its many possible consequences, makes one cautious about what can be expected from such measures.

A concluding example: methodological pluralism in practice

I will conclude with an example of some good practice in the sphere of evidence-based psychotherapeutic intervention. Sometimes it does prove possible to categorise patients productively in relation to an 'ideal typical' configuration, established within a definite theoretical framework, and to develop interventions based on these explanatory ideas.

Take the example of mothers whose depression after the birth of their infants is interfering with their capacity to care for their babies. There will be many factors in a situation which will affect whether and to what degree a mother is depressed, whether she can accept and benefit from therapeutic help, and whether she can stay out of depression once an intervention has ended. Some of these causes will lie in the previous generation of parenting and identify the relevance of preventive intervention in one generation intended to help the next. But for all the possible differences, this field of post-partum maternal depression is one where some good 'evidence-based' therapeutic interventions have been developed by Lynne Murray (1998) and her colleagues in the Winnicott Research Centre now at Reading University. These interventions have shown that counselling which promotes the sharing and understanding of emotional states is usually beneficial to mothers and their babies, and also that this function can be incorporated within the normal role of health visitors who have routine contact with mothers of newborns. This is one example of the successful application of theoretical insights derived both from attachment theory and psychoanalytic ideas. What such interventions make possible is the resumption of a normal developmental process in which the uniqueness of the relationship between mother and infant can be enjoyed.

It is worth noting, however, that this intervention was based on psychological understandings gained of 'pure' or ideal-typical configurations, informed by psychoanalytic understanding of early relationships as well as by their laboratory observation.

It was only once these primary understandings had been gained that it seems to have been possible to devise procedures in which their usefulness could be tested, as they now have been, in these practical ways.

Notes

1 The four types are: secure (type B), avoidant (type A), anger and passivity (type C) and disorganised-ambivalent (type D).

2 Longitudinal studies of birth cohorts subsequently revealed that children who had been exposed to hospitalisation was a factor increasing their risk of later developmental difficulties.

3 Analysis of narratives which depends on measures of coherence is also the central methodological principle of the socio-biographical method developed by Gabriele Rosenthal and followed in the Social Strategies in Risk Society research project at the University of East London and elsewhere.

   Both these methods of analysis of text can be seen as reflections or effects of the broader 'linguistic turn' in the social sciences over the past two or three decades, in which the philosophy of Wittgenstein, Austin, Searle and others has had profound effects. There have been comparable developments in Francophone social science, whose agenda has been dominated since the war by different kinds of cultural interpretation, in 'structuralist' (Saussure,

Lévi-Strauss), 'action-oriented' (Touraine, Bourdieu) and post-structuralist (Lacan, Foucault, Derrida) forms.

4   The fundamental importance of meaning and interpretation in psychological science is described by Charles Taylor (1985). The centrality of the 'interpretive' self in Western culture is explored in Taylor (1989).

5   Where the 'medical model' in psychiatry sought to impose normalising ideas derived from physical medicine onto the mind, 'holistic' and alternative medicines attempt a move in the reverse direction, asking that physical medicines themselves become 'person-sensitive' or 'identity-related'.

References

Barnes, B., Bloor, D. and Henry, J. (1996) *Scientific Knowledge: A Sociological Analysis*. London: Athlone.

Bick, E. (1968) 'The experience of the skin in early object-relations', *International Journal of Psychoanalysis* 49.

Bion, W.R. (1970) *Attention and Interpretation*. London: Tavistock Publications.

Brazelton, T.B. and Cramer, B.G. (1990) *The Earliest Relationship*. Reading, Mass: Addison-Wesley.

Collins, H.J. and Pinch, T. (1993) *The Golem: What Everyone Should Know About Science*. Cambridge: Cambridge University Press.

Damasio, A. (1994) *Descartes' Error*. New York: Grosset/Putnam.

Damasio, A. (2000) *The Feeling of What Happens: Body, Emotion and the Making of Consciousness*. London: Heinemann.

Edelman, G. (1992) *Bright Air, Brilliant Fire*. New York: Basic Books.

Fonagy, P., Steele, M. and Steele, H. (1991) Maternal representations during pregnancy predict the organisation of mother–infant attachment at one year of age. *Child Development* 62: 891–905.

Fonagy, P., Steele, M., Steele, H., Higgitt, A. and Target, M. (1994) 'The theory and practice of resilience', *Journal of Child Psychology and Psychiatry* 35 (2).

Fraiberg, S.H., Adelson, E. and Shapiro, V. (1975) 'Ghosts in the nursery: a psychoanalytic approach to the problems of impaired infant–mother relationships', *Journal of the American Academy of Child Psychology* 14.

Galison, P. and Stump, D.J. (eds) (1996) *The Disunity of Science*. Stanford: Stanford University Press.

Harré, R. (1993) *Social Being*. Oxford: Blackwell.

Heimann, P. (1950) 'On counter-transference', *International Journal of Psychoanalysis* 31 (1/2).

Holmes, J. (1993) *John Bowlby and Attachment Theory*. London: Routledge.

International Journal of Psycho-Analysis (*IJP*) (1994) 'The conceptualisation and communication of clinical facts in psychoanalysis', 75 (5/6). (Special 75th Anniversary edition.)

King, P. and Steiner, R. (1991) *The Freud–Klein Controversies 1941–45*. London: Routledge/Institute of Psychoanalysis.

Latour, B. (1987) *Science in Action*. Cambridge, Mass.: Harvard University Press.

Murray, L. (1998) 'The early mother–infant relationship and child development: a research perspective', *Infant Observation* 1 (1).

Parkes, C.M., Stevenson-Hinde, J. and Marris, P. (eds) (1991) *Attachment Across the Life-Cycle*. London: Routledge.

Rustin, M.J. (1997) 'The generation of psychoanalytical knowledge: sociological and clinical perspectives Part 1: Give me a consulting room', *British Journal of Psychotherapy* 13 (4).

Rustin, M.J. (1998) 'What do we see in the nursery? Infant observation as 'laboratory work', *Infant Observation* 1 (1).

Shuttleworth, J. (1998) 'Theories of mental development', *Infant Observation* 1 (2).

Spence, D.P. (1994) 'The special nature of psychoanalytic facts', *International Journal of Psychoanalysis* 75 (5/6).

Stern, D.N. (1985) *The Interpersonal World of the Infant: A View from Psychoanalysis and Developmental Psychology*. New York: Basic Books.

Stern, D.N. (1994) *The Motherhood Constellation: A Unified View of Parent–Infant Psychotherapy*. New York: Basic Books.

Taylor, C. (1985) *Human Agency and Language: Philosophical Papers Vol. 1*. Cambridge: Cambridge University Press.

Taylor, C. (1989) *Sources of the Self: The Making of Modern Identity*. Cambridge: Cambridge University Press.

Trevarthen, C. (1979) 'Communication and cooperation in early infancy: a description of primary intersubjectivity', in Bullowa, M. (ed.) *Development of Communication: Social and Pragmatic Factors in Language Acquisition*. Chichester: Wiley.

Trevarthen, C., Aitken, K., Papoudi, D. and Roberts, J. (1998) *Children with Autism* (second edition). London: Jessica Kingsley.

Chapter 4

Randomised controlled trials

The gold standard?

Simon Wessely

Previous contributions (Chapters 1 and 2) have addressed the question 'what is evidence?' in the broadest sense. Originally my presentation at the meeting which forms the basis of this book was concerned solely with the problem of assessing treatment efficacy and the role of the randomised controlled trial, but before doing so it is instructive to continue the theme of evidence in a wider sense, and indeed to refer specifically, as do the previous contributions, to matters arising when one is asked to give evidence in a legal context.

When we do that, it is interesting that we are usually asked to answer a specific question. Putting aside the type of questions asked of forensic psychiatrists (and I am no longer one), which is usually on the lines of 'why did A do B?', many psychiatrists usually give evidence in personal injury cases, in which case we are asked 'did A cause B?' And if we are honest, we often conclude 'a bit', which is why lawyers hate us, as indeed Chapter 2 confirms.

I start with the nature of evidence about causation and the problem of uncertainty already highlighted. The question that plaintiffs, lawyers and others ask is 'did my road accident cause my illness?', or 'was it stress at work that gave me ME?' And these are important questions. If the answer is 51 per cent, the case is won and compensation follows, but if the answer is 49 per cent, then the case is lost and all of us have to pick up the legal aid bill. That 2 per cent is important to the patient and to the lawyer.

But psychiatric causation is never that simple. Psychiatric diagnoses are descriptive not aetiological. Psychiatric diagnoses do not tell you why that illness happened; they tell you about its symptoms, about what may happen to the patient and perhaps to what treatments they may respond, which I will come to. But they do not tell you why they are ill, with one possible exception. In the whole of ICD-10 there is only one diagnosis that is aetiological – post-traumatic stress disorder (PTSD), which is why it is such an uncomfortable, difficult and in many respects unsatisfactory diagnosis because it breaks all the other rules of causation in psychiatry.

PTSD was created as a conscious effort to atone for the sins of Vietnam (Scott, 1990). It was not created on the basis of epidemiological surveys, or serendipitous inquiry. It was created for a purpose and the research to support it followed it. The research that we cite to support the concept of PTSD came after PTSD was created.

In reality, we know that people develop illnesses after trauma for all sorts of reasons because of who they are, because of their genetic background, their life experiences, their childhood, their social support, other life situations, what happened to them afterwards, their families and many other reasons. Trauma is a piece of this jigsaw, but it is not the whole picture.

So, there is little difference between depression that occurs after a life event and PTSD after trauma, except that in the latter we assume unifactorial aetiology. This happens most particularly when we give evidence in court, because that is what the lawyers want. That is also why lawyers and psychiatrists come to grief, because we have completely different rules of evidence. In science and epidemiology we sometimes use the Bradford Hill criteria, which gives us the rules by which either exposure or event A is the cause of illness B.

Having said that, I do have colleagues who are able to look at the judge and say with a straight face: 'in my expert opinion the accident caused 20 per cent of this person's disability – not 10 per cent or 30 per cent, but 20 per cent', and that is what lawyers like to hear. This is nonsense, but we all do it.

Evidence and treatment

When we talk about evidence we should remember there are all sorts of types of evidence. There is evidence that we use when we try and talk about causation, and evidence that we use when we decide what treatment we should give our patients.

An outsider might expect that in our profession we should by now be in a position to answer with considerable accuracy most questions about what treatments work for which of our patients. We have been doing the kind of things that we do for long enough. With the exception of atypical antipsychotics there haven't been any new treatments in psychiatry for at least 20 or 30 years. So by now we should be able to say, 'Yes, treatment X works, but for God's sake don't use treatment Y'. But we can't. We have precious little evidence on which to base this most fundamental decision of all, which is how to treat our patients.

But before I can address the question of what evidence we need, one must first consider the question of whether we need any evidence at all.

Do we need evidence at all?

Do we need evidence? There are those who have argued that what we do in psychiatry or psychotherapy is simply not amenable to be answered by questions about evidence. However, this is not a view I share. We need evidence, and our patients require us to have that evidence, as much as any person practising in any discipline that claims to be able to help people.

Let me quote an extract from the magazine *Hospital Doctor*, written by the editor, who is also a doctor (Anon., 1990). It is about the Bristol Cancer Centre Study (Bagenal *et al.* 1990), which caused such a furore a few years ago:

> At the end of the day it is the faith of those NHS doctors mostly closely involved with the work of the Cancer Centre . . . which provides us with the most meaningful statistic of all. That when both patients and their doctors can testify to the intrinsic worth of something they are unlikely to be proved wrong.

I am afraid this is untrue. Doctors almost invariably believe that what they are doing is right for the patient, or they wouldn't be doing it. Therapists, who are perhaps more reflective than some doctors, usually believe they are right as well. Both doctors and therapists are well-meaning people who believe they do their best and that what they do is reasonably successful. They couldn't work otherwise. And usually they are right, because most illnesses, especially the ones we see, usually do improve. If not, they at least wax and wane, to give the illusion of improvement – like depression or asthma. Patients come to see us when they are at their worst and providing you don't mess things up they are likely to improve anyway – this is called 'regression to the mean' or the 'physician's friend'. From the patients' perspective providing they meet a doctor or therapist who is nice, courteous and respectful things are not normally too bad. Most patients report good outcomes because they may have got better anyway, and because they like their doctor or therapist.

Let me use another example, one which draws on my passion for something called chronic fatigue syndrome (CFS), otherwise known in the press as ME. We recently carried out a randomised controlled trial of cognitive-behaviour therapy (CBT) for CFS, which we compared with relaxation (Deale *et al.*, 1997). We used relaxation because we wanted to control for the general effects of therapists' time, being nice to patients and giving them an explanation for their symptoms – sometimes called the non-specific effects of treatment. And it proved very popular – hardly anyone dropped out of relaxation, and the patient satisfaction ratings were high. Except for one small thing, which was that it didn't work. At least it didn't work in the way we wanted it to work, which was to help patients over their fatigue, their functional disability, and perhaps help them get back to work. Relaxation was not very good at all in achieving this, unlike CBT. Patient satisfaction is not a good outcome measure. It does not tell you whether your treatment is doing what you claim it will do.

Let me give you another example. We are still in the world of chronic fatigue syndrome, but this time under its earlier label of neurasthenia (Wessely *et al.*, 1998b). I want to introduce a man named Willie Lane. He was a Barts surgeon at the beginning of the century. Willie Lane used to treat patients with neurasthenia. He had a flourishing private practice. He also had a theory. His theory was that the products of the colon leak through the colonic wall into the body and bloodstream, and it is these toxic products that made his patients ill. It was called autointoxication (Lane, 1921). This was Willie Lane's big idea. Like all ideas it is not intrinsically bad, and indeed it survives to this day in colonic lavage clinics still frequented by some of the good and the great. Unfortunately Willie Lane was a surgeon, and surgeons then (and now) have an almost irresistible desire to take soft organs out of depressed women. Willie probably did at least 1,500 colectomies for neurasthenic women, and it nearly always was women. And it worked. Some of them got better, and one can find accounts by women who lost their colons and said that since then they have never felt better. But the operative mortality of colectomies was then 10 per cent. Ten per cent of these women with neurasthenia, most of whom we would now called anxious or depressed, died. It didn't do any harm to Willie Lane. He became Sir Arbuthnot Lane, Surgeon to the King, and to his dying day he continually reaffirmed the doctrine of autointoxication and the need to perform colectomies.

So why a clinical trial?

In our own time doctors still cling to treatments. If we had not done clinical trials we would still be giving insulin coma to schizophrenics. Those of you who were medically trained in my time will remember being house officers, and the standard treatment for septicaemic shock. This was high dose steroids. We now know, because of randomised controlled trials, that more people die when you give them steroids than when you don't.

Likewise, at the time I qualified the treatment of cerebral malaria was high dose steroids, except that trials showed that, too, killed more people than it cured. After my house jobs I worked as a senior house officer on Coronary Care. We used to give a drug called lignocaine, which is a local anaesthetic agent, to people whose ECGs showed plenty of ventricular ectopics. It had to be given slowly, I recall, but it did work, since it suppressed the ventricular ectopics, which was thought to be a good thing. Except it wasn't. Again the trials showed that more people died from being given lignocaine than those not receiving it. How could that have been shown except by a clinical trial with random allocation of treatment? Let's say that one of my patients, to whom I had just given lignocaine, went and died. As a true believer in lignocaine I would say: 'Well, not surprising, since this is a coronary care unit, people here have had heart attacks, and lots do die.' I could have gone on for years in the same way. It is only in a randomised trial that you can actually spot the fact that your treatment may be doing more harm than good.

Let us turn to the fields of psychiatry and psychotherapy. At the moment, the management of victims of disasters is a big thing. Whenever disaster strikes the call goes out for the trained counsellors. They perform what has become known as 'psychological debriefing', or 'critical incident stress debriefing', usually a single session, which can be delivered in an individual or group format. And it seems to be very sensible. What harm could possibly come from talking to someone who has been exposed to a trauma? 'Better out than in' my mother used to say. Who could possibly think this is not a good idea? Very few, judging by the number of indications for stress debriefing – I have found over 56 different scenarios in which stress debriefing is used or advocated.

Yet there are now nine randomised controlled trials of stress debriefing to the victims of accidents – accessible in the Cochrane Library and regularly updated (Wessely *et al.*, 1998a). These studies are all remarkably similar – it doesn't work. It doesn't prevent post-traumatic stress disorder, nor does it reduce distress. Indeed, the biggest and longest trial showed the opposite – a statistically significant increase in the rate of PTSD at one year in those who received debriefing (Bisson *et al.*, 1997). Armed with that information we can all come up with lots of explanations of why it may not work, and why it might make you worse. Perhaps it is the medicalisation of distress, or maybe the intervention interferes with the normal processes of healing and prevents people from using their own social networks, or perhaps it actually increases the expectancy of psychiatric distress. Who knows? But my point is that without those trials we would still all be giving debriefing happily enough, safe in the knowledge that regression to the mean will ensure that most get better anyway, and that those that don't – well, they were indeed exposed to something nasty so perhaps they were going to get PTSD whatever we did.

And it is worse than that, because in some parts of this country, and in Australia as well, some people are given compulsory debriefing. People who work in banks and are involved in armed robberies often get compulsory debriefing the next day. In some police authorities there is compulsory debriefing for all officers involved in firearms incidents. One reason why some organisations are so keen on debriefing is to reduce the risk of litigation afterwards. A Chief Constable may believe that he is less likely to be sued when one of his officers developed PTSD if he insisted that they receive debriefing. It will be interesting to watch the first case of an officer suing because he or she received debriefing.

So now, armed with the evidence of the trials, we can start to express some scepticism about the role of debriefing. But if you had said this a few years ago nobody would have believed you. Debriefing is very popular, almost a social movement, and unless and until someone started to publish randomised controlled trials it would have been impossible to mount such a debate.

Please note I am not suggesting we should not treat the victims of trauma; but we must do so only in the knowledge of who actually is a victim, who is going to get sick unless they are treated, and what is the correct treatment. It seems to me, watching the literature, that the most successful interventions are those that are targeted only at those with clear-cut psychological distress, and in which the intervention lasts for several sessions and follows standard cognitive-behavioural principles, when given by an appropriately trained professional (André *et al.*, 1997; Bryant *et al.*, 1998).

So trials have the potential to tell us things that are difficult, unpopular and unexpected (Tyrell *et al.*, 1999). They sometimes tell us that what we are doing is not as good as we think it is. And that is uncomfortable for all of us. Trials can challenge conventional wisdom. For example, one of the earliest clinical trials ever undertaken took place in 1939 and involved delinquent boys. They were randomly allocated to two treatments by a straight toss of the coin (a method which would now be frowned upon). Active treatment sounded absolutely great – counselling, tuition, camps, boy scouts, community programmes, and so on. All the poor controls got was an interview with a psychologist.

Thirty years later Jean McCord followed them up to see what had happened to them (McCord, 1978). The intervention didn't prevent juvenile delinquency, or criminality – but perhaps that was asking too much. But the two groups did indeed differ. One group was more likely to be alcoholic, less likely to have got skilled jobs, more likely to report stress, and so on. However, those with the worse outcome were those who had received the active programme. Once again, there was difficulty in getting these unpopular results published, and some suggested that McCord had somehow got the codes the wrong way round. She hadn't.

If we need trials, why do they have to be randomised?

Randomised controlled trials are the best way to really know if my treatment does more good than harm. But why? Why is randomisation so important? Because randomisation is the only way of dealing with what we call confounding (Kleijnen *et al.*, 1997). Confounding is an alternative explanation. There are many famous examples of confounding. When the Samaritans opened offices in many towns in Great Britain the suicide rate fell, often quite dramatically. But what happened where there was no Samaritan branch? The suicide rate fell equally in both those towns with branches of the Samaritans and those without (Jennings *et al.*, 1978; see Figure 4.1).

The reason is that the confounder was the change from coal to natural gas. A confounder is something that happened at the same time as the intervention we are interested in (in this case the Samaritans) and also affected the outcome we are monitoring (the suicide rate). Hence the switch to natural gas confounded the observed association between the Samaritans setting up shop and the suicide rate falling.

Randomisation deals with confounders by ensuring that they are distributed between the two groups in an unbiased fashion. Because we need to ensure that those who make up our comparison group (i.e., those that we compare our treatment with) are the same in terms of prognosis and treatment responsiveness as those who receive the treatment. Clearly if those who are the controls are in some way different it is not a fair test of our treatment. And the only claim, the special claim, the unique claim that can be made for randomisation is that it ensures that allocation to treatment is unbiased in respect of prognosis and responsiveness to treatment. No other way exists of doing that with any certainty – only randomisation (Kleijnen *et al.*, 1997).

There are short cuts. You can try things like matching. However, you can only match on a small number of variables – anyone who has actually done research will know just how difficult it is to match on anything more

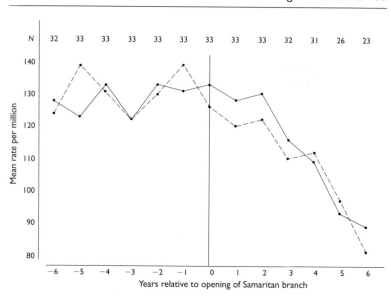

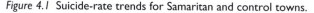

Figure 4.1 Suicide-rate trends for Samaritan and control towns.

Key: •——•, Samaritan towns; • - - - •, control towns

Source: After Jennings *et al.* (1978), published with permission of *Psychological Medicine*.

than gender or age. Second, you can only match for things that you think about at the time. You can't match for things that you forget, or that your referees point out later. You can't match for prognostic factors that you simply don't know about, and there are plenty of those. Indeed, when we talk about treatment response, there are probably more things we don't know than we do know. Randomisation, then, is the only way of ensuring that things that we don't know or can't measure are distributed in an unbiased fashion between the groups.

What happens when we don't randomise? The answer is that we are more likely to come up with the wrong answer. The late Tom Chalmers was one of the first to point out the many ways in which non-randomised evidence could provide insidious, and not so insidious, biases. For example, he and his colleagues reviewed trials of anticoagulation after heart attacks (Chalmers *et al.*, 1977). They looked at what actually happened to the controls, and showed that regardless of the treatment the controls themselves had a much higher case mortality rate. In other words the controls had a worse prognosis from the start, presumably because in some way non-randomly chosen controls tend to be sicker than those who get the new treatment. In a series of papers he confirmed that non-randomised trials were considerably more likely to give more positive results than randomised ones, and that this was because the controls tended to have more poor prognostic factors. Tom Chalmers later compared the results of randomised controlled trials with trials that used historical controls (Sacks *et al.*, 1982). A historical control is when you take 100 patients who had the old treatment and then compare them with the next 100 who had the new treatment. Of the studies that compared the new treatment with the historical control, 80 per cent of them reported that the new treatment worked, whereas only 20 per cent of those that used a randomised design found any advantage to the new treatment.

Others went on to look at how randomisation was performed, and in particular how easy it was for the researchers to cheat, whether unconsciously or consciously. One of the ways in which randomised control trials can be compromised, and indeed the reason that they usually are, is actually at the moment of randomisation, known as allocation concealment. Some trials allocate patients to the different treatments by methods in which it is possible to influence the decision. These might be coin tossing, alternate numbers or envelopes that you can hold up to the light and see what is in them. I can recall an occasion when a trial was being run, and the nurses on the unit had the task of opening the envelope to decide which treatment should be given. However, one of the senior nurses was convinced that the treatment was a bad idea. She used to open the envelopes, have a look, and if the person was randomised to the treatment and looked sick she made sure the patient was excluded.

Ken Schulz and his colleagues published a paper looking at how allocation concealment influenced the results (Schultz *et al.*, 1995). In studies where it was possible to influence the allocation, the results were four times more likely to be positive than those in which it was not possible. If you didn't randomise at all, then nearly all the studies were positive. Instead, nowadays we go for methods such as random numbers, telephone or computer allocation where the person running the trial really can't influence the decision – in other words can't cheat. The Schulz paper could mean that when doctors do trials with non-random assignment, or alternatively a design where it is possible to cheat, they are for some bizarre reason dealing with treatments that are more powerful and are more likely to work. That seems totally implausible. Instead what it does mean is that forms of assessing treatment are amenable to bias, the better the study design, the more likely it is that you are getting a true reflection of the effects of your treatment and less likely that you are getting a biased result due to other factors.

There are cases where clearly you don't need to do any of this. You would not do a trial of defibrillation for cardiac arrest, or penicillin for bacterial meningitis. In situations where the natural history of the illness is known, inevitable and deadly, you would never do a randomised trial. But I submit that in psychiatry there are no such examples. We are by definition dealing with illnesses which are not like that. Our kind of problems are not automatically fatal, where the kind of treatment effects we are looking for are probably quite subtle. This in itself gives us another reason for doing clinical trials. Mental disorder and psychological distress is very common and very debilitating. Cardiologists think it worth while to do trials on 20,000 people in order to demonstrate a 10 per cent decrease in mortality. If we could show that a new treatment in psychiatry was 10 per cent better than the old, then because our illnesses are so common, we could easily justify the expense of a trial to prove that. But we don't. Instead, most of our trials are pathetically small.

It is because of the size problem that clinical trials in psychiatry have not had the impact in changing practice that they should. That is not the fault of trials, this is our fault. For example, there is a debate about the relative merits of old versus new drugs – the tricyclics versus the Selective Serotonin Reuptake Inhibitors (SSRIs). My colleague Matthew Hotopf did a study and looked at 130 trials comparing SSRIs and old antidepressants (Hotopf *et al.*, 1997). What he said was this: let us say for the sake of argument that SSRIs are a perfect treatment (i.e., they get a 100 per cent response rate). In other words they are greatest thing since sliced bread and a revolution in psychiatry. How many of those 130 trials could have picked this up? Only half could have done. Half of them couldn't even have shown the new drug was perfect. Then he said: 'Let's be more realistic; let's say the new drug is 20 per cent better than the old.' This would still be a seriously good improvement, and an advance well worth knowing about. How many trials could pick up a 20 per cent difference? The answer was one out of 130. Again, the fault is not that of the clinical trial, the fault is ours in performing small trials that cannot answer the questions that we want them to answer.

Do trials tell me anything about my patients?

Another criticism of clinical trials is that they are non-representative. They only take place in perfect patients who only exist in places like Oxford. Hence the results are not realistic. The kind of patients who take part in clinical trials are simply not those out there. In the real world patients have multiple problems, complex disorders, often drink and usually do not comply with treatment. Those who sponsor trials often make them impossibly complex as well (Yusuf, 1999). I once started a trial of an antidepressant in physical illness and the sponsors were so petrified that someone might die during the course of the trial that the exclusion criteria for the trial excluded nearly every known physical illness. Not surprisingly, we never recruited enough patients.

This issue of generalisation – that patients that are in trials are not representative of real life – is a very valid point (Licht *et al.*, 1997; McKee *et al.*, 1999). But again it is not a criticism of trials, but of us. We do not do the proper big, pragmatic trials that would really answer questions that we want to ask (Hotopf *et al.*, 1999). Instead, we do small trials on atypical patients seen in specialist care. True, the results don't really inform our practice; but there is nothing wrong with the RCT methodology, it is the way we apply it.

It is also not easy to do trials because of the emphasis on informed consent we now have, which is gradually strangling the representiveness of clinical trials (Chalmers and Lindley, in press). Here of course I am writing something that will be anathema in some quarters. But at present we have the ludicrous situation where the doctor or therapist can carry out just about any treatment he or she chooses, so long as he or she doesn't actually sleep with the patients. The mistake is to admit uncertainty and wanting to do something about it. When the doctor actually admits being uncertain, and attempts a clinical trial in order really to find out what is the best thing to do for the patient, then the trouble can start. Provided I give the same treatment to all my patients, I am rarely subject to any critical scrutiny, but should I decide to give the same treatment to 50% of them, the world seems full of people telling me why this is impossible, impractical, undesirable or unethical (Chalmers and Lindley, in press).

I draw attention to the problems surgeons such as Hedley Atkins and Michael Baum have encountered with their seminal trials of breast cancer treatment. As surgeons they could have gone on doing radical mastectomies for their entire careers, and no one would have said anything. Only when surgeons started to allocate patients to lumpectomies or mastectomies randomly were they accused of using patients as guinea pigs, and so on. No matter that these trials ended the widespread and inappropriate use of radical mastectomies (Early Breast Cancer Trials Group, 1995).

Other people say that randomised trials are fine for new drugs, or surgery, but not for my clinical practice as a psychotherapist. My treatment, my therapy, perhaps it may not work as well as I claim, but it couldn't possibly do any harm, could it? But, again, nonsense. The only treatments that can't do harm are those that don't involve any treatment at all. Show me a truly harmless treatment and I suggest you are looking at an ineffective one. The question is not 'Could my treatment do harm?'; all effective treatments have the potential to do harm. The question is simply, 'Does my treatment do more good than harm?' We don't stop doing things because they have side effects. We take an informed judgement about the balance of those side effects. Is the treatment worth while? I do not know a treatment that is both effective and has no capacity whatsoever to do harm – and that certainly does not apply to psychotherapy, as the readers of this volume will know well. Randomisation is the only way in which you can disentangle the side effects of treatment from those of the illness itself.

And finally people say that RCTs are no good because my treatment is too individual. Each patient is so different that there is nothing that I can do, there is no inference I can make from the treatment of one patient to apply to the other. It is true that all treatments have individual aspects unique to that particular person and those cannot be addressed in a randomised controlled trial or indeed any evaluation. But all treatments must also have something in common which can be assessed. If that were not the case then what is the purpose of training? What is the purpose of jumping through all the hurdles and hoops that our professions force upon us if it was not to acquire some specific skill that we bring to patients when we use a certain set of rules and assumptions when dealing with specific disorders and specific problems – and that we can test. It is indeed easier to test an antidepressant, but it is not conceptually different if we are talking about a non-drug therapy, where we are talking about testing the common elements of our treatment which must be there.

In saying this I realise I am preaching to the converted, since the record of our disciplines in assessing what we do is honourable. It is rare now to find a voice that genuinely disagrees with the need to justify what we do, and the need to provide evidence better than the purely anecdotal. Indeed, psychologists are at the forefront of developing new ways of carrying out clinical trials, such as the patient preference method (Brewin and Bradley, 1989), and it was psychologists who pioneered modern methods of research synthesis and first used the term 'meta analysis' (Glass, 1976).

Trials and clinical freedom

Another criticism is that trials spell the end of clinical freedom. To some extent this is true. But is this a criticism? We shouldn't have the freedom to take out the colons of anxious or depressed women just because we think it is a good thing. We should not have clinical freedom to do everything we please simply because I am doctor and I know best. The public expect to be protected from Willie Lane, and rightly so.

There are limitations to randomised controlled trials, and particularly the emphasis on overall results as opposed to individual outcomes. They can't differentiate necessarily between the wide variations that occur in practice, but they can tell you overall whether treatment does more harm than good. And as we try and construct a health service in which resources are allocated fairly, and in which patients are not given treatments that are more likely to do them harm, then we have to rely on evidence of clinical trials. There are many other ways of assessing treatments, and many valid designs other than the randomised controlled trial. However, the hierarchy of evidence that we teach to medical students that places the evidence from randomised trials at the top of the pyramid, because it provides evidence that is least likely to be contaminated by bias, has never been seriously challenged.

So I conclude, then, that it is not for those of us who do clinical trials to justify what we do. I think it is the other way round. It is for those who do not do clinical trials to justify why they don't.

Acknowledgements

I thank Sir Iain Chalmers for commenting on the manuscript and Stirling Moorey for assisting in altering a talk to a chapter.

References

André, C., Lelord, F., Legeron, P., Reignier, A. and Delattre, A. (1997) 'Étude contrôlée sur l'efficacité à 6 mois d'une prise en charge précoce de 132 conducteurs d'autobus victimes d'agression', *L'encephale* 23: 65–71.

Anon. (1990) 'Flawed study's mixed effects', *Hospital Doctor*, 18 Oct.

Bagenal, F., Easton, D., Harris, E., Chilvers, C. and McElwain, T. (1990) 'Survival of patients with breast cancer attending Bristol Cancer Help Centre', *Lancet* 336: 606–610.

Bisson, J., Jenkins, P., Alexander, J. and Bannister, C. (1997) 'Randomised controlled trial of psychological debriefing for victims of acute burn trauma', *British Journal of Psychiatry* 171: 78–81.

Brewin, C. and Bradley, C. (1989) 'Patient preferences and randomised clinical trials', *British Medical Journal* 299: 313–315.

Bryant, R., Harvey, A., Dang, S. and Sackville, T. (1998) 'Treatment of acute stress disorder: a comparison of cognitive-behavioral therapy and supportive counselling', *Journal of Consulting and Clinical Psychology* 66: 862–866.

Chalmers, I. and Lindley, R. (in press) 'Double standards on informed consent to treatment: ignored for a quarter of a century by most professional medical ethicists', in Doyal, L. and Tobias, J. (eds) *Informed Consent: Respecting Patients' Rights in Research, Teaching and Practice*. London: BMJ Publications.

Chalmers, T., Matta, R., Smith, J. and Kunzler, A. (1977) 'Evidence favouring the use of anticoagulants in the hospital phase of acute myocardial infarction', *New England Journal of Medicine* 297: 1091–1096.

Deale, A., Chalder, T., Marks, I. and Wessely, S. (1997) 'A randomised controlled trial of cognitive behaviour versus relaxation therapy for chronic fatigue syndrome', *American Journal of Psychiatry* 154: 408–414.

Early Breast Cancer Trials Group (1995) 'Effects of radiotherapy and surgery in early breast cancer: an overview of randomised controlled trials', *New England Journal of Medicine* 333: 1444–1445.

Glass, G. (1976) 'Primary, secondary, and meta-analysis of research', *Educational Research* 5: 3–8.

Hotopf, M., Churchill, R. and Lewis, G. (1999) 'Pragmatic randomised controlled trials in psychiatry', *British Journal of Psychiatry* 187: 217–223.

Hotopf, M., Lewis, G. and Normand, C. (1997) 'Putting trials on trial: the costs and consequences of small trials in depression – a systematic review of methodology', *Journal of Epidemiology and Community Health* 51: 354–358.

Jennings, C., Barraclough, B. and Moss, J.R. (1978) 'Have the Samaritans lowered the suicide rate?', *Psychological Medicine* 8: 413–422.

Kleijnen, J., Gotzsche, P., Kunz, R., Oxman, A. and Chalmers, I. (1997) 'So what's so special about randomisation?', in Maynard, A. and Chalmers, I. (eds) *Non-random Reflections on Health Services Research*. London: BMJ Publications.

Lane, A. (1921) 'Reflections on the evolution of disease', *Lancet* ii: 1117–1123.

Licht, R., Gouliaev, G., Vestergaard, P. and Frydenberg, M. (1997) 'Generalisability of results from randomised drug trials', *British Journal of Psychiatry* 170: 264–267.

McCord, J. (1978) 'A thirty year follow-up of treatment effects', *American Psychologist* 33: 284–289.

McKee, M., Britton, A., Black, N., McPherson, K., Sanderson, C. and Bain, C. (1999) 'Interpreting the evidence: choosing between randomised and non-randomised studies', *British Medical Journal* 319: 312–315.

Sacks, H., Chalmers, T. and Smith, H. (1982) 'Randomized versus historical controls for clinical trials', *American Journal of Medicine* 72: 233–240.

Schultz, K., Chalmers, I., Hayes, R. and Altman, D. (1995) 'Empirical evidence of bias: dimensions of methodological quality associated with estimates of treatments effects in controlled trials', *Journal of the American Medical Association* 273: 408–412.

Scott, W. (1990) 'PTSD in DSM-III: a case in the politics of diagnosis and disease', *Social Problems* 37: 294–310.

Tyrell, I., Winn, D., Chalmers, I. and Adams, C. (1999) 'Treatment on trial', *The Therapist* 6: 24–32.

Wessely, S., Bisson, J. and Rose, S., (1998a) 'A systematic review of brief psychological interventions ("debriefing") for the treatment of immediate trauma related symptoms and the prevention of post traumatic stress disorder', in Oakley-Browne, M., Churchill, R., Gill, D., Trivedi, M. and Wessely, S. (eds) *Depression, Anxiety and Neurosis Module of the Cochrane Database of Systematic Reviews* (Issue 2). Oxford: Update Software.

Wessely, S., Hotopf, M. and Sharpe, M. (1998b) *Chronic Fatigue and its Syndromes*. Oxford: Oxford University Press.

Yusuf, S. (1999) 'Randomised controlled trials in cardiovascular medicine: past achievements, future challenges', *British Medical Journal* 319: 564–568.

Chapter 5

Evidence, influence or evaluation?

Fact and value in clinical science

Paul Sturdee

This chapter aims to stimulate debate about the evidential status of scientific research outcomes in mental health. The intention is not to undermine science, but rather to claim that the credibility of science rests on the transparency with which evidential claims are argued.

I will argue that scientific research in psychological fields cannot be viewed as providing objective knowledge about phenomena which are themselves unproblematic, and that we should instead view the outcomes of research as being themselves inherently problematic and open to interpretation. The approach taken will be to examine what concept of evidence is appropriate to psychiatry; understanding this will have implications for the closely related fields of clinical psychology and psychotherapy. I will argue that scientific evidence cannot provide proof, it can only affirm our commitment to the conceptual structures and theoretical constructs provided by the paradigm within which what counts as evidence has already been defined.

The proponents of scientific psychiatry, especially those who champion evidence-based medicine (EBM) trade, implicitly, on the *realisability* of an ideal of science as the impartial, disinterested seeking after truth resulting in objective knowledge – although, as I shall try to demonstrate, this realisability is illusory. Science is an inherently social activity with its own ends and means, and those ends and means are circumscribed by the interests and concerns of those who control the signification and dissemination of information and knowledge. I will argue that the epistemic status of scientific evidence (in natural science) should not be understood within a legalistic model of proof (see, e.g., Twining, 1985), but instead needs to be assessed within a model which sets different aspects of the knowledge-generating process in tension: informational inputs versus cognitive structures, expectations versus outcomes, meanings versus purposes, and theory versus data. In short, I will argue for the view that there are no proofs (in terms of evidence) to be had in scientific psychiatry, only demonstrations of the construct validity of specific concepts in the context of the theoretical paradigm within which they are conceived.

I will use as a case-example the way in which much scientific research into mental health problems has been sponsored and exploited by the pharmaceutical industry. I will show how scientific outcomes in this context can be properly understood only within a framework of judgement and interpretation which acknowledges the role of assessment and evaluation within the context of the interests and concerns of the individuals and groups involved in the generation and dissemination of such information. There are three sets of questions that should be asked of every scientific research outcome in psychiatry:

1   Who decides what counts as evidence?
     What status should an outcome be given?
2   What is the best way to use this information?
     Who will be the principal exploiter of it?
3   What is the likely impact of this information?
     Who will benefit the most from it?

In attempting to address these questions it will become clear that there is a nexus of interests operating to shape the reception and understanding of research outcomes which is very difficult to disentangle. This nexus is composed of industrial interests (pharmaceuticals, suppliers, etc.), academics (researchers, research departments) and practitioners. Yet these three groups are separable only on a conceptual level – in reality a circulation of elites and an interpenetration of interests render it almost impossible to claim of any one interest that it is isolatable from the others. But what is important is the way in which the more powerful of these interests can shape our conception of the phenomena in question and our expectations of the data generated by research. This is amply demonstrated by the history of the research into, and the production and marketing of, antidepressants, and is also true, I believe, of other pharmaceutical products. In effect, pharmaceutical companies are influencing our conception of what counts as an 'important' disease entity, and what counts as a worthwhile approach to its treatment, and they do this by defining what counts as evidence in support of the applicability of the disease concept itself, and the efficacy of the treatment they manufacture.

I will argue that to minimise the exploitation of the current enthusiasm for EBM by vested interests what is needed is a requirement for all participants in the knowledge-generating process to set out their interests and concerns alongside reports of research which they sponsored, are involved in, or are disseminating. Even more important, an open debate is needed about the way in which the evidential status of scientific research outcomes should be assessed and evaluated to minimise the effects of bias. I will conclude by identifying the likely winners and losers from the current enthusiasm for EBM.

Scientific research outcomes in psychiatry as manufactured products

In commercial terms, scientific knowledge and evidence has a market, and it is a market which centres on the promotion of goods (e.g., drugs) supported by scientific knowledge and evidence. What has happened, in the last 40 years or so, is that scientific knowledge and evidence has itself become the focus of promotion and marketing, so that it is now itself a commercial product in its own right. It has a value to its commercial sponsors which is equivalent to its worth as an advertisement for products which have a high profit potential, such as psychotropic drugs.

These are provocative claims, and deliberately so. I will support them by drawing on the history of the pharmaceutical industry as related in David Healy's recent book *The Antidepressant Era* (1997a).

In 1952 the anti-psychotic drug, chlorpromazine, was discovered, or rather its properties useful in psychiatry were discovered, the compound itself having been worked on for some years by the Swiss pharmaceutical giant, Geigy. During the same period, another member of the iminodibenzyl family, the one closest to chlorpromazine in structure, and later to be called imipramine, was being investigated for its therapeutic potential. However, it was not realised until the mid-1950s that the primary importance of imipramine was in the treatment of depression, because the research up until that time focused on testing whether it had properties similar to those of chlorpromazine.

This underscores the extent to which selection and signification occur very early on in the research process. That is, questions are asked, interpretations and judgements are made, which affect the way in which data is collected and understood. For example, one of the psychiatrists asked by Geigy to conduct clinical trials on imipramine in the mid-1950s was Roland Kuhn. When Kuhn published the results of his trials, his interpretation of the significance of the outcomes was highly selective. Healy writes:

> Despite the observations that certain patients had become manic whilst taking the drug, Kuhn declared that imipramine was an antidepressant but not a euphoriant. He picked out the features of a syndrome that he felt was particularly likely to respond; a state that for some time had been called endogenous depression, vital depression, or melancholia.
>
> (Healy 1997a: 52)

The manufacturers of imipramine, Geigy, did not, however, rush into the market with the new drug. There was uncertainty as to whether it would be as effective as ECT in treating depression; they did not know whether the size of the market would justify the commercial risk; and they were hampered by Kuhn's assertion that imipramine was not a stimulant (at the time the market for stimulants was booming).

In the end, Geigy was pushed into launching imipramine commercially by the emergence of a competitor – in April 1957 its commercial rival, Roche, launched the first MAOI, iproniazid. Even then, the sales campaign failed to produce impressive results compared with the sales of chlorpromazine, which had taken off rapidly following its introduction only five years before. It was the appearance of another competitor to imipramine, amitriptyline, produced by Merck, which stimulated the demand for antidepressants. Merck had the bright idea of ordering and distributing, along with their sales literature, 50,000 copies of a new scientific treatise on the treatment of depression, *Recognizing the Depressed Patient*, by Frank Ayd (1961). Healy takes up the story:

> It was the discovery of amitriptyline which finally led to the acceptance of imipramine. With the emergence of the tricyclic group of antidepressants, and the later eclipse of the MAOI's, a premium was put on ideas that were congruent with the proposal that these were treatments that were specific for depressive illness in contrast to ideas of nonspecific psychic energizing. In the 1960's a number of figures, such as Martin Roth, Max Hamilton, Herman van Praag, later to become some of the best-known names in international psychiatry, came up with formulations [of disease processes] that appeared to coincide with the action profile of the tricyclics. Hamilton produced a rating scale that became the gold standard for the assessment of antidepressant effects, which is generally conceded to fit almost

hand-in-glove with the profile of imipramine, so much so that there are concerns that its use as a standard rating instrument may be inhibiting the development of compounds that are unlike imipramine.

(Healy 1997a: 76)

In effect, the 1960s saw the development of a nexus of interests between pharmaceutical companies, academics, and practitioners, in which all parties viewed the association as serving the benefit of the patient. And there can be no doubt that many hundreds of thousands, if not millions, of patients did indeed benefit.

But there is a disturbing side to this story. By the late 1970s psychiatric disease classification was in turmoil, and many of the older, more general, terms for mental disorder (which were really disease *concepts* rather than naming specific disorders) were being replaced by highly specific terms carrying connotations of disease *entities*. Healy provides the example of the old 'anxiety neurosis' being replaced by 'Panic Disorder', 'Obsessive Compulsive Disorder' and 'Social Phobia' (Healy 1997b: 30). The drug companies have jumped on the scientific bandwagon by actively promoting their drugs as treatments for specific disease entities. In effect, they promote the evidence in favour of the construct validity of the disease entity which suits the therapeutic profile of their product, along with the scientific research outcomes which support the efficacy of their drug in treating that disease entity. Upjohn did this with Panic Disorder and alprazolam, and Ciba-Geigy did it with Obsessive Compulsive Disorder and clomipramine. As a result, the number estimated to suffer from such conditions has skyrocketed, along with prescriptions for the drugs.

This activity on the part of the drug companies might be viewed as the legitimate promulgation of scientific data for the benefit of all concerned. Why should we be worried about this?

Distorting the perception of science

What is happening amounts to a distortion of our perception of science, and of the evidential status of scientific research outcomes. The distortion comes about because the carefully targeted marketing of science (as a validator of knowledge claims) may serve to obscure what is really important about science itself, and about the evidential status of scientific research outcomes. What is interesting here is that those who seek to promote a conception of science as affording epistemic authority are usually keen to have us believe that natural science is characterised by a set of features which I will here call the 'traditional view of science':

1   An aim of arriving at objective knowledge.
2   The impartial, disinterested seeking after truth.
3   Unified, progressive development of systematic theories, method-
    ologies and knowledge.
4   A conception of factual data as being value-free and independent of
    theory.

This view of science has been heavily compromised by developments in
both science and philosophy during the past century or so, and I suspect
very few scientists or supporters of science would explicitly support
it unconditionally. But it is this view of science which is appealed to
by those who use science as a source of epistemic authority in the service
of interests *other* than the pursuit of knowledge, and which is implicitly
endorsed by those who champion EBM. For example, take the following
definition from one of its most eloquent advocates, Professor David
Sackett, as presented in his 1996 Office of Health Economics Lecture. In
his view:

> [EBM is] the conscientious, explicit and judicious use of current best
> evidence in making decisions about the care of individual patients
> [by] integrating individual clinical expertise with the best available
> external clinical evidence from systematic research.
>
> (Sackett, quoted in Black 1998: 23)

Note the use of heavily value-laden terms ('conscientious', 'judicious',
'systematic'), and, more worryingly, of superlatives ('current best
evidence', 'best available external clinical evidence').

   Underlying this view of EBM is the implicit assumption that 'systematic research' can afford clear, precise and unambiguous evidence for
knowledge-claims which can then be unproblematically applied in
practice through the 'conscientious, explicit and judicious' use of the 'best'
evidence. Later in this chapter I will offer an argument as to why this view
is dangerously misleading.

   A more appropriate view of science might be something like:

1   An aim of arriving at defensible knowledge-claims which aspire to
    objectivity.
2   An aspiration to a guiding ideal of science as the impartial,
    disinterested seeking after truth, a commitment to which is expressed
    by being transparent about one's value-commitments, concerns and
    interests.

3   A unified, progressive development of systematic theories, method-
    ologies and knowledge within an identifiable paradigm, with an
    openness to cross-paradigm challenges.
4   A conception of factual data as being defined by theory and imbued
    with value.
5   An acknowledgement that scientific data and knowledge must
    be viewed as provisional in its epistemic status, since it cannot be
    known in advance whether it will turn out to be justified (e.g., data
    might later be shown to be inaccurate, or knowledge-claims later
    disconfirmed by further evidence).

The significance of all this for the present argument is that research
outcomes can mean more than one thing. They need interpreting within
a context of theory, applicability, and possible utilisability – and it is
important that their openness to interpretation and disconfirmation is not
obscured through clever marketing by parties whose primary concern is
in serving their own interests (e.g., making a profit) rather than furthering
the development of scientific knowledge.

The issue is one about how science and its outcomes are presented and
used, and how we should go about protecting a certain ideal of science (as
something to which we should all aspire), and protecting those activities
which aspire to such an ideal from being diverted by other activities
which are of questionable value scientifically. In saying this I am not
casting aspersions on the scientific standards or ethics of any commercial
organisation, or any other interest group. It may well be the case that all
such organisations and interest groups achieve and maintain the highest
standards of scientific propriety. But it is my belief that the issue should
be raised, if only to ensure that it is out in the open, and an acceptable
matter for debate. It is precisely when such issues are *not* recognised
as being acceptable matters for debate that the real danger is present –
and currently, because of the enthusiasm for EBM, there is a serious
risk that these issues will become simply unfashionable, or, worse still,
unpublishable.

In fact, this danger is becoming more and more obvious as enthusiasm
for evidence-based medicine grows. EBM is already becoming a social
movement, and as such the effect is to narrow and perhaps even close
down areas of debate which are taken to be antithetical to it. The difficulty
is that academic scientists, and those mental health practitioners who see
themselves as being primarily scientists, are not actually very comfortable
with addressing the questions which need to be asked. And because of
this, there is a serious risk that those commercial and other interests who

have always used science for their own ends will seize upon the marketing opportunity presented by evidence-based medicine to promote their products and services to the detriment of both our understanding of science and the process of mental healthcare.

A case example of alternative values

The pharmaceutical industry, to which reference has already been made, provides a case example of how competing values can influence 'evidence'. Pharmaceutical companies generally have clear aims that can be summarised in terms of the ideal commercial profile of a pharmaceutical preparation:

1   It should be clear-cut and unambiguous in its therapeutic effect.
2   It should have nil or minimal side-effects.
3   It should be efficacious in the management (NB: not 'cure') of a specific disease entity for which there is a high public interest in a cure.
4   It should be profitably marketable at a price which can be sustained by its market position, and its likely market position as competitors appear.
5   It should stimulate a high level of repeat business.
6   It should be capable of further development to enable its patent to be renewed.
7   It should be supportable by the outcomes of scientific research demonstrating its efficacy, and its advantages over its competitors.

A preparation possessing all these characteristics is easily marketable, and is likely to generate very high profits for the manufacturer. Moreover, it is marketable as a 'cost-limited' treatment (i.e., the cost is limited to the price of the prescription), unlike some other forms of treatment, such as psychotherapy, in which the eventual cost is unknown at the time of commencement of therapy.

The implication of this sort of 'ideal profile' is that pharmaceutical companies need to be highly capitalised, committed to a long-term view in terms of research effort and business strategy, and be prepared to commit themselves to products which have a high development cost and, at least initially, an uncertain future but with a high potential for generating very high profits. In consequence, successful pharmaceutical companies are enormously powerful economically, and use science as a means to an end in the development and marketing of their products. Science, like almost anything else which is useful in the promotion of a product, becomes a marketable product in its own right. In effect, the message is: 'Science is intrinsically impartial, disinterested and objective. If our product is supported by scientific research outcomes, then it must be good – you can rely on science to get at the truth.'

In presenting such a pessimistic view of the influence of commercial interests on science I am not claiming that the drug companies are doing anything ethically wrong. Far from it. They are participating in a social activity in which competing claims are set against one another and the arbitration between them is on the basis of the best judgement of the appropriate experts, using the best available evidence. But it is exactly this kind of process which is being misrepresented when a view of science as an impartial, disinterested seeking after truth is, implicitly, promoted by other interests.

Science is fundamentally a human social activity – there is no such abstract entity ('science') to which we can appeal when shortcomings in the practice of science are identified, allowing us to claim that the problems exist with human activities and not with 'science' itself. Actual practice is all there is. Science exists either as (relatively speaking) 'good' or 'bad' science, and the goal must be 'good' science. Progress in science is reliant upon the intersubjective agreement of a majority of the most influential figures in any field of inquiry. Because of this, we should be concerned about ways in which our perception of science can be distorted when our ideas about disease concepts and the outcomes of scientific research are actively marketed by other powerful interests.

Evidence-based medicine: from concept to social movement

A golden opportunity for vested interests to use science for other ends is evident in the current enthusiasm for evidence-based medicine as it develops into a social movement. As this focuses attention on some issues in psychiatry at the expense of others, our conception of what is worthwhile science, and what is not, can be distorted. The distortion is both subtle and pervasive. Some disease entities are likely to achieve a much higher diagnostic profile than others, simply because they are actively publicised by their (commercial) supporters (schizophrenia is a very good example); other entities, which are not helpful to commercial interests, lose out in the competition for research funding and diagnostic popularity – the disability and distress represented by 'personality disorder' being one example here.

Perhaps even more worrying is that research into the effects of psychotropic drugs upon normal cognitive functions has declined as the manufacturers have seized marketing opportunities elsewhere. It is almost as if science is being held hostage by economic interests which stand to gain little from the truly impartial, disinterested pursuit of truth. The fact remains that the raw materials for this type of commercially disengaged research (i.e., the drugs) must be supplied by manufacturers. It is also the case that much of the research funding also comes (perhaps indirectly) from the same source. Consequently, if the commercial potential is small, both the raw material and the funding are likely to dry up.

I do not want to give the impression that anything wrong or unethical is going on here. The problem lies both in (a) the way in which unequal competition between different interests is disadvantaging research into, and patients suffering from, problems which are not at present easily captured by the current enthusiasm for evidence-based medicine, and (b) the way in which our perception of science is being distorted. The ideal of science as an impartial, disinterested seeking after truth is being presented, implicitly, as the reality of a situation guided by other (commercial) values. The evidential status of research outcomes (as confirming a theoretical prediction, or supporting a knowledge-claim) are used as a means to an end which owes only an instrumental loyalty to either science or psychiatry.

Unequal competition between different interests exists because their resources are not fairly matched, and the problems they address differ in the extent to which they present conceptual and practical difficulties in the context of EBM. For example, the psychotherapy community has actively promoted an intellectual and professional culture in which dissociative phenomena are seen as a recognised, and expected, consequence of some experiences of childhood sexual abuse. But the financial resources they can bring to bear on the funding of research and the dissemination of its results is but a drop in the ocean compared to the amounts available to, and from, the drug companies for research into disorders which are seen as likely targets for their products. The effect is that research into mental health problems is increasingly being weighted towards those problems which offer at least the possibility of profitable marketing opportunities for commercial vested interests. Only certain problems are addressed, only certain questions are asked, only certain results are actively marketed.

One of the key concepts whose meaning is being actively distorted is that of evidence – especially in the term 'evidence-based medicine'. As a concept, 'evidence-based medicine' is simply medicine which cites the support of good-quality research outcomes to legitimate practice. This seems innocuous enough. It is perfectly reasonable that one should be able to cite scientific research outcomes to legitimate clinical practices. That is, until one realises that in doing so one contributes to a climate of opinion in which research efforts and clinical approaches which are easy to support with such citations will be favoured over other research efforts and clinical approaches, which, although addressing equally difficult and perhaps more fundamental problems, are currently less easy to support with citations from scientific research although they have other justifications.

An obvious comparison in this context is between the use of drug treatments for psychological conditions versus the use of non-drug treatments like psychotherapy. The effect is to create a social movement away from a liberal conception of psychiatric practice (in which science is an adjunct) towards a more oppressive conception of psychiatric practice as being dominated by scientific considerations (in which the practitioner is defined in terms of the practices and products of science). Whatever the merits of these two views of psychiatric practice, a crucial question which must be asked here is what concept of evidence should apply in this context? Other concepts of evidence than those currently adopted might serve to balance unequal competition between different interests, and at the same time render the assessment and evaluation of scientific research outcomes more transparent.

What concept of evidence is appropriate to scientific psychiatry?

That there is an actual (as opposed to merely academic) problem here for scientific psychiatry is demonstrated by the fact that it has not yet been possible to characterise the phenomena which constitute the objects of investigation for scientific psychiatry in a way which enables the generation of theoretical constructs which work as we would like them to – one has only to consider the problems of application of DSM-IV in this context. Take the example of cross-cultural studies into the validation of the conceptual schema of DSM-IV, using tests of diagnostic consistency. It is arguable that studies into the consistency of application of diagnostic criteria across cultures reveal more about the adequacy of training (in applying the diagnostic criteria) of the clinicians involved than the validity of the theoretical constructs underlying the diagnostic criteria. It is even possible that, in this way, science creates spurious support for the very phenomena it seeks to study. For example, the disease concepts which epistemically motivate DSM-IV are dominated by a Western paradigm about the 'mental', and, notwithstanding representation of eminent psychopathologists of many different nationalities on the consulting board of DSM-IV, the ideas about mental pathology it expresses are intrinsically products of Western intellectual culture.

The fact that we can find evidence to support these diagnostic concepts shows that it is possible to identify phenomena which are consistent with such ideas – but this cannot on its own constitute a claim that the data generated can be understood as *proving* that the underlying reality is as we think it is. The relationship between evidence and the world (or, in this case, the mind) must be taken to be considerably more complex. Since what counts as evidence for any specific knowledge-claim is, in fact, defined by the theoretical paradigm the terms of which are used in framing the knowledge-claim, evidence for the knowledge-claim is not 'proof' at all – it is merely a *demonstration* that the knowledge-claim is framed correctly within the terms of the paradigm being used.

Evidence as 'fit'

I am therefore going to suggest that we should view the evidential status of scientific research outcomes in psychiatry in terms of a 'best fit' model. The argument for this rests on how we might understand the concept of knowledge. What we call 'knowledge' is not some objective entity but the product of a relation between the object of knowledge and the knowing subject. The knowing subject is constrained to approach the object of knowledge from a 'point of view' – there is no 'view from nowhere' (Nagel, 1986). This does not, of course, prevent us from aspiring to objectivity – it means only that we should not assume that attaining objectivity is a straightforward matter. Theoretical models are abstractions from the common features of several points of view. Their status as 'knowledge', or even as candidates for knowledge, is highly problematic, as is the evidential status of experiences, observations, observation-statements, and so on, which appear to confirm them. Nowhere is this more true than of our ideas about the mind.

This is not to devalue science, but to put it in its proper place as, ideally, a systematic and rigorous method of generating useful information about the world. We are sometimes motivated to call this information knowledge.[1] But, in themselves, the theories of science are not meaningful as knowledge-claims. They acquire meaning as knowledge-claims only within the context of the relation between a knowing subject and an object of knowledge – a relation which is realisable only by demonstrating that there is evidence supporting the knowledge-claims. Because the theories of science are useful to us – either in satisfying our curiosity or enabling us to achieve ends which we value – we look for evidence which might indicate just *how* satisfying or useful they might be. It makes sense, therefore, to understand evidence as being concerned with the 'fit' between different aspects of the knowledge-generating process.

Evidence is thus intelligible in terms of 'fit' – what we call 'evidence' is constituted by observations, observation-statements, measurements, data (depending upon one's view of the epistemic process of science) which establish on a firmer footing the relation between different elements of the knowledge-generating process. Thus, rather than adopting a legalistic concept of proof as a model for evidence, we would do better to examine the concept of evidence using a model which sets different aspects of the knowledge-generating process in tension – one which establishes a requirement for the *demonstrability* of the appropriate relation between the different elements of the model. I propose a model in which there are four elements, and all four elements stand in tension with one another, as well as possessing internal tensions which, if minimised, can be understood as contributing to the evidential status of a scientific research outcome. The four elements are:

1   Informational inputs versus cognitive structures.
2   Expectations versus outcomes.
3   Meanings versus purposes.
4   Theory versus data.

In each case, the degree of 'fit' is constituted by compatibility between an aspect of a feature on one side of the 'versus', and an aspect of a feature on the other side. The order in which each pair of features of the knowledge-generating process is represented above is not arbitrary, and reveals something fundamentally problematic about our perception of science as a knowledge-generating process. Basically, the intellectual credibility of natural science (as conceived of under the 'traditional view', and also under the 'more enlightened view' I outlined at the beginning of this chapter) rests on its ability to provide not only an objective account of the way the world is but also an account of how the knowing subject is capable of developing such an account. The best candidate for this is a theory which ties together informational inputs with the cognitive structures of the mind. So we might understand the concept of evidence in terms of the degree of 'fit' between certain informational inputs and the appropriate cognitive structures which enable the knowing subject to register that information as evidence for something's being the case.

Facts are inextricably imbued with values, and the facts of psychiatric science are so heavily imbued with values that the two are best understood as being heavily interpenetrative (see, e.g., Fulford, 1989). Much the same is now being said of the very concepts which we employ in our attempts at understanding how and why things go wrong with the mind – our evaluative commitments are a fundamental component of our epistemic commitments (see, e.g., Sadler, 1995, 1997). Perhaps most important of all, values are intrinsic to our evaluation of research outcomes. Push the right value 'button' and you will get the positive response you are after – this is exactly how the drug companies approach the marketing of their products. It is certainly not 'hard sell', but it is systematic, carefully conducted, and very precisely targeted. It is this kind of process that can be used to create a 'halo' of scientific respectability for a drug (by showing how efficacious it is, how few side-effects it has, how much better it is than other treatments), at the same time as scientific evidence is gathered that the drug provides a disease-specific treatment. As I have argued already, this approach has been enormously helped by the adoption in disease classification systems of 'disease-entity' concepts of disorder.

How might the concept of 'evidence' I have been proposing here allow research outcomes to be evaluated more transparently?

Evaluating research outcomes

I want to raise an issue which it is not usually raised in the standard vehicles for scientific debate (i.e., scientific journals, conferences and symposia). The reasons for this are probably complex, but scientists are, in the main, simply not very good at reflecting upon the nature of science or even the process of science. Yet they need to be debated, not only so that the scientific credentials of research findings may be scrutinised but also so that the non-scientific aspects of science which impact upon our under-standing of data, and of scientific concepts, can be carefully examined. Without this discussion, we are likely to be led astray by partisan conceptions or claims about science and its findings.

This means that researchers and their organisational and financial sponsors should be prepared to reveal where their interests lie (i.e., not merely where the funding comes from – the content of most 'declarations of interest' – but what it is in their interests to know, and why). They should also make freely available information about research funding, research design and methodology, and also experimental data, which might otherwise be withheld from the published report on the basis that it was not relevant to the results. Only if such information is freely available is it possible to question the judgement and interpretation of the researchers; and it is only then that we can assess and evaluate the true significance of the research in the light of the interests and concerns which *we* as its consumers bring to the matter (after all, that is why we are interested in scientific research outcomes in the first place – because we have a point of view on the matter). If conducted in this way critical scrutiny allows scientific research outcomes to be assessed for their evidential status, taking into account the full range of interests impacting upon the interpretation of information at every turn in the processes and procedures of the production and dissemination of knowledge-claims. If assessment in these terms is successful (i.e., it identifies and renders explicit all the interests which have impacted upon the research process and dissemination of the outcomes), then the intellectual cloak of science is much less likely to be able to disguise and lend respectability to claims that are not motivated by the goals and values of science.

In practical terms, it means that journal editors, and conference and symposia organisers, need to impose certain conditions upon the publication of research: that the original research proposals should be made available if required, that records be kept of the methodology and progress of the research, and that any unused/unpublished data be made available to other researchers or interested parties. Further, that the published record of the research should contain explicit information about the evaluative commitments of the researchers and their sponsors, and that there should be a climate of openness concerning the possible significance of the data (both published and unpublished). The importance of what I am proposing should not be underemphasised: most published research papers represent the only available information that survives about the projects they report – and yet, as I have argued above, this information is highly biased. Normally the only clues as to the nature of the bias lie in the unpublished material – this is illustrated by the example of Roland Kuhn's reporting of his study on the effects of imipramine, in Healy's book (1997a). Unfortunately, there is no obligation upon researchers to preserve their unpublished material, still less to deposit it in a secure repository from which it can be accessed by scholars seeking to investigate possible bias.

Assessing the nature of scientific research outcomes more objectively

This chapter identifies an issue which, like the issue of the value of a free press in a democratic society, must be raised if only to demonstrate that good faith exists on the part of those who might otherwise seek to suppress it. I have done so not to undermine science (still less the reputation of the pharmaceutical industry), but to promote the proper use of science and its positive benefits in psychiatry. The effect of taking the issue seriously would, I believe, increase our ability to assess the nature of scientific research outcomes more objectively – that is, with the full recognition of the effect our own concerns and interests had upon our interpretation of the information involved.

Let us return to the three sets of questions I asked at the beginning of this chapter:

1   Who decides what counts as evidence?
    What status should an outcome be given?
2   What is the best way to use this information?
    Who will be the principal exploiter of it?
3   What is the likely impact of this information?
    Who will benefit the most from it?

It is quite clear that the answers one might give to these questions depend fundamentally on the values, beliefs, ideals, interests and concerns which motivate one to address the question in the first place. It might be that some intersubjective agreement is possible about there being an objective answer to such questions. But what actually turns out to be the case will, in some important respects, rest upon the commitment of the individuals involved that things *should* turn out that way. In other words, we simply cannot get away from the evaluative aspects of science and the assessment of scientific research outcomes in evaluative terms.

The point I draw from this is that science should not be allowed to drive the values and activities of mental health practice, still less should they be distorted by the commercial interests of those who seek to exploit science for profit. Over the years I have met many psychiatrists, psychiatric scientists, and mental health practitioners, who see their professional loyalties as being fundamentally to a 'hard-nosed' view of natural science. I believe that such a view is not only inappropriate but a distortion of what actually matters in mental healthcare. The reasons one ostensibly wishes to know more about the mind and the ways in which it might or does go wrong are motivated by a commitment to an evaluative conception of human beings, as having an intrinsic and unconditional value which transcends all other values. Now, it may be the case that such matters (i.e., such commitments) are not often subject to scrutiny by mental health professionals (although I believe they should be), but the inescapable point is that mental health practice has its own values, ideals, beliefs, concerns and interests (quite separate from those of science), and it is these which should drive practice. This means that they should also motivate the use of science in practice. The values, ideals, beliefs, concerns and interests of science should not motivate practice, still less the values, ideals, beliefs, concerns and interests of those who would use science for the purpose of furthering their own ends where those ends are not fully congruent with the ends of mental healthcare practice.

In psychiatry, science is a means to an end – the alleviation of a certain sort of human suffering – and it is this end which should determine the nature of science appropriate to psychiatry (the work of Karl Jaspers is poignantly appropriate in this context – especially as his most insightful work on the nature of a *human* science has all but been ignored by those who champion EBM).

Likely winners and losers from evidence-based medicine

I entered a promissory note at the beginning of this chapter that I would identify the likely winners and losers in psychiatry from the current enthusiasm for EBM. Basically, at a general level, we can divide possible winners and losers into three categories: concepts and ideas of disorder/ disease; clinical activities and practices; and lastly, groups or interests. It is always risky to attempt to foresee the future, but such is the potential for disaster with EBM that I am prompted to put my neck on the block of history.

The categorisation of concepts and ideas about disorder/disease will, I believe, come to show marked effects from EBM. What is congenial to EBM is the availability of specific disease-entity concepts which can be related to specific treatment methodologies. So specific disease-entity concepts (like schizophrenia, and organic mental disorders) are likely to flourish under EBM. On the other hand, psychological problems, such as personality disorders and anxiety-related illnesses, which are less amenable to conceptualisation as specific disease-entities, will struggle to survive as concepts (not least because research into their use as diagnostic constructs, and into their treatment, will have greater difficulty in attracting funds).

Clinical activities and practices will also, I predict, respond to the current enthusiasm for EBM. Those practices and activities, such as the prescribing of certain drug treatments for specific disease-entities, will thrive, whereas those practices and activities which are problematic when studied by the research methods favoured by EBM (such as randomised controlled trials) will not do well – and I think clinical psychotherapy (as a stand-alone service) may well come into this group.

Finally, what will happen to all the different groups and interests which compete for a slice of the pie of resources dedicated to mental healthcare? I predict that those groups and interests which can cite unequivocal scientific research outcomes in their favour will do very well indeed out of EBM (these will include 'hard-nosed' scientific researchers and research programmes, and those who exploit the epistemic value commitments involved, such as the drug companies), whereas those which have difficulty in providing unequivocal scientific support for their continuing influence will lose credibility and ultimately decline (I think this will be true of psychotherapists as a group, and possibly other groups such as commercially disengaged scientific researchers).

If my predictions turn out to be correct, mental healthcare will develop into a loose collaboration of disciplines competing for scientific credibility and status, according to the edicts of the champions of EBM. Some of the most fundamental issues in mental health, concerning the evaluative aspects of mental health concepts and practices, and also ethical issues concerning the basis on which claims of value in mental health are defensible, will be seriously distorted and rendered mere adjuncts to scientific psychiatry in what the more dogmatic supporters of EBM see as a triumph of objectivity over myth. The uncomfortable truth, for all of us, is that the kind of objectivity they champion is itself a myth, and we would do well to pay more heed to the way in which concepts like 'evidence' acquire their own mythology. If we do not grasp the nettle now, or in the very near future, and engage in an open debate about the evidential status of scientific research outcomes in psychiatry, the influence of powerful vested interests may become so embedded that the debate is no longer a possibility. If that happens, we will all be the losers.

Note

1   This is not to adopt unconditionally a pragmatic conception of knowledge or evidence, which, as I have argued earlier, has its own problems. However, I believe it is important to acknowledge that to assert a knowledge-claim presupposes an interest in it turning out true, if only because the intellectual credibility of the assertor rests on such an outcome. On a psychological level, the ideal of science as an impartial, disinterested seeking after truth seems to me to be fundamentally an expression of a need to satisfy a certain sort of intellectual curiosity in which the inquirer, ideally, wishes to claim neutrality (i.e., lack of personal interest) concerning the outcome. Whilst this is a worthwhile ideal, it clearly cannot be allowed to obscure the fact that, in practice, scientific research is not interest-free, or value-free.

References

Aronowitz, S. (1988) *Science as Power*. Basingstoke: Macmillan.

Ayd, F.J. (1961) *Recognizing the Depressed Patient*. New York: Grune & Stratton.

Black, D. (1998) 'The limitations of evidence', *Journal of the Royal College of Physicians of London* 32 (1): 23–26.

Fulford, K.W.M. (1989) *Moral Theory and Medical Practice*. Cambridge: Cambridge University Press.

Healy, D. (1997a) *The Antidepressant Era*. Cambridge, MA: Harvard University Press.

Healy, D. (1997b) 'Architects of the Great Depression', *The Times Higher Education Supplement*, 30 May, p. 30.

Nagel, T. (1986) *The View from Nowhere*. Oxford: Oxford University Press.

Sadler, J.Z. (1995) 'Diseases, functions, values, and psychiatric classification', *Philosophy, Psychiatry & Psychology* 2: 219–232.

Sadler, J.Z. (1997) 'Recognizing values: a descriptive-causal method for medical/scientific discourses', *The Journal of Medicine and Philosophy* 22: 541–565.

Twining, W. (1985) *Theories of Evidence: Bentham and Wigmore*. London: Weidenfeld & Nicolson.

Chapter 6

Evident causes

The nature of reason in psychotherapy

Digby Tantam

Rycroft was one of the first psychotherapists to point out that an understanding of the difference between the meaning of something and the cause of something was essential to an understanding of the effects of psychotherapy (Rycroft, 1966). Philosophy has been much preoccupied by the different implications of these two kinds of explanation (Puttnam, 1973), but whilst there has been a considerable discussion within medicine about what constitutes evidence of cause, there has been much less about what constitutes evidence of meaning (Grünbaum, 1990).

Part of the problem is that if meaning has no causal properties it seems to be a matter of indifference what meaning is given to any particular event. In this chapter, based on a workshop at the AUTP/ UPA/ College conference on evidence in psychotherapy, I argue that meanings do have causal properties but that these are distinct from the causal properties of events which produce their effects by a physical process. One habit that confuses thinking in this area is that the reasons that people give for their actions may be of either character. I may say that the reason that I was late is that my car broke down, or that the reason that I was late was that I was reluctant to come. For clarity, I shall refer to these reasons as reasons1 and reasons2, respectively.

Causes

Causes were succinctly defined by Hume in the following terms: 'a cause is said to be an object followed by another, where all the objects similar to the first are followed by objects similar to the second, and where, if the first object had not been, the second had not existed' (Hume, 1748: 76–77). Very many glosses on this statement have established the fact that causes rarely act alone, and that a particular cause may have an indeterminate effect because of the multitude of other causes also contributing to that effect. But this has not weakened the principle of constant conjunction, that wherever there is an effect, a particular cause has preceded it.

If I say that the reason he passed the examination was that he had read the right books, I am stating a proposition about the cause. I do not imply that reading the right books is sufficient to pass the examination, but that passing the examination is always preceded by reading the right books. I could equally have said 'the reason that he did not pass the exam was that he did not read the right books'.

I suppose that a minority of reasons that are given for things are of this type (which I have called reasons1). Many more reasons are of the type 'The reason that he did not pass the exam was that he could never allow himself to succeed.' These reasons2 explain events in terms of goals, intentions, or motives. They are similar to what Fincham and Jaspars (1980) call justifications.

It is often assumed that goals, intentions, etc., although they may be different in many ways from other causes, do at least precede their effects. It is my contention that this assumption is not unjustified. Indeed, that there are good reasons for thinking that they follow their effects. If this is true, then some important consequences follow.

In the example given, it is a proposition ('I never allow myself to succeed') which is the candidate causal agent. Can propositions ever be causal? Let us take the case of a violent patient who has assaulted someone and afterwards says, 'I thought, "he's the devil and he's come to hurt me". So I lashed out first.' Are we prepared to accept, following Hume's precept, that had the proposition 'He's the devil . . . ' not been thought, the assault would not have followed? Clinicians might think that it's not all or nothing. Assaults happen without that sort of thought preceding them. The thought might be something that is elaborated in retrospect in response to questioning, or might be an attempt at exculpation. We are all familiar with the parallel case of aiming at one goal – a winning cross-court shot at tennis, perhaps, and achieving it, but not in the expected way (the shot turns out to be a passing shot to the back of the court, maybe). There is a temptation to claim the credit for intending the passing shot after all, a temptation which may be translated into a conviction that we were *really* aiming at that. We might even say that our tennis brain took over and placed the shot without our consciously being aware of it. In this case, it cannot be said that the deliberate intention to make a cross-court shot was causal, because it certainly cannot be said that the occurrence of the passing shot would not have occurred had there been no intention to make a cross-court shot.

Let us look again at the statement, 'he could never allow himself to succeed', which is taken to describe the cause of examination failure in the earlier example. Let us further imagine the candidate sitting his examination, fully in a position to succeed, but not allowing himself to do so. Does the proposition, 'If I carry on like this I will pass, but I never allow myself to succeed, and so I must start to answer a few questions wrongly' come into his mind? Has the generalisation, 'I never allow myself to succeed' ever been formulated by the candidate at all? I think that the answer in almost all cases must be 'no'. What actually happens is that a person panics before the exam, or their mind goes blank, or they make some sort of mistake in choosing the questions. It is this which causes them to fail: the meaning of that failure is attributed after.

What is the relation of the proposition 'he could never allow himself to succeed' to the anxiety that the candidate feels? Could it precede the anxiety, but be unconscious? Two widely held views about consciousness (with which I agree) are that propositions are language-dependent, and that 'being conscious of something' and 'speaking about something' can be used interchangeably. This seems to have been Freud's view. He made verbalisability the cardinal distinction between conscious and unconscious processes. This view, too, seems to continue to be upheld by modern-day psychoanalysts, despite Lacan's mysterious remark that the unconscious is structured like a language.

I have tried to show that propositions which are supposedly caused like 'he could never allow himself to succeed' are rarely consciously in mind before an action, and cannot be unconsciously in mind, either before or after. It follows that such propositions do not meet Hume's criterion that the cause precedes the effect.

The causal properties of *post hoc* reasons

Do reasons2 – reasons which attribute cause to a proposition – have any causal properties at all? Consider this illustration, an account of an interpretation by the leader of a therapy group, taken from Cohen (1997). 'They [Pam and Beth] want to be cared about and accepted by one another, but they are afraid to trust one another because they each have been hurt so badly by their mothers.' If my previous argument is accepted, the proposition 'I have been hurt badly by my mother' does not precede instances of not trusting Pam (or Beth). It is not causal. It is not a necessary antecedent but a contingent relation. Does it have any truth-value at all? Can it be refuted, for example, by finding evidence against it?

Suppose that either Pam or Beth said that they had not been hurt badly by their mothers. There would still be room for thinking – and many therapists would probably think – that they were forgetting or denying or idealising. Suppose, however, that Pam and Beth both admitted that they had been hurt by their mothers, but that it also turned out that they did trust each other. I think that would be a refutation of the interpretation. It would be a refutation because of the failure of Hume's constant conjunction if, that is, the proposition 'they have been hurt so badly by their mothers' is *caused* by the observation that they did not trust one another.

This presumes that reasons2 are reasons which refer to causal statements in which the meaning element attributed to the event is really a proposition whose formulation is caused by the event, not the cause of it. In the case of the exam example this is not a demanding reinterpretation. 'He said "you never allow yourself to succeed" because the student failed his examination' is only a condensation of 'Because the student failed his examination, he said "the student failed his examination because he never allowed himself to succeed".' These propositions which are the effects of some action or non-verbalised event are reminiscent of Wittgenstein's pain statements which he said were symptoms of pain, like a groan, and not comments about the pain.

In a psychotherapy context, this reinterpretation has more significance. Let us take some more examples. 'He could never get on with his bosses because his Oedipal conflicts were unresolved.' There is first the cause, the observation that the patient could never get on with his bosses. Then there is the effect: the therapist says, or thinks, that the patient's Oedipal conflicts are unresolved. Or, 'He could never get on with his bosses because he had a negative schema about authority.' At first sight, this may not seem to be a reason2 but an ordinary causal statement. However, later on in the cognitive therapy it emerges that a negative schema about authority is an enduring belief which can be expressed as a proposition about authority, such as 'They're all in it for themselves.' Other modalities of psychotherapy are explicit about their basis in propositions. Ryle states, in summarising the CAT model of psychotherapy, that 'Human beings are "dialogic": every act or statement is addressed, implicitly or explicitly, to a real or imagined other' (Ryle, 1988: 304).

When we look for evidence to support interpretations or negative schemata, we should not therefore look to find them causing the events with which they are linked, but being caused by them. The relevant evidence is whether or not the event, or problem or symptom, caused the therapist's comment. This may not always be so. A therapist may reply wildly, or randomly, or because he or she has misheard. If we consider these occurrences unlikely, we might remember that a therapist may respond because of some internal state of his or her own.

Relevant evidence might be that the effect, which may be the interpretation that 'the patient has an unresolved Oedipal conflict', is caused in most psychotherapists with an analytic background by the observation that 'the patient never gets on with his bosses'. However, as one cause may have different effects depending on other influences operating at the time, we should expect that a number of different interpretations are each validly caused by the observation that the patient never gets on with his bosses.

Psychotherapeutic formulations are caused by the actions that they explain, and are not representations of the causes of the actions.

Evidence and truth

Supposing that we want to find evidence to support, or to refute, the notion that catastrophic interpretations of physical symptoms cause panic. A possible experiment might be to have ten people interview ten other people who have suffered panic, asking about the antecedents of a panic attack. Let us suppose – and this is merely a thought experiment – that five people said that all ten panickers had experienced catastrophic thoughts before their attacks, and five people said they had not. As a proponent of the catastrophisation hypothesis, I might argue that this experiment was flawed because the interviewers were unselected. Only interviewers who had some experience of interviewing people about their faulty thinking should be used, I might legitimately claim.

Evidence should be sought and appraised by competent observers: in the example above by people with some training in cognitive analysis. However, looking for the evidence that a particular reason2 is true of a particular action comes down to finding out whether the same reason2 would be given for the action by all competent observers. Competent observers might be the proverbial travellers on the Clapham omnibus who, as members of a jury, are considered able to divine the reasons for the actions of the defendant or, as more often applies to evidence in psychotherapy, the competent observers might be well-trained cognitive therapists or well-analysed psychoanalysts.

It has been central to my argument so far that the competent observers of panickers do not discover a causal proposition that precedes panic, but arrive at a reason2 for a person's panic in terms of catastrophic thoughts. This way of looking at matters is analogous to Wittgenstein's treatment of pain:

244. How do words *refer* to sensations? . . . Here is one possibility: words are connected with the primitive, the natural, expressions of the sensation and used in their place. A child has hurt himself and he cries; and then adults talk to him and teach him exclamations and, later, sentences. They teach the child new pain-behaviour.

(Wittgenstein, 1958: 89)

In fact, whether or not there is a cause to be labelled and given as a reason1 or whether the event causes a reason2, competent observers are required for the relation to be discerned, although the criteria of competence may be different.

He means, it means

Consider the question, 'What does he mean?', asked by a Spaniard with no English about what an English speaker has just said. A sufficient answer to this question is a translation into Spanish from the English. A useful simplification is to suppose that this translation is a matter of operating rules, rules which can in fact be instantiated in a computer program. If the statement is of some importance, the Spaniard may wonder whether what he heard in Spanish was really what the English speaker meant and fall to considering the evidence. There will be a flavour to the English utterance, conveyed by tone of voice, gesture and so on, which should be consistent with the flavour of the Spanish statement. Beyond that, all the evidence that the Spaniard will have is the good intentions of the translator (that he or she was doing their best to provide a correct translation) and the competence of the translator (that they had an accurate grasp of the rules of conversion between English and Spanish). The Spaniard can get reasonable evidence about the translator's fluency in Spanish from conversation and about the translator's fluency in English from observing conversation with the English speaker.

An event causing an explanation is more like an interpretation than a translation. But in searching for evidence of the explanation we are even more likely to have to rely on the goodwill and competence of the explainer, as well as the compatibility of the flavour of the event and of the explanation.

Efficacy

I have argued that the reasons that psychotherapists give for behaviour are usually reasons2: that is, they are of the same kind as justifications or attributions of meaning. I have also argued that it might be useful to consider these reasons2 as being caused by the events that they explain, and not as pictures of the causes of those events.

I want to consider finally what efficacy reasons2 might have. If I say that someone is fleeing from the awareness of death and that is why they act as they do, and by this I mean that there is a fear of death which is a cause of that person's behaviour, then I can use ordinary causal reasoning to devise further intervention. For example, I can tackle the fear of death directly. If this explanation is a consequence of a person's behaviour, and not a cause, its efficacy is not so obvious. Maybe there is an emotional reaction which the explanation produces, so that the person might feel criticised or encouraged in their behaviour. Maybe, too, they feel that I am kindly disposed to them, or not, depending on the explanations that I give. But whether or not the explanation is true does not seem to influence the efficacy of my response.

Previously, I suggested that the evidence of the truth of a reason2 was taken from its flavour, the goodwill of the explainant, and the competence of the person doing the explaining. In the previous paragraph I noted that the flavour of an explanation and the goodwill of the explainant were emotionally efficacious. Is this all there is to it? Has this line of thought collapsed into an extreme post-modernist or narrative kind of solipsism in which there is no reason other than palatability to prefer one explanation, one narrative, from another?

This danger is made present by the apparent absence of adhesions between reasons2 and reality. Reasons1 are about actual causes, reasons2 are not. Nor are reasons2 translations which can be shown to be true or false according to linguistic rules.

It is sometimes claimed that a certain person knows 'the truth' because of their spiritual status, and that this status is itself evidence that what they say is 'the truth'. Psychotherapists have an ambivalent relationship to this kind of authority. On the one hand, it seems phoney and it is all too easy to find false prophets. One the other, it is integral to psychotherapists' reverence for personal characteristics like age, charisma, and experience.

Psychotherapists badly need some external criteria for judging therapist competence in providing truthful reasons2, and badly need a model of how a therapist's competence in giving reasons2 produces personal change. This seems to me to be the single most important intellectual challenge facing psychotherapy as an academic discipline.

A developmental narrative

Imagine a son who says to his mother, when he first knowingly hears a cuckoo, 'What is that?', and then, when the mother says that it was a cuckoo, asks, 'Why does it make that noise?'

The mother, an ornithologist, might say, 'Because it belongs to the Cuculidae and they all have a song which is a brief phrase with a transition from one note to another.' It is unlikely that she would, though, because any mother would give a reason2 to the question, knowing it to be one about meaning. She might therefore say, 'Because the sound carries a long way and this is important for solitary birds who are widely scattered in their habitat'; or she might say, 'Because that is the way one cuckoo attracts another.' Or she might say, 'Because the spring is coming.' All of these reasons2 may be accepted by the child without much reflection. But let us suppose that the child, in being answered in that way by its mother, is sufficiently identified with her that he glimpses the concept of spring, with all the changes that it entails. From this small starting point, each successive year may bring a clearer awareness in the child of what spring is, and a greater response to the sound of the cuckoo as the harbinger of that transformation. Supposing that the child, and then the man, is susceptible, the sound of the cuckoo may become magical. It will conjure up that special time with mother, the springs of past years and the springs of poetry and novels, the quintessence of longing and yearning.

In the prepared mind, the sound of the cuckoo becomes somewhat like the organiser of an embryo. Memories, thoughts, ideas, experiences, and feelings about spring become yoked together because the sound of the cuckoo evokes them and because they in turn evoke the sound of the cuckoo.

Of course, this description of the impact of hearing the first cuckoo of spring may fail to move many readers, but they will find, I suspect, that they can replace it with another emblem which has the same effect for them.

An argument by analogy for the factors that make some therapeutic interventions preferable to others

The causal power of these emblems, these reasons2 for things, comes about because of their capacity to organise past and present experience and in so organising it to influence what actions or perceptions that experience tends to. I put this forward as model of psychotherapy intervention or interventions: they act, too, as organisers of experience and change the tendencies to action or perception as a result.

If the analogy of the sound of the cuckoo – or whichever other emblem the reader has chosen – holds further, does it tell us anything about what might constitute an effective psychotherapy intervention?

Before considering this, it needs to be established whether or not such interventions all involve reasons2. This is almost apodeictic in the case of an interpretation which is framed by the therapist as an explanation of why someone acted as they did. It may be less obvious in the case of other forms of therapy which seek to uncover basic assumptions, self-deception, or the effects of hidden dilemmas or scripts (to take a few concepts from cognitive, existential, cognitive-analytic and transactional analytic therapies). Some psychotherapists might argue that relationship change is what mediates the effect. I suspect that a person's perceived reasons for their own actions, and the reasons that they attribute to others, do always change as a result of psychotherapy even if they are not the apparent targets of the therapy. I suspect that such changes are integral to the process of therapeutic change. However, I do not have the opportunity to demonstrate this here. So the reader should assume that subsequent discussion of therapeutic intervention is applicable to interpretations, but less certainly applicable to other interventions.

The harbinger of spring (reason2) for the cuckoo's call is inductively true. Throughout its range the cuckoo calls at the beginning of spring. The bird is sufficiently prevalent that most northern Europeans will hear it most years at this time. However, the harbinger of spring (reason2) is not the only one that is inductively true: the cuckoo also calls to attract a mate. Other considerations are therefore needed to provide an explanation of why the harbinger of spring explanation bites so deeply into some (many?) people's consciousness. I suggest that there are several others that are important.

First, the call of the cuckoo is distinctive. Almost everyone can recognise it. This salience lends itself to emblem formation. The equivalent for a therapeutic intervention would be the event which sticks in the mind. There are many candidates: the first time that something happens, the last time it happens, 'that terrible day when . . . ', or 'that wonderful day when . . . ', to name but a few.

Almost everyone knows another thing about the cuckoo, as well as its call: its obnoxious dependency on other birds for the survival of its young. This is deprecated almost as much as the vernal character of the cuckoo is lauded. I think that this combination of good and bad characteristics in a 'flavour' gives objects with this flavour a special status and importance. Teddy bears, toy trains, jokes about excretion, and many Kleinian interpretations all have this same character. They contain references to dangerous objects (bears, trains, and so on), but combined with another flavour which makes them an antidote to danger rather than being dangerous in themselves.

The conversation about cuckoos and spring I have imagined to be between a mother and her son. Conversations between parents and children, between lovers, between revered teachers and their pupils are among that class of conversations in which what is said is particularly remembered and regularly recalled. This location in a special relationship is likely to be of importance to the genesis of the cuckoo's emblematic quality, and equally likely to be important in the genesis of a potent therapeutic intervention.

The final characteristic of the harbinger of spring reason2 for the cuckoo's call is that it points to a mysterious connection between the activity of birds and the cycle of nature which suggests a hidden order behind natural phenomena. There is, too, something intoxicating about the human ability to infer large events from small beginnings. Or, at least, both of these assertions are true of me and how I think of my place in the world. They are statements of some of my fundamental values. The fact that the harbinger of spring reason2 for the cuckoo's call supports these values is one of the reasons that I am moved by hearing the first cuckoo of spring. If the analogy of the cuckoo's call to the therapist's intervention has held the reader to this point, then I hope that this final parallel will be considered. A final factor that determines that one therapeutic intervention, one reason2 given by the therapist for her or his client's actions, is preferred over another is that this reason2 springs from fundamental values which are deeply held by the client.

Summary and conclusions

I have argued that reasons do have causal properties but that certain reasons, reasons2, have these properties not because they determine the actions that they rationalise but because they retrospectively interpret these actions and therefore modify the consequences of the actions. I have further argued that interventions in psychotherapy act by providing or uncovering reasons2 and that they should not be judged according to evidential criteria for causes but by a special sort of evidence akin to the evidence taken in court or provided in other arguments about motive.

I have suggested, on the basis of a long analogy, that preferred explanations in psychotherapy, as in other settings, will be those which have turned on some salient event, have a complex flavour, reflect the personal significance of a relationship, and point to shared values. Whether or not these factors turn out to be the important determinants of 'good' therapeutic interventions, or whether they are the only ones, may be less important than the fact that there is a debate as to what a good intervention is. The drug-metaphor of psychotherapy has broken down empirically (Stiles and Shapiro, 1994) as well as conceptually. If we can no longer maintain that causal efficacy is the criterion of our work as psychotherapists we must consider the criteria we are working to. We cannot maintain that one intervention is as good as another, or that as non-judgemental therapists it is not our place to judge what is better or worse. We cannot say either 'I just do what works'. Psychotherapists must pay urgent attention to the nature of the evidence that they wish others to use in judging their work. In the absence of evidential criteria, others will conclude that there is no evidence. That conclusion, in this era of evidence-based practice, is tantamount to oblivion in a service funded by the public or other third-party payer.

References

Cohen, S. (1997) 'Working with resistance to experiencing and expressing emotions in group therapy', *International Journal of Group Psychotherapy* 47: 443–458.

Fincham, F. and Jaspars, J. (1980) 'Attribution of responsibility. From man-as-scientist to man-as-lawyer', in L. Berkowitz (ed.) *Advances in Experimental Social Psychology*, Vol. 13. New York: Academic Press.

Grünbaum, A. (1990) 'Meaning connections and causal connections in the human sciences: the poverty of hermeneutic philosophy', *Journal of the American Psychoanalytic Association* 38: 559–578.

Hume, D. (1748) *Enquiries Concerning Human Understanding and Concerning the Principles of Morals*. London: Millar.

Puttnam, H. (1973) 'Meaning and reference', *Journal of Philosophy* 70: 699–711.

Rycroft, C. (ed.) (1966) 'Causes and meaning', in *Psychoanalysis Observed*. London: Constable.

Ryle, A. (1988) 'Transferences and countertransferences: the cognitive analytic therapy perspective', *British Journal of Psychotherapy* 14: 303–309.

Stiles, W.B. and Shapiro, D.A. (1994) 'Disabuse of the drug metaphor: psychotherapy process–outcome correlations', *Journal of Consulting & Clinical Psychology* 62: 942–948.

Wittgenstein, L. (1958) *Philosophical Investigations* (trans. G.E. Anscombe) (2nd edn). Oxford: Basil Blackwell.

Chapter 7

Single case methodology and psychotherapy evaluation

From research to practice

Graham Turpin

Introduction

The well-described case study has been a cornerstone of the development of psychotherapy since the publication of Freud's detailed accounts of therapy during the early years of the twentieth century. Indeed, the discussion of case materials arising from therapy sessions has formed the basis for supervision, training and the general dissemination of knowledge throughout the psychotherapeutic world. Advances in therapeutic thinking and specific techniques have usually been heralded by published case studies detailing innovations in therapy. Given the focus of this book and the current climate of 'evidence-based medicine' whereby pressures exist on therapists to justify the efficacy of their therapeutic techniques, it would be reasonable to reappraise the standing of the 'case study' as one such means of demonstrating treatment efficacy. The aims, therefore, of the present chapter are to review the development of single case methods in general and to provide a brief overview and evaluation of their practical application to psychotherapy research. As is discussed below, a variety of different single case approaches may be identified. However, this chapter will focus mainly on single case experimental designs (SCEDs) which have been developed in order to evaluate the impact of clinical and educational interventions.

Single case methodology represents a wide range of methods that have been used extensively across many different areas of study. Essentially they can be defined, with respect to psychotherapy, as a collection of techniques for evaluating the efficacy of a specific intervention(s) within a single or series of clinical cases. However, the study of the individual, as opposed to the usual nomothetic approach of studying groups of individuals, may be generally identified throughout a range of different areas of study. Although the clinical case study is widely used within medicine and other clinical disciplines, individually focused research strategies are also commonplace within educational research (Hegarty and Evans, 1985), experimental psychology (Valsiner, 1986), neuro-psychology (Dywan and Segalowitz, 1986; Shallice *et al.*, 1991) and sociology (Stake, 1995; Yin, 1994). Indeed, although it is common within psychology as a discipline to criticise single case idiographic approaches on the grounds that they fail to generalise to groups of individuals, many basic laws of behaviour have evolved within psychology, and particularly in psychophysics, by the careful and intensive study of just a few selected and usually well-trained individuals.

The range of applications of single case approaches is also reflected in a diversity of methods. Even the 'case study' ranges from anecdotal reports of therapy published in books through to the publication of brief clinical reports in journals, and the formal presentation of case studies. The latter are frequently used as assessments of assumed clinical competence within many forms of psychotherapy training. However, the traditional clinical case study has been criticised for being biased and unscientific (Kazdin, 1981) and has given way to a range of more scientifically focused techniques which are commonly described as 'single case experimental designs' (Hayes, 1981; Hilliard, 1993). These approaches commonly involve the comparison of data derived from a baseline period prior to when no intervention has been offered, with data obtained from an intervention period. The use of a follow-up assessment some months or years following the treatment is also frequently undertaken. These approaches are often termed AB designs, the letters referring, rather confusingly, to baseline (A) and intervention (B) respectively. Since they usually involve the collection of large amounts of continuous data collected daily over several months, they are also referred to as 'time series' designs. The comparison between baseline and treatment is also frequently repeated, either giving rise to 'ABAB' designs or the use of several different measures concurrently which are termed 'multiple baseline or phase designs'. Occasionally, SCEDs will be repeated across a small series of individuals and this approach is called 'a small N design'. The latter approach is common in educational research when data from a group of children are assessed both individually and as a small group (see Hegarty and Evans, 1985). In the latter case, care is taken to compensate for the lack of statistical power arising from the small subject numbers, by careful experimental design and the control of confounding variables.

In addition to the quantitative experimental approaches described above, the case study has also been developed to yield a range of quali-tative methods which are commonly adopted within sociology. Indeed, classic case studies of particular services or institutions have resulted in dramatic changes in attitudes and models of understanding. Well known examples include Goffman's (1961) ethnographic studies of institutional life. Although qualitative approaches are not the main focus of this chapter, their potential for understanding therapeutic processes are becoming increasingly recognised (Smith, 1996; Stiles, 1993). For further details of qualitative approaches, the interested reader should consult Stake (1995) and Yin (1994). A particular bibliographically based approach which has also been applied clinically is described by Bromley (1986).

Research and clinical applications

Single case experimental designs have a range of applications which should attract both researchers and practitioners. From a research perspective, it could be argued that evaluating efficacy within a single clinical case is the bottom line as regards 'evidence-based medicine'. How can we reliably and objectively demonstrate clinical change within the individual? On a day-to-day basis the effectiveness of our interventions are demonstrated via our own perceptions of what seems to be effective; the satisfaction of the client which may be expressed verbally in terms of compliments or complaints; behaviourally by gifts, non-attendance and the unplanned discontinuation of therapy; by comments from carers and relatives; or by peer evaluations during the process of 'supervision' or clinical audit. However, do these sources of information really constitute evidence of effectiveness? Even if clinical change is observed, how confident are we that it was our own specific intervention, as opposed to a myriad of other influences ranging from the client's family through to other possible interventions of the multidisciplinary team, that brought about the real change. Single case experimental designs have been developed in an attempt to provide proof of effectiveness within the individual. Accordingly, it can be argued that these techniques should provide therapists with an objective means of demonstrating the efficacy of their interventions. As such, they represent one approach to evidence-based practice which the psychotherapist might exploit in order to demonstrate their own effectiveness to a sometimes sceptical world.

The evidence-based psychotherapist has to justify their use of specific therapies with respect to the published research literature and also provide some evidence supporting their own clinical effectiveness. This is not to say that every piece of clinical work should be treated as a potential piece of psychotherapy outcome research. Instead, there may be situations when the therapist has a particular reason for evaluating their work and publishing the outcome within the public domain. The most common reason for employing SCED is when the therapist is engaged in an innovative approach to therapy and wishes to disseminate through scientific publication the results of this new treatment approach. Single cases have provided the starting points for many commonly used therapeutic techniques which are widely employed throughout clinical practice today. For example, the cognitive treatment of panic disorder owes its origins to a series of single case studies on the use of rebreathing and re-attribution techniques published by David Clark and his colleagues some 15 years ago (Clark *et al.*, 1985). Similarly, the cognitive management of psychotic symptoms was first published by Birchwood as a single case series (Chadwick and Birchwood, 1994). Although these publications by themselves do not meet the full rigours of evidence-based medicine they have provided useful starting points for more systematic approaches to therapy. Indeed, in the case of both approaches, evidence from single case studies has now been superseded by the findings from randomly controlled trials (Drury *et al.*, 1996; Kuipers, *et al.*, 1997; Barlow, 1997). Within psychotherapy outcome research, therefore, the single case plays a pivotal position as providing a starting point for the development of new therapies within the range of evaluative approaches to psychotherapy research as identified by Kazdin (1992). It is also seen as a means by which regular practitioners may involve themselves in research since the demands of SCED tend to be less resource-hungry than psychotherapy group evaluations. Accordingly, many have suggested that SCED may provide a route for everyday clinicians to follow if they are to continue to involve themselves in research after training (Hayes, 1981; Stanley, 1985).

Another reason for employing single cases includes the study of rare clinical conditions whereby the limited availability of clients precludes a group evaluation approach, especially in the first instance. Examples of this particular strategy include the evaluation of behavioural treatments of tic disorders (Turpin, 1983) and the in-depth investigation of neuropsychological patients with specific and unique head injuries (Dywan and Segalowitz, 1986). Single cases can also provide important illustrative material about the implementation of new treatment approaches. Such accounts are frequently to be found in the appendices of published studies which have relied upon more traditional group evaluative approaches to outcome research. One particularly important area for the use of such case material is when therapy is ineffective. Although an evidence-based approach emphasises identifying efficacious interventions, no single treatment will be effective for all clients. Breakthroughs in knowledge surrounding psychotherapy frequently arise from the detailed investigation of why certain forms of treatment are ineffective for some clients (e.g., Foa and Emmelkamp, 1983). Single case approaches have much to offer the study of treatment-resistant cases. However, the degree to which unsuccessful cases are published and discussed tends to be limited by the implicit bias of scientific journals only to publish positive results. This form of bias may seriously distort the perceived efficacy of treatments which have been evaluated using single case approaches. It is usual, therefore, that only positive accounts of new treatment strategies are published at the expense of negative findings. Typical examples of this involve some specific psychological interventions for Tourette's syndrome and the use of 'ear plugs' to control auditory hallucinations in psychosis. Singularly and enthusiastically published positive results have tended to give way to the later publication of more sceptical and negative case series within both these clinical areas (Birchwood, 1986; Turpin, 1983).

The adoption of a SCED approach to clinical work may also have some benefits for clinical practice outside of a research setting. These approaches can be employed to demonstrate individual effectiveness of a particular approach to sceptical colleagues or managers. Within the context of cognitive-behavioural work, using single case approaches to data collection facilitates a collaborative relationship between therapist and client which can enhance both the client's motivation and 'self efficacy'. The approach enables client and therapist to sit down together to identify agreed treatment goals, decide upon how individual outcomes should be assessed, and how the impact of therapy can be monitored. It is acknowledged that such an open and goal-directed approach to treatment would not be consistent or appropriate for all forms of psychotherapy.

Finally, the demonstration of clinical change using objective measures can be particularly important when working indirectly with care staff. Woods and Cullen (1983) demonstrated that staffs' subjective perception of clinical change is frequently biased and may not match more objective change measures, especially for chronic problems. They suggest that this is due to 'recency effects' whereby care staffs' perceptions are determined by recent events which then makes it difficult for them to track change accurately over an extended period of time. The use of SCED allows a more objective assessment to take place. This can be particularly useful in motivating and informing staff that their efforts do yield positive effects, particularly with individuals with challenging and chronic or even deteriorating problems who have previously been resistant to change.

It is commonly believed that SCED can only be used by therapists working in either a behavioural or cognitive-behavioural framework. Although it is undoubtedly the case that many examples of single case work are published within behaviourally oriented journals, this doesn't have to be the case (Aeschleman, 1991; Crane, 1985; Hayes, 1981). As Long and Hollin (1995) have identified, single cases have been studied using a wide variety of different therapeutic frameworks. What is required, however, are that certain goals of therapy can be established, that they are measurable is some way, and that there is a framework (e.g., formulation) that links the therapeutic model to intervention, together with some hypotheses relating to clinical change. The basic principles underlying single case work will be further elaborated in the next section.

Basic principles underlying single case experimental designs

Single case experimental deigns rely on several widely recognised and important principles (Kazdin, 1982; Hayes, 1981). These are usually described as: (a) repeated measurement, (b) stable baselines, (c) single and well-specified treatments, (d) reversibility and (e) generalisability. In order to understand the implementation of single case designs it is essential to appreciate the relevance of these principles. Moreover, it is these characteristics that distinguish the SCED from the ordinary case study. If a clinical study is unable to address the above principles, it is likely that it will be classified as a case study.

Before expanding on the relevance of the above principles it is important to understand what a single case design is attempting to accomplish. As emphasised by Kazdin and others, the traditional case study is flawed since it relies on *post hoc* explanations and interpretations which can be subjected to different sources of bias. The purpose of single case design is to identify these potential sources of bias, and control for their influence, and in so doing to eliminate them as potential alternative explanations for the observed pattern of results that constitutes the case study. What potential sources of confounding might obscure the interpretation that a particular intervention has had a specific effect within a client on a particular outcome? For example, if during the course of therapy a client's relationship breaks down or a colleague alters the level of prescribed medication, to what extent is any clinical change a function of the therapy provided, the relationship difficulty experienced by the client, the change in medication or a combination/interaction of all three? Although some might argue that to attempt to disentangle these factors may be totally artificial, the SCED attempts to place on the case study certain limits or boundaries which might distinguish or minimise the impact of these confounding variables.

Threats to the validity of a case study

One of the foundations of experimental design in psychology is the identification of confounding variables which need to be controlled in order to rule out alternative accounts or interpretations of a study designed to test a particular hypothesis. These sources of confounding have been described as threats to internal and external validity by Cook and Campbell (1979) in their classic text on quasi-experimental design. Internal validity concerns the extent to which the findings can be interpreted in support of the proposition that an intervention had a *specific* effect on the clinical outcome. They list a series of possible scenarios which if present would severely compromise the study and limit the validity of the conclusions drawn. These circumstances include:

- *History*. Here extraneous concurrent events (e.g., relationship break-up, change in medication) may happen alongside the clinical intervention studied. These events may either be known or unknown to the experimenter.
- *Maturation*. This refers to a change process which may be endogenous to the client and independent of the applied experimental intervention or treatment. For example, neuropsychologists and physiotherapists frequently attempt early interventions aimed at facilitating recovery from brain injuries such as a stroke or a closed head injury. However, if left 'untreated' most individuals with head injuries show a degree of spontaneous recovery in functioning following the injury. Any measurement of clinical change must, therefore, be interpreted against a moving baseline of endogenous change associated with recovery.
- *Testing (reactivity)*. The exposure of a client to the assessment process itself is not a neutral act, particularly when structured forms of assessment such as questionnaires or self-monitoring diaries are employed. The very task of inviting the client to self-assess requires a possible shift in self-awareness and focusing on possible new information. The nature of questionnaires might seek to clarify a client's understanding or attribution of events and, by doing so, challenge their existing attributions and explanations. Thus, the very act of participation and assessment within a case study may bring about therapeutic change.

Indeed, such changes are frequently observed during the baseline phase prior to the introduction of any *formal* intervention.

- *Instrumentation (reliability)*. Nearly every assessment tool which a clinician will employ will have some error of measurement associated with it. If a client's depression is assessed using a BDI as 12 on one occasion and 14 on the next, is this a significant and meaningful change? Given that all measurement devices will have some associated error of measurement, it is important that these incidental changes in measures across time are not misinterpreted as specific treatment effects.

Other sources of confounding include regression to the mean, multiple intervention problems and instability. The interested reader should consult Cook and Campbell (1979) for a more in-depth account of these threats to internal validity.

Threats to external validity were also identified by Cook and Campbell as important sources of confounding which require experimental control. External validity concerns the extent to which experimenters can generalise their findings from one particular set of observations to another. With respect to case studies, generalisation refers to the degree to which a finding observed within a single individual can be extended to other individuals and in other settings. Essentially, two sources of bias which might limit generalisability may be identified:

- *Selected individuals/samples*. The degree to which individuals or samples are specifically identified will limit the generalisability of the findings. The more heterogeneous the sample from which individual cases are drawn, the more likely that the results will generalise across individuals. In the case of psychotherapy, the importance of generalising across variables such as social class, education, gender and ethnicity will be important for establishing the widespread applicability or otherwise of psychotherapeutic approaches throughout the NHS.
- *Biased interventions/settings*. The setting or the specific manner in which an intervention is delivered might affect the specific outcome within a particular individual. For case studies, the issue here is one of clinical replication. Are results obtained within specialised research clinics by presumably highly trained therapists generalisable to practitioners attempting to replicate similar interventions within routine clinical practice?

The above threats to validity identified by Cook and Campbell need to be carefully considered by researchers wishing to employ SCEDs. Only by being aware of these threats, can the researcher consider and exclude common alternative explanations regarding the relationship between intervention and outcome. As Kazdin (1981) has argued, the use of a traditional case study exposes the researcher to a variety of interpretative biases which, at best, have to be accounted for when interpreting the results and, at worst, may be confounded with specific treatment effects leading to misleading conclusions. Moreover, Hayes (1981) has extended this argument to support the use of specific experimental designs which control for or minimise these threats to internal validity. For example, a common control for historical concurrent extraneous events is to repeat or replicate the treatment effect. If a specific treatment–outcome relationship can be observed, and this result is repeated a number of times on different occasions, it is unlikely that some other event *unrelated* to the intervention will have occurred successively in order to account for this particular repeating pattern of results. The more consistent the replication of the finding, the less likely it is that some other concurrent event has occurred alongside the specific intervention. Traditionally, group evaluation designs address historical threats to validity by examining the replication of findings over a sample of different individuals. For single case research the replication is over different occasions within the same individual. Another example of designing against threats to validity concerns maturational effects. As discussed above, such endogenous changes may take the form of recovery functions. They may be distinguished experimentally from intervention effects by observing within an individual the form of the recovery function under baseline conditions in the absence of an intervention and comparing it following the introduction of the intervention. A specific treatment effect would predict a change in the gradient of any pre-existing recovery function.

Design principles

The following principles have been evolved for SCEDs in order to control for threats to validity and include repeated measurement, stable baselines, single well-specified treatments, reversibility and generalisability. In order to understand the rationales underlying these principles, it needs to be acknowledged that their origins extend back to experimental studies of animal learning conducted largely in the middle of the twentieth century. Essentially, psychologists interested in animal learning conducted single subject/animal experiments to investigate the effects of changes in various environmmental contingencies on patterns in animal behaviour. Hence, the knowledge base of animal learning derives very much from single case experimental studies, together with replications, and has relied predominantly on the visual analysis of the graphical displays of results. This is in marked contrast to group nomothetic approaches, used elsewhere within psychology, and the reliance on statistical testing. The methodology underlying this approach was summarised in Sidman's (1960) classic handbook.

It is these basic principles which have been extended to single case experimental designs. An obvious reason for this extension was the application of learning theory in the form of Applied Behavior Analysis to a whole range of human problems, but particularly within the fields of learning disabilities and special education within the USA. This resulted in learning theory paradigms and methodologies being transferred into the clincal domain. It has to be emphasised, however, that the single case approaches that these methods have inspired are frequently used to evaluate interventions which are no longer associated with learning theory. In these circumstances, it is likely that rationales developed on the basis of learning theory may no longer apply. An example which we will return to is the use of either withdrawal or reversal techniques to demonstrate the specificity of an intervention. From a learning theory perspective, strong evidence of an environmemtal effect can be demonstrated if the contingencies can be manipulated to obtain withdrawal effects or reversals in the pattern of responding observed. Hence, a particular environmental event (e.g., social praise) could be shown to reinforce particular desirable behaviours (e.g., social interaction) in a young person with learning disabilitities, if the behaviours increase when the praise is contingently offered but remain constant when the praise is withheld. Observation of a direct and repeated effect between the behaviours and the environmental effects provides evidence that the contingencies are reinforcing the behaviour. However, this is based on certain learning theory assumptions concerning both the short-term and reversible nature of environmental contingencies. As we will discuss later, these assumptions do not apply to the vast majority of internventions that are employed within psychotherapy. The evidence, therefore, that can be gathered from reversal or withdrawal designs is limited only to situations whereby the intervention will have short-term and reversible effects, and if these assumptions cannot be made then the utility of reversal designs as a principle underlying single case methodology is markedly curtailed (see also Hayes, 1981; Morley, 1996).

Bearing in mind the origins and possible limitations of the design principles underlying single case designs, each principle will now be briefly reviewed.

Repeated measurement

Perhaps the most important distinguishing feature between a case study and a SCED is the number of observations or data points that have been obtained. A basic aim of a SCED is to demonstrate within each subject intrasubject change using repeated measures. It is hypothesised that when comparing within a subject measures obtained prior to treatment with those during and following treatment, some therapeutic effect will be observed. The greater number of repeated measures obtained, and the greater the consistency of change across these measures, the more confidence that an effect has taken place. This is analogous to a group design comparing, say, therapeutic and placebo groups whereby the repeated measures are obtained across the different individuals constituting the groups, as opposed to the single case whereby the repeated measures are derived from a single individual but at many different points in time.

In order to achieve repeated observations, the measures used have to be easily replicable. This means that they can easily be repeatedly administered, reliable and relatively free of error or bias. This may discount many traditional forms of psychotherapy outcome evaluation that use extensive psychometric questionnaires or interviews designed only to be used on a single or infrequent sessional basis. Instead, daily measures derived from structured self-report diaries or staff observational schedules are frequently employed. Hence the case study which includes only a single psychometric measure of pre- and post-intervention change should not be considered a SCED design. However, the inclusion of additional repeated daily diary measures would allow a SCED evaluation to be made. The question arises, therefore, as to what is the minimun number of repeated measures to be obtained in order for a study to be considered as a SCED. The strict minimum is probably at least three baseline and three intervention observations per single measure (see Barlow and Hersen, 1984). The number of observations constituting an adequate baseline is dealt with in the next section. For a greater discussion of different measures and issues of reliability readers might consult Turpin *et al.* (in press) or the recent review of Primavera *et al.* (1996).

Stable baselines

The basic premise for using repeated measures is that clinical change will be self-evident following the introduction of some therapeutic intervention. The degree to which change is discernible depends both on the magnitude of the therapeutic impact and on the nature of the pre-intervention baseline. The greatest confidence about therapeutic impact can only be made when a stable baseline has been obtained (see Figure 7.1). If the baseline is unstable (i.e., it displays an existing trend or slope, cyclical variability or excessive variability or noise), the confidence of detecting therapeutic change is much reduced. It is frequently suggested that baselines should be collected until they demonstrate stability. However, this may not be practical within the psycotherapeutic situation

Baselines should be stable (mean level) with low variability. Problems arise if baselines display:

(a) Linear trends:

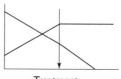

Treatment

(b) Higher-order trends:

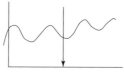

Treatment

(c) High variability

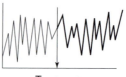

Treatment

Figure 7.1 Stable baselines.

Note: The presence of (a), (b) or (c) makes both visual or mathematical analysis difficult.

and a frequent question posed concerns the minimum length of baseline acceptable. Huitema (1985) has reported that the most frequent baseline size used in 881 studies published in the *Journal of Applied Behavior Analysis* ranged between three and ten observations. In practice, it is likely that baselines will be obtained perhaps within the second and third sessions as part of an overall assessment process. If derived from daily ratings it is feasible to collect baseline data ranging from 7–20 or so observations across a period of a few weeks, which ought to be more than sufficient, although this will depend ultimately upon the type of analysis to be employed.

Treatments are well specified and documented

In order to assess the effects of an intervention, it is important that essentially only a single treatment is applied at any one time and that its nature can be specified. Many therapists have difficulties with this limitation since it forces the therapist to assess and formulate the case and prescibe a particular therapeutic approach in advance (see Morley, 1996). However, this doesn't mean that case reformulation and changes in therapy cannot occur; if possible, they need to be anticipated and incorporated into the design. Another issue of contention is exactly how is 'a single intervention' defined? Again this is the responsibility of the therapist and depends largely on why the case is being evaluated in the first place. Therapists frequently argue that they plan to use a combination of different treament strategies or techniques. If the aim of the evaluation is to assess the overall impact of this package of strategies, then the package, if it can be defined, becomes synonymous with a 'single treatment'. Another problem frequently encountered is the presence of other therapeutic work such as medication or other inputs from a multidisciplinary team. Two possible approaches to this common problem are available: to negotiate keeping external therapeutic inputs constant (i.e., no planned changes in medication regime), or directly involving the other therapists in the design and attempting to evaluate the comparative effectiveness of these other approaches with respect to the psychotherapeutic intervention.

Replications, reversibility and withdrawals

It is argued that greater confidence in the impact of treatment on intrasubject change can be demonstrated if the effects can be replicated within repeated measures, across different phases of a design, and that the effect of the intervention on the measures can be directly manipulated through either reversals or withdrawals. Replication is largely a means to protect against either historical or maturational threats to internal validity. Hence, if the results from the simplest AB design (Baseline vs Treatment) can be replicated, then it is less likely that some extraneous event can account for the original but replicated change from baseline to treatment. This is in essence the logic of the ABAB design (see Figure 7.2) which is frequently advocated as a standard for SCED. However, within the context of many psychological therapies such designs have important limitations. Essentially, their rationale depends upon reversible treatment effects analogous to contingency manipulations employed within applied behavioural analysis. Fortunately, at least for the client, many interventions are considered as long-lasting and hopefully resistant to reversal, relying on dynamic intrapersonal changes (e.g., cognitive therapy will promote schema changes). It is, therefore, neither theoretically likely nor ethically desirable that a positive treatment effect can be reversed. Hence, ABAB or ABA designs have their limitations since replication due to withdrawal of treatment and return to baseline may not actually be predicted due to the irreversible nature of the intervention employed. Non-reversible treatments that are usually identified include psycho-educational approaches, skills-based therapies, schema-directed therapies, altered therapeutic environments, staff attitudes and training, surgical or long-term pharmacological interventions. Nevertheless, the introduction of a brief second baseline can be useful to assess and demonstrate the permanence or otherwise of therapeutic change. This can be practically incorporated into 'therapeutic holidays' whereby clients are encouraged to assess progress by putting aside what has recently been learnt or temporarily suspending homework exercises or self-coping techniques.

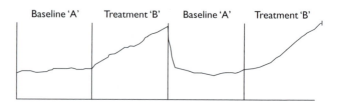

The ideal case of intrasubject replicability is the withdrawal design:

Baseline 'A'   Treatment 'B'   Baseline 'A'   Treatment 'B'

Figure 7.2 Withdrawal designs.

Ethically this is defensible on the principle of demonstrating efficacy to the client of an intensive therapeutic regime. It is also likely that a second baseline will be introduced at the termination of treatment in the form of a follow-up specifically to assess the permanence and stability of change. If there has been a deterioration in therapeutic improvement, this might argue for the introduction of 'booster sessions': such a protocol would result in baseline and treament phases not that indistinct from a classic ABAB design. Further discussions of issues surrounding ethical and clinical implications of withdrawal designs are available in the literature (Hayes, 1981; Long and Hollin, 1995; Svenson and Chassan, 1967).

Generalisability

A common misconception about SCEDs is that they invole only a single subject (Aeschleman, 1991). In order to derive general explanations or laws of behaviour change, effects should be generalisable. The converse of this is that these laws ought to account for known sources of variability, and this is often obscured in group designs. Although a single N=1 design has limited generalisability, a series of N=1 designs should identify sources of variability and lead to greater generalisability (see Barlow and Hersen, 1984; Kratochwill and Williams, 1988; Sidman, 1960). Different types of generalisability include: across individual clients or clients with similar attributes, across different therapists and across different settings or situations. The issue of generalisability is resolved, therefore, through replication across different clients, therapists and settings. Hence, N=1 studies lead on to N=1 series, small N designs with homogeneous subjects and well-controlled conditions. Finally, it is also important to ensure that single case research is not only generalisable but also clinically replicable within ordinary clinical settings.

Practical considerations and examples

Limitations of space prevent a detailed account of the practical implementation of these ideas to psychotherapy evaluation. However, since there exist many reviews and texts devoted generally to this subject (e.g., Franklin et al., 1996; Barlow and Hersen, 1984; Kazdin, 1982; Kratochwill, 1978; Kratochwill and Levin, 1992; Morley, 1996; Ottenbacher, 1986; Turpin et al., in press), only a cursory summary of the issues will be given. Nevertheless, some of the more important questions that researchers wishing to use SCED should ask themselves are

Table 7.1 Practical issues to be addressed

Design stage	Specific question
Identifying clinical questions and hypotheses	• Can it be clearly stated? • Have you a clear formulation that links assessment, theory and intervention? • Can therapeutic predictions be made? • Can these be operationalised and measured? • Is the question worth while – who will benefit (client, peers, etc.)?
Identifying materials and resources	• What measures are required to assess therapeutic aims and goals? • Are they suitable for a SCED? • Do they assess symptoms and functioning? • Are they acceptable to the client? • Have I the co-operation of staff and colleagues to collect data, if required?
Choosing an appropriate design	• Identify threats to validity which need to be controlled for by the design. • Ensure that treatment phases can be identified, clearly specified and are independent. • Are the effects reversible? • Should a withdrawal phase be included? • Should multiple baselines or measures be included?
Data collection and supervision of the study	• Is the overall design acceptable to the client and have I obtained informed consent, especially for subsequent publication? • Have all staff been adequately trained or briefed? • Is it necessary to perform reliability checks? • Manipulation checks – ensure that intervention is being applied in the manner desired. • Is data being reliably collected and stored confidentially?
Analysis	• Visual versus statistical? • Clinical or statistical significance? • How are the results to be used – for publication or as clinical communication?
Interpretation	• What are the main changes or effects? • How do they correspond to predictions? • Are they valid given the design?

Table 7.1 continued

	• What alternative explanations (i.e., threats to validity) are there? • Are the effects reliable or clinically significant? • Are they generalisible or clinically replicable?
Communication and dissemination	• To whom should I communicate the findings? • Is it appropriate to share the findings with the client? • What level of understanding is required by the audience? • What format is suitable – clinical forum or journal article? • What are the implications for the client and the service? • Have I thanked client and staff?

summarised in Table 7.1. These will be illustrated with respect to a published SCED (Kellett and Beail, 1997) which adopted this approach in order to evaluate the efficacy of a psychodynamic-interpersonal style psychotherapeutic intervention for an unusual Post-Traumatic Stress Disorder (PTSD) condition.

As is indicated in Table 7.1, before embarking on the use of a SCED, the rationale for using this approach in relation to the actual clinical case and the research question posed should be clearly established. In the case of Kellett and Beail (1997), the rationale concerned an atypical presentation of PTSD, together with the opportunity to explore the efficacy of a psychodynamically oriented approach to PTSD which had not previously been reported in the literature. The case concerned a woman suffering a traumatised reaction to a road traffic accident and subsequently experiencing repeated bizzare nightmares. They hypothesised that 'psychodynamic-interpersonal psychotherapy', based on a manualised version (Shapiro and Firth, 1985), would reduce the frequency and intensity of nightmares for this client, together with improvements in depression and anxiety.

Once suitable hypotheses have been formulated, appropriate measures have to be identified. In this particular case, a daily diary was designed to record the frequency and intensity of nightmares, the degree of fear and upset experienced (using a 7-point Likert scale), and the time to recover from each nightmare and return to sleep. In addition, various psychometric measures (i.e., Beck Depression Inventory, Inventory of Interpersonal Problems and the Symptom Check-List: SCL 90r) were obtained at assessment, during treatment and at follow-up.

Assuming the measures to have been appropriately chosen, it is then necessary to adopt a design. As has already been discussed, a great variety of different designs have already been reviewed in the literature (e.g., Barlow and Hersen, 1984; Hayes, 1981; Kearns, 1986; Ottenbacher, 1986). However, many of these designs have only been illustrated using behaviour modification examples. Accordingly, Morleys' (1996) chapter is also to be recommended since it provides an easy-to-follow introduction to different design types, and includes examples from adult psychotherapy. In the present example, a simple AB design, together with a six-month follow-up, was chosen and conducted simultaneously across a set of multiple measures. The baselines consisted of the weekly averages of two weeks of daily ratings obtained prior to the formal initiation of therapy.

Once the design has been finalised and the client has consented to participate in the study, the data can be collected. It is at this stage that the design and study frequently break down. Common problems include inappropriate, inaccessible or excessive measures; poor therapeutic alliance and lack of client co-operation; failure of other staff to fulfil participation in the study, and many other pitfalls.

Assuming that an appropriate data set has been collected, an analytic strategy can be identified. The major decision to be made concerns the use of techniques for statistical analysis. Traditionally, single case data have been analysed visually using graphical presentation, together with some simple descriptive statistics such as mean or medians (see Morley and Adams, 1989, 1991; Ottenbacher, 1986; Parsonson and Baer, 1986). However, some authors have argued for a more systematic approach to statistical evaluation (e.g., Edgington, 1984; Gorman and Allison, 1996). Unfortunately, due to a unique statistical feature of single subject data termed 'serial dependency', the assumptions underlying most of the commonly used statistical tests are violated (Wampold, 1988); this severely limits their application. In the present clinical example, graphs displaying the changes in the various measures were plotted and visually inspected. As can be seen in Figure 7.3, reductions occur within most of the symptom ratings following the intervention. In addition, clinical significance was also evaluated according to Jacobson's (1988) definition.

Finally, the results have to be interpreted and appropriately disseminated, which in this particular case led to publication in an appropriate journal.

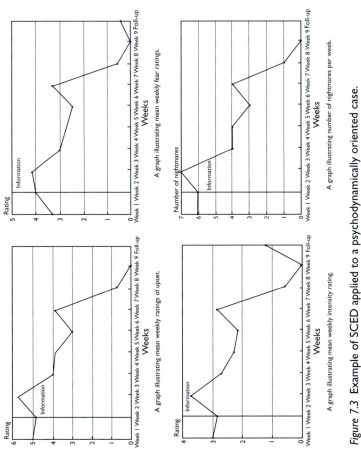

Figure 7.3 Example of SCED applied to a psychodynamically oriented case.

Source: Kellett and Beail (1997), published with permission from the *British Journal of Medical Psychology*.

Conclusions

The purpose of this chapter has been to review the general principles underlying SCED and to suggest that they might play a role in helping to establish the efficacy of psychotherapeutic interventions. Such a methodology might assist psychotherapists to address the agenda established by the 'evidence-based medicine' movement and, in doing so, encourage practising clinicians to evaluate their clinical work and engage with clinical research. However, it should be recognised that much of the work published using SCED has derived from more experimentally based psychotherapies and that many of the fundemental principles underlying this approach might be antithetical to some psychotherapies, especially those that are more dynamically oriented. Notwithstanding these potential obstacles to the implementation of single case approaches, I should like to invite interested therapists to explore how these approaches might be integrated with their own therapeutic work. To achieve this, it will be important to identify clear clinical formulations which link to therapeutic strategies. These strategies need to identify various therapeutic goals which can then be assessed as clinical outcomes and reliably and repeatedly measured. In addition, clinicians will need to be disciplined in order to follow a predetermined therapeutic strategy, but also sufficiently flexible so as to engage the client and be ready to reformulate and redirect the therapy as the therapeutic process unfolds.

Acknowledgement

This chapter is based on ideas and examples published within Turpin *et al.* (in press).

References

Aeschleman, S.R. (1991) 'Single-subject research designs: some misconceptions', *Rehabiliation Psychology* 36: 43–49.

Barlow, D.H. (1997) 'Cognitive-behavioral therapy for panic disorders: current status', *Journal of Clinical Psychiatry* 58 Suppl. 2: 32–36.

Barlow, D.H. and Hersen, M. (1984) *Single Case Experimental Designs: Strategies for Studying Behaviour Change* (2nd edn). New York: Pergamon.

Birchwood, M. (1986) 'Control of auditory hallucinations through occlusion of monaural auditory input', *British Journal of Psychiatry* 149: 104–107.

Bromley, D.R. (1986) *The Case Study Method in Psychology and Related Disciplines*. Chichester: Wiley.

Chadwick, P.D.J. and Birchwood, M.J. (1994) 'The omnipotence of voices – a cognitive approach to auditory hallucinations', *British Journal of Psychiatry* 164: 190–201.

Clark, D.M., Salkovskis, P.M. and Chalkley, A.J. (1985) 'Respiratory control as a treatment for panic attacks', *Journal of Behavior Therapy and Experimental Psychology* 16: 23–30.

Cook, T.D. and Campbell, D.T. (1979) *Quasi Experimentation: Design and Analysis Issues in Field Settings.* Chicago: Rand McNally.

Crane, D.R. (1985) 'Single-case experimental designs in family therapy research: limitations and considerations', *Family Process* 24: 69–77.

Drury, V., Birchwood, M., Cochrane, R. and Macmillan, F. (1996) 'Cognitive therapy and recovery from acute psychosis: a controlled trial. 1: Impact on psychotic symptoms', *British Journal of Psychiatry* 169: 593–601.

Dywan, J. and Segalowitz, S.J. (1986) 'The role of the case study in neuropsychological research', in Valsiner, J. (ed.) *The Individual Subject and Scientific Psychology.* New York: Plenum Press.

Edgington, E.S. (1984) 'Statistics and single case designs', *Progress in Behaviour Modification* 16: 93–119.

Foa, E. and Emmelkamp, P.M.G. (1983) *Failures in Behaviour Therapy.* New York: Wiley.

Franklin, R.D., Allison, D.B. and Gorman, B.S. (1996) *Design and Analysis of Single-Case Research.* Hillsdale, N.J.: Lawrence Erlbaum.

Goffman, I. (1961) *Asylums: Essays on the Social Situation of Mental Patients and Other Inmates.* Chicago: Aldine.

Gorman, B.S. and Allison, D.B. (1996) 'Statistical alternatives for single-case designs', in Franklin, R.D., Allison, D.B. and Gorman, B.S. (eds) *Design and Analysis of Single-case Research.* Hillsdale, N.J.: Lawrence Erlbaum.

Hayes, S.C. (1981) 'Single case experimental design and empirical clinical practice', *Journal of Consulting and Clinical Psychology* 49: 193–211.

Hegarty, S. and Evans, P (1985) *Research and Evaluation Methods in Special Education.* Windsor: NFER-Nelson.

Hilliard, R.B. (1993) 'Single case methodology in psychotherapy process and outcome research', *Journal of Consulting and Child Psychology* 61: 373–380.

Huitema, B. (1985) 'Autocorrelation in applied behavior analysis: a myth', *Behavioral Assessment* 7: 109–120.

Jacobson, N.S. (1988) 'Defining clinically significant change: an introduction', *Behavioral Assessment* 10: 131–132.

Kazdin, A.E. (1981) 'Drawing valid inferences from case studies', *Journal of Consulting and Clinical Psychology* 49: 183–192.

Kazdin, A.E. (1982) *Single-case Research Designs: Methods for Clinical and Applied Settings.* New York: Oxford University Press.

Kazdin, A.E. (1992) *Research Design in Clinical Psychology* (2nd edn). New York: Macmillan.

Kearns, K.P. (1986) 'Flexibility of single-subject experimental designs. Part II:

Design selection and arrangement of experimental phases', *Journal of Speech and Hearing Disorders* 51: 204–214.

Kellett, S and Beail, N. (1997) 'The treatment of chronic post-traumatic nightmares using psychodynamic-interpersonal psychotherapy: a single-case study', *British Journal of Medical Psychology* 70: 35–49.

Kratochwill, T.R. (ed.) (1978) *Single Subject Research: Strategies for Evaluating Change*. New York: Academic Press.

Kratochwill, T.R. and Levin, J.R. (1992) *Single Case Research Design and Analysis: New Directions for Psychology and Education*. Hillsdale, N.J.: Lawrence Erlbaum.

Kratochwill, T.R. and Williams, B.L. (1988) 'Perspectives on pitfalls and hassles in single-subject research', *Journal of the Association of Severe Handicaps* 13: 147–154.

Kuipers, E., Garety, P., Fowler, D., Dunn, G., Bebbington, P., Freeman, D. and Hadley, C. (1997) 'London–East Anglia randomised controlled trial of cognitive behavioual therapy for psychosis. 1: Effects of the treatment phase', *British Journal of Psychiatry* 171: 319–327.

Long, C.G. and Hollin C.R. (1995) 'Single case design: a critique of methodology and analysis of recent trends', *Clinical Psychology and Psychotherapy* 2: 177–191.

Morley, S. (1996) 'Single case research', in Parry, G. and Watts, F.N. (eds) *Behavioural and Mental Health Research: A Handbook of Skills and Methods* (2nd edn). Hove, UK: Psychology Press.

Morley, S. and Adams, M. (1989) 'Some simple statistical tests for exploring single case time series data', *British Journal of Clinical Psychology* 28: 1–18.

Morley, S. and Adams, M. (1991) 'Graphical analysis of single case time series data', *British Journal of Clinical Psychology* 30: 97–115.

Ottenbacher, K.J. (1986) *Evaluating Clinical Change*. Baltimore: Williams and Wilkins.

Parsonson, B.S. and Baer, D.M. (1986) 'The graphic analysis of data', in Poling, A. and Fuqua, R.W. (eds) *Research Methods in Behavior Analysis*. New York: Plenum Press.

Primavera, L.H., Allison, D.B. and Alfonson, V.C. (1996) 'Measurement of dependent variables', in Franklin, R.D., Allison, D.B. and Gorman, B.S. (eds) *Design and Analysis of Single-case Research*. Hillsdale, N.J.: Lawrence Erlbaum.

Shallice, R., Burgess, P.W. and Frith, C.D. (1991) 'Can the neuropsychological case-study approach be applied to schizophrenia?', *Psychological Medicine* 21: 661–673.

Shapiro, D.A. and Firth, J. (1985) 'Exploratory therapy manual for the Sheffield Psychotherapy Project', Sheffield Applied Psychology Unit Memo, no. 733, University of Sheffield.

Sidman, M. (1960) *Tactics of Scientific Research: Evaluating Experimental Data in Psychology*. New York: Basic Books.

Smith, J.A. (1996) 'Qualitative methodology: analysing participants' perspectives', *Current Opinion in Psychiatry* 9: 417–421.

Stake, R.E. (1995) *The Art of Case Study Research*. Thousand Oaks, Calif.: Sage.

Stanley, B. (1985) 'Towards "applicable" single case research', *Bulletin of the British Psychological Society* 38: 33–35.

Stiles, W.B. (1993) 'Quality control in qualitative research', *Clinical Psychology Review* 13: 593–618.

Svenson, S.E. and Chassan, J.B. (1967) 'A note on ethics and patient consent in single-case design', *Journal of Nervous and Mental Disease* 145: 206–207.

Turpin, G. (1983) 'The behavioural management of tic disorders: critical review', *Advances in Behavioural Research and Therapy* 5: 203–245.

Turpin, G., Morley, S. and Adams, M. (in press) *Single Case Methodology: A Practitioner's Guide*. London: Sage.

Valsiner, J. (1986) *The Individual Subject and Scientific Psychology*. New York: Plenum.

Wampold, B.E. (1988) 'Special mini-series on autocorrelation', *Behavioral Assessment* 10: 227–297.

Woods, P.A. and Cullen, C. (1983) 'Determinants of staff behaviour in long-term care', *Behavioural Psychotherapy* 11: 4–17.

Yin, R.K. (1994) *Case Study Research: Design and Methods*. Beverly Hills: Sage.

Chapter 8

Working hypotheses in psychoanalytic psychotherapy

Kevin Healy

Introduction

W.B. Yeats wrote of the impossibility of telling apart 'the dancer from the dance'. I suggest it is equally difficult to distinguish the working hypotheses from the workers. In this chapter I will present Jane's clinical story, and discuss possible working hypotheses generated from a psychoanalytic perspective.

Working hypotheses generated by workers are greatly influenced by their personalities and styles. Jon Stokes in his chapter in the book *The Unconscious at Work* (Stokes, 1994), writes of underlying predispositions that lead us to do the work we do. He proposed that doctors and nurses are drawn to their profession by unresolved issues relating to dependency. Social workers are attracted to their work by issues related to the basic assumption fight/flight. Therapists are attracted by the basic assumption of pairing. Similarly, I suggest we may be attracted to particular theoretical orientations because of issues that remain active within our mental life, whether conscious or unconscious. It may be that the propositions and hypotheses we espouse may just as readily be determined by our own particular struggles and problems, as by our resort to reason and rational argument.

The work of therapy must be seen within its context. There are boundaries around all pieces of work, which both contain the work and consequently limit the work involved. A therapist may be the sole person with whom a patient discusses or re-enacts their problems. Other patients will have family and friends with whom they may recreate the difficulties and find some solutions. Other patients will be, for example, in-patients at the Cassel Hospital, where the psychotherapy is seen as one active ingredient of the treatment package, alongside active psychosocial working, and the experience of living as part of a therapeutic community.

In any context the resources available largely determine the work of the therapy, and greatly influence the mode of therapy employed.

I suggest that the patient is also a worker, who needs to be actively engaged in generating working hypotheses. These hypotheses may be linked with the patient's particular problems and difficulties. They probably also reflect personality and living styles. Such hypotheses need to tap into a patient's strengths and resources if they are indeed to be effective and truly working.

The professional worker

I turn now to the therapist involved in the work I will shortly describe – myself. There are many issues of a personal nature that greatly determine the type of working hypotheses *I* can generate. I have inherited a genetic potential (nature), which has developed within the context of my life experiences (nurture). I recognise personal struggles around dependency and independence. I was raised as a Roman Catholic in Ireland, and remain influenced by social, political and cultural aspects of my early and current environment. I am a curious, inquisitive person, with a clear philosophy of life. I came to London to pursue a personal psychoanalysis and a training at the Institute of Psychoanalysis. I am now greatly influenced by my wife and partner of twenty years, and by my two young children, who bring so many extra dimensions to my daily life. I have many interests which at times amount to passions, and which no doubt shape and determine the style and content of my hypothesising.

In 1997 I came across an article entitled 'Research-informed Psychotherapy' by Claus Grawe, in the journal of the Society for Psychotherapy Research. Research-informed psychotherapy (or RIP) is about the death of older concepts and slavish adherence to various theoretical schools. Grawe introduces research-based concepts and procedures, and proposes that psychotherapy is now in transition from faith to fact. Grawe proposes that on the basis of his extensive work on the process and outcome of psychotherapy, he has recognised four basic mechanisms of change in psychotherapy. These are:

1   mastery/coping;
2   clarification of meaning;
3   problem actuation;
4   resource activation.

I shall use these mechanisms of change when discussing my work with Jane.

Jane's clinical story

Jane was a 26-year-old woman, who spent 15 months as an in-patient on the Adult Unit at the Cassel Hospital approximately ten years ago. She was referred by her GP because of severe self-mutilation, terrifying nightmares and persistent relationship difficulties. She had been damaging herself since the age of eight, frequently head-banging, and hitting her arms against walls (leading to fractures on three occasions). She had repeatedly cut herself on her wrists, legs and stomach with razor-blades. She had spent the greater part of her life between the ages of five and ten years in hospital after surgery on her eyes, having traumatised her eye with a pencil as a 5-year-old.

Prior to referral, she had found it increasingly difficult to work as a trainee solicitor, and contrary to expectations had failed her recent exams. She felt lonely, isolated and had very few friends. She had become very anxious in social situations, and was terrified of sleeping at night-time because of the consequent horrifying nightmares she experienced. She was seen by a child psychiatrist at the age of 12 because of difficulties adjusting to school. She refused to talk there, and stopped going after six sessions. She again saw a counsellor during her time reading Sociology at college. She did not find then that talking helped. She was being treated with benzodiazepines by her general practitioner for anxiety.

She was the youngest of three children. Her brother was four years older, her sister two years older than she. Her father was a violent, alcoholic man, and left the family home when she was two years old. Her family remembers him as 'a bad ogre'. Her mother had been agoraphobic for many years. Jane felt she had to protect her mother from many problems throughout her life. Jane's brother, John, who was four years older, took on a father-figure role in the household. Like father, he too became violent to his younger sister, while at the same time being the apple of his mother's eye. Jane and John had a close, emotional, intense relationship, which progressed from closeness and violence to sexual contact and intimacy, which persisted throughout Jane's adolescent and early adult life. Following assessment at the Cassel, and while awaiting admission, Jane cut her wrists severely, and took an overdose, and was admitted to her local psychiatric hospital. While there, she had the status of 'a special patient'. She came and went from the ward as she pleased, attending work during the day. She decided on her own medication. Her consultant psychiatrist was on a first-name basis with her, and gave her a lift home in her car on one occasion. Jane had also had a close relationship with her general practitioner, coming to know her GP's family, and going on cycling trips with her female GP on occasions.

Working hypotheses

It is possible to create working hypotheses from a number of different perspectives. The hypotheses generated will be a function of the 'professional worker's' personality, professional background and personal interests. They will also be determined by the treatment resources available at the time. Finally, the 'patient worker's' personality, personal interests, difficulties and strengths, will also influence the working hypotheses generated. In the following paragraphs I will specify the hypotheses generated by the differing workers involved with Jane's assessment and treatment at the Cassel. Her GP referred her with some urgency, following self-inflicted injuries consisting of marks on her head and face, and superficial wrist cuts. After giving some information about her background, family situation and current situation, the GP wrote of her 'continuing to punish herself physically, and people consequently becoming frightened of her. I would be grateful for your expert help as soon as possible.'

Her assessor wrote of how terrified Jane was in coming to see her, and of Jane's increasing difficulty in retaining control over her life and herself. She was frightened that this self-mutilation might get out of control and lead to her suicide. Jane's brother, John, had stepped into the same role as father throughout Jane's childhood, abusing her physically and sexually. As the apple of his mother's eye, Jane was never able to complain about the treatment she received from her brother, and instead became the family scapegoat, who then started to punish herself. Jane had no difficulty in understanding the connection between her current symptoms and her past life, although in her desperate need for caring support she was terrified of blaming her mother for events. Jane felt that talking about her difficulties only made them worse. This was the reason for the decision to admit her for treatment on an in-patient basis.

Jane herself wrote of having been damaging herself physically since about the age of eight:

> I sometimes go for periods at a time when I do not do this, but recently it has reverted back to more serious injury, like when I was twelve, and at university. The injuries are in the nature of cutting my head, arms and wrists, and hitting the same areas against the wall, sometimes resulting in fractures. It frightens me at the moment, because of the seriousness of the injuries, and because of trying to conceal them from others, and that they will think I am really mental and have me committed before I have a chance to sort them out myself. I hyperventilate when I am out with large groups of people; again this

is not every time I go out, but at the present time it often happens when I'm on my own. I am worried at the moment because I used to be able to rationalise difficulties, and now they are getting more out of control, and consequently I spend more time on my own, and I hate being alone.

Jane wrote of being frightened of her mother, and frightened of disappointing her. She wrote of feeling guilty about her problems because she feels responsible for them, and for her mother. She described her father as a very violent man, who features fiercely in her recurring nightmares. In response to the question, 'In what ways do you expect treatment to help you?', Jane wrote:

> I feel that I cannot go on injuring myself and hyperventilating, and that although I always thought I could rationalise my behaviour and deal with it, I realise that I cannot do so. I hope that treatment can help me to deal with the confusion and conflict and fear that I feel, so that I can build relationships with people, and not feel guilty about everything I do, and become less nervous. I feel that unlike previously, when I could isolate the excessive behaviour from the other part of my life and my past, I am now confused and it is all jumbled up. I hope I can sort it out, but I am frightened of dealing with it on my own.

This was Jane's own formulation.

The nurse who visited her at home prior to admission, wrote,

> I feel that Jane is going to find admission particularly stressful, and feel she is being somewhat unrealistic when she says that if she has people to talk to she won't need to 'act out'. I think that she will be accepted by members of the community, because she seems pleasant and likeable. However, the patients have expressed anxiety about her acting out, and I feel unsure as to how much they or staff will be able to tolerate, and feel it important to stress to her and me that she will be here for assessment. During the visit, I noticed Jane's left wrist to be heavily bandaged, and when I asked her about it towards the end of the visit, she revealed that she had cut her wrist on the Monday, and had needed eleven stitches. I was concerned that I had to ask about this, and that she probably would not have told me. Despite liking her, I felt quite overwhelmed by the degree of disturbance that she seems to display, and feel concerned about her ability to cope with the pressure of life at the Cassel.

The same nurse wrote the following, four weeks after Jane's admission to the Cassel:

> I feel that Jane should be offered treatment here, as I feel she is making use of some of the structures available to her. I feel some concern at the possibility of her acting out her self-destructive behaviour after being accepted for admission. I feel that a very encouraging sign is that Jane, apart from one incident at the weekend, has been able to cope with the admission here so far, and has not resorted to acting out in a self-destructive manner. However, on speaking with Jane about this, she does feel that she is being self-destructive in a less harmful way by not eating. My nursing aim with Jane is difficult to formulate, as I shall be moving Units in the near future. However, I feel that her difficulties need to become more public in some way, in that Jane would like us to forget that she hurts herself, or has a disturbed past, as she would like to forget herself.

At the same time, her individual psychotherapist wrote:

> It appears that Jane experienced profound anxiety and lack of security in her early childhood, in the context of intense parental argument and violence. There was no resolution of this when her father left, because her brother took on his father's role, and Jane became the family victim. She describes vividly the discrepancy between physical violence in the family, and ideas the family had of itself as a safe, close place, in contrast to the dangers of the external world. Outsiders were painted as ogres, and Jane was discouraged from having contact with them. In this context Jane has only been able to develop the most immature sense of self, and is often extremely confused and doubting about her feelings. In her relationships with others, there is a profound lack of trust that they will be reliable or caring or concerned, and she constantly fears rejection and punishment, which she will inflict on herself if her objects do not oblige. Intense feelings of rage are countered by intense loyalty towards her family, and the wish to protect her mother at all costs. Jane's one avenue of escape from this emotional nightmare has been her studies and her work, into which she has poured enormous effort, which has been productive until very recently. She has been living away from home, but her social relationships have obviously been extremely problematic, her experiences with her father and brother have led her to be extremely fearful of men, with whom there seem to have been no close relationships. She admits to feeling disgusted about sexual matters.

In her assessment meeting, Jane's ability readily to make contact with staff members and other residents was noted. The Unit Consultant Psychiatrist noted that before her admission it had been felt that Jane would inculcate herself into a special position within the hospital, and that boundaries would be broken. He also made a prediction that her acceptance for in-patient treatment would probably precipitate further boundary testing, and likened this to her family situation, in which external conformity belied the internal violence. There was unanimous agreement in the staff group for Jane to continue treatment at the Cassel. It was felt she should concentrate on specifying the small steps of the here and now, and that these need to be worked out between her and her nurse – for example, in relation to weekends and smoking. It was recommended that she urgently sorts out the position concerning her work, and that there should be discussion sharing with her the potential dilemmas between her nurse and her therapist in relation to her. At her next review meeting, two months later, Jane was noted to make her nurse and therapist feel tied up, and unable to make any moves with her treatment because she presents as being so damaged and terrorised. There was a lively discussion around whether Jane is recreating the past at times like meal-times, to deny what the reality of the present situation is making her feel. It was felt that this then stops people from working with the reality of her relationships. In feedback to Jane, it was acknowledged how difficult it is to have ordinary expectations and interactions with her, because of the fear of making things worse for her.

I am not highlighting specifically the systemic and institutional dynamics within the Cassel Hospital in relation to Jane. However, at that time there were three separate in-patient Units, Families and two Adult, and an active patient and staff community. Tensions between Units, and between Units and the in-patient community, were manifest at that time, just as they continue to be today. These dynamics were often important in influencing, or in turn were often influenced by, more specific dynamics relating to Jane and her relationships.

I do not propose, either, to dwell on the network dynamics or hypotheses that may be created in relation to Jane's treatment. There were important negotiations between the Cassel Hospital and her catchment area psychiatrist, in order to contain Jane in treatment by having recourse to a back-up psychiatric bed if necessary. Jane also needed to negotiate actively with her employers in relation to carrying on part-time work during her treatment at the Cassel.

Working hypotheses in the individual therapy work

I propose to examine a number of the working hypotheses generated in the individual psychotherapy work at the time, by returning to the headings of the mechanisms of change in psychotherapy outlined by Grawe. I will be looking at a number of hypotheses, under the headings of mastery and coping, clarification of meaning, problem actuation and resource activation.

I took over as Jane's therapist five months into her treatment, and saw her for twice-weekly, 50-minute individual therapy sessions for the next ten months. Allowing for holidays, breaks, etc., there were a total of 67 sessions in all. Initially Jane spoke of feeling responsible for the departure of her previous therapist, and responsible for making others anxious and angry. Initially she spoke of me being an ogre like her father and brother, but in sessions did not appear to be in touch with the dread associated with this. She spoke of her need to be the worst patient in the hospital, as a way of protecting everybody else from harm. As the weeks progressed, she felt guilty about the breakdown of treatment of a patient to whom I had been therapist on another Unit. She felt it was her fault because she had taken me away from this patient. She moved from a position of pleasantly attacking and castrating me in sessions, to openly expressing her anger. She felt that it was I who let her down, and also let down other patients to whom I am therapist. She felt that I remind her of her father and brother, and also of her mother who ignored her, and that I am somebody who expects her to cope, and did not really understand how she feels. As the sessions progressed, there was a tendency for things to become more sexualised, and I hypothesised the re-creation of a mixed but abusive relationship. She began to fear my going mad and attacking her in an angry and sexual way. She feared that her nurse was just like a patient, and may be cracking up. She was angry at me expecting her to cope, and expressed the desire of just wanting to be hugged. She began to focus more on her sexuality, which became linked with my getting inside her. It was very difficult for me and her nurse to co-exist together in Jane's mind.

While in hospital Jane cut or harmed herself on at least 16 occasions. The self-mutilation frequently happened on a Friday evening, after Jane returned home from the work of the week at the Cassel Hospital. There seemed to be a powerful connection in Jane's mind between finishing treatment at the Cassel on Friday and an urge to mutilate and punish herself. She spoke of her image of a cruel big me, which contrasted with her image of a caring me lying beside her in bed. In sessions she wished to stand up or sit on the floor or shout and scream at me. Sessions became sexually exciting and charged, as she spoke of her past experiences;

she feared that her mother would kill herself if she knew about the past. She linked her image of a sadistic grinning me with that of her brother, John. In one session I arrived five minutes late at the hospital, with brolly in hand. I took my coat off in front of her, and I closed the door, in contrast to her usually closing the door in the room when she came in last. She went on to speak of her fear of me as an ogre, and noted my closing the door. She spoke of her left arm being dead, and not knowing why. She only gets particular satisfaction from cutting her left arm. I wondered if there was some connection with sexual intimacies with her brother. She told me on one occasion she had literally nearly cut off her hand, and wished it was dead. In the next session she wondered if I was frightened of her, and was afraid I might kill myself, like she feared about her brother and mother at times. She spoke of a man knowing a woman inside, and spoke of imagining my having breakfast with my wife, rather than being with her in her early morning session.

Mastery/coping

Throughout her therapy and her treatment at the Cassel Hospital, Jane developed a capacity to relate more to herself and her own feelings. She found a way of coping with intense feelings that had hitherto been camouflaged by her anxiety and her immediate urge to act destructively as a way of dealing with this tension. Some of my working hypotheses evolved from favourite theoretical positions. For example, I like to enable patients to recognise their ambivalence and mixed feelings towards others and towards me in therapy; also, following on Winnicott (1963), I believe that I recognise the importance for patients of attacking me as therapist, while at the same time wishing me to survive as therapist. Some of my working hypotheses were less based on theoretical positions, and represented more real situations of trial and error. Jane was talking in Session 51 about her sister informing her mother about Jane and John experimenting sexually as children. At a party on the previous Saturday Jane had spoken to John. He had told her that their sexual relationship stopped when Jane said so, and said that it shouldn't happen between brother and sister. He felt rejected. Jane spoke angrily about everybody in the hospital thinking she can do so much in firm and community meetings. We don't realise how awful she feels. It was her birthday, and she ought to be happy, not miserable. However, she wished that I would push her more in the sessions. She recalled my saying that I would leave it up to her to talk about things, but said angrily that if she could she would. I commented that I also spoke of her perhaps feeling abused by my explicit questioning. She replied, 'Well if I do, I do. I'll let you know. I think you and staff are afraid of me and my anger.' I commented on her wish to share things with me, and that she had made a suggestion how we might proceed. I agreed to try it. She said, however, 'Not today, there isn't time. I want to be happy on my birthday.'

In the following session she told me of her being drunk on the previous night, banging her head, kicking the wall, being restrained by staff from jumping downstairs, and needing to be specialled overnight. This also coincided with a family meeting in which all was eventually revealed. I hypothesised that she had been angry at me for not being more aware, pushing her and finding out and preventing her self-abuse, as if like a mother who doesn't care. We spoke of her mixture of love and hate for me and for her brother, John. She spoke of feeling confused, of not feeling real, and sat pulling at her skin, where she had previously cut. She told me of a nightmare she had, where I and her family were trying to convince her to kill herself. She had woken frightened, but feeling, 'No, I won't.'

The above interactions do represent some development of mastery and coping, both on her part and on my part, as we both struggled to face more difficult issues within the therapy.

Clarification of meaning

In Session 55, Jane was speaking of how she feels when with men and with women. She spoke of her wish to flirt, and of being unsure how to behave in the session with me. I noted that she was pulling at her wrist/sweatband, and opening and closing the top button on her shirt. I commented on being aware of her wristband and her cut wrist. She spoke of wondering if she could show it to me as a safe person. I commented on her previously asking me to push her, and that she felt confident that she could tell me that enough was enough. I asked to see her cut. She exposed her wrist and her cuts. I asked if she could leave off the sweatband in future in her sessions. She went on to talk more about links between men and women, and exposing her vulnerability. I commented on her different images of me, as either caring, lying gently beside her in bed, or as the cruel ogre me. She felt I was not being cruel now. On leaving she had difficulty opening the door, and said, 'Your door is stuck.' In the next session, she experienced the cruel ogre me, and felt this was so if she showed me her wrist, if she created a boundary and said no, and in her sexual fantasy. She described a sequence of a caring, cuddling me, leading to sexual excitement, leading to an image of an attacking ogre me. Session 58 was the final session before my three-week holiday. We discussed a plan to keep her safe by having a back-up bed in another psychiatric hospital, should the need arise over the coming weeks. She spoke of having a nightmare the previous night, even before I had gone. In it, she had pictured my asking to see her, and two other patients. One of the nurses had said I had something for them. She recalled wanting something of mine to remember me by (e.g., a pen). She came to my big room. I was cooking for her. I then beat her up, pinned her down on the floor, with her hands behind her back. The night orderly said, 'Stop, she doesn't know what she's saying.' She then went to her mother's. She was scared and shouting at me. She couldn't find the right platform. I don't think I got a chance to work out an hypothesis about this dream in the rest of the session. However, she linked it with her wish for me to care, love her, mother her and nourish her, while at the same time hating me for caring and leaving her for three weeks to fend for herself.

Problem actuation

This is a potent mechanism for change when working psychoanalytically with the transference. An abusive relationship was re-created and enacted between Jane and myself over the course of her sessions. In Session 41, she was describing herself as sarcastic and a stroppy baby. I suggested that she really hates me, and sees me as sadistically grinning and leering now on picking her up. She agreed that she feels like that most of the time now, and the previous Friday she had been in a firm meeting and tried to look at me arrive in my car for work. She felt I was a monster. She felt she hated me, and hated everybody, but said this quietly. I commented on her being very polite. She said she would like to shout it, and blamed me for stopping her shouting. I suggested that things were perhaps more complicated because she also spoke previously of having longing and loving feelings towards me. She spoke of thinking of me at her sister's flat. She is unable to sleep at night, and wishes I was there. She feels it's OK for me because I'm married. So's her brother, John. We've both got someone else. She had seen my wife at Christmas, and at the hospital sale of work. She had felt we both looked very happy. She spoke of thinking of me especially in bed at her sister's. She doesn't do it here in the hospital, only there. She sat forward and looked embarrassed, and didn't look at me. I wondered aloud if she masturbated when thinking of me. She said, 'Yes, I feel awful.' She said, 'If I look at you, I'll see the monster.' Two sessions later I commented on my being in the hospital over the weekend, and her being in bed. She said she had wanted to show me her cut arms, but was afraid she'd have to show more. She cut herself to show me her inside. I commented that this sounded quite sexual, and involved a man knowing a woman's inside. She felt she could not talk about this. She didn't know whether I could understand what it was like for her. In the next session, she spoke of her anger at me, and at other staff. I commented on it being difficult for her being a patient, and it had apparently been difficult for her being a child. She recalled her mother got attention and was looked after because of her agoraphobia, but no one cared about us. She spoke of her own sexual excitement, and of thinking of me before and after but not during it. I wondered what she meant by this. She spoke of seeing other couples, reading about things in books, or seeing things in films. She spoke of a bloke doing it to a woman, it being a one-way transaction. She enjoys it, and gets aroused, but afterwards feels bad. Some ten sessions later, she spoke of being cared for and then feeling attacked by me, by her brother John, and indeed by the nurses at the Cassel. She regularly expects to be attacked by me, and feels abandoned at the end of sessions and in facing her forthcoming leaving treatment. She has images of attacking me, of flattening and squashing my penis. She wants to shout, 'Stop, leave me alone, I've had enough', and feels she could shout this at me or at her brother, John. She is very anxious to get away at the end of a session, and get away from the attack from me. At her third to last session with me she wears a black skirt for the first time. She spoke of being afraid of my reaction, that I might sexually use her, or attack her with my interpretations. She was afraid of my interpreting too quickly, and not letting her speak for herself. She feels guilty about being thought of as seducing her brother, John. She loved him as a brother and as a male. She spoke of having very mixed feelings towards me, seeing me at times as attacking her, recognising her need and want for me, having a sexual image of me in her. She wasn't sure whether she could hold onto the images with me, and the hateful destructive feelings stirred up as a result.

Resource activation

The various examples given, I think, have highlighted Jane's finding strengths within herself to face hitherto unbearable images and feelings. In this sense, resources were activated within her. I think the examples also illustrate my growth as a therapist, and my finding resources within myself and within my relationship with Jane, to try out new things, discover new questions, and discover some new answers. The whole treatment must be seen in the context of resources activated within the Adult in-patient unit, staff and patients, the Cassel Hospital as a whole therapeutic community, and the network of family and professionals involved in Jane's care.

Conclusion

In this chapter I have highlighted some of the different perspectives from which working hypotheses are generated. In particular I have looked at the detailed work of the psychoanalytic psychotherapy sessions which were a central part of Jane's treatment in the psychotherapeutic community at the Cassel Hospital. I have outlined various working hypotheses generated by Jane, by myself as her therapist and by us both jointly in the sessions. I propose that such working hypotheses sustain the clinical work and make it possible for mechanisms of change in psychotherapy to then come into play.

This was the case with Jane. After 15 months of in-patient treatment within the psychotherapeutic community at the Cassel Hospital, Jane was discharged. She continued to train as a solicitor and has since progressed in her career. She has not self-harmed since discharge from treatment and has succeeded in establishing satisfactory personal relationships. She sees her time in treatment at the Cassel Hospital as a turning point in her life.

Note

In the interests of anonymity, identifying biographical details were amended in this account of "Jane".

References

Grawe, K. (1997) 'Research-informed psychotherapy', *Psychotherapy Research* 7 (1): 1–19.

Stokes, J. (1994) 'The unconscious at work in groups and teams', in Obholzer, A. and Roberts, V.Z. (eds) *The Unconscious at Work: Individuals and Organisational Stress in the Human Services*. London: Routledge.

Winnicott, D.W. (1963) *The Maturational Processes and the Facilitating Environment*. London: Hogarth Press.

Chapter 9

Hypothesis testing in cognitive-behaviour therapy

Simon Jakes

In this chapter I want to describe three major types of hypotheses which are used in cognitive-behaviour therapy and to discuss some issues that arise about the testing of these hypotheses. The three types of hypothesis I will consider are those developed within three different cognitive-behavioural models. These are (1) functional analysis, (2) traditonal Beckian cognitive therapy and (3) schema-focused cognitive-therapy. I will place this discussion in the context of a discussion of hypothesis testing in general. I will argue that one problem which can infect the discussion is the mistaken identification of the scientific method with hypothesis testing. This can have serious implications in what is considered to be evidence and can, therefore, affect our practice. I will argue that an oversimplified view of how we test our ideas has been prevelant in cognitive-behaviour therapy and in psychotherapy generally. I also argue that many of our hypotheses are maintained by non-rational factors (e.g., professional identity) and this also needs to be acknowledged. Hypotheses (that is, tentative statements) can be constructed about any matter of fact at all. Two situations in which hypotheses are tested in cognitive psychotherapy are (1) to establish that a particular causal model is true, and (2) to establish the effectiveness of a particular treatment technique. In both cases it is a valuable activity. However I want to begin by exploring the limitations of hypothesis testing. I will argue (1) that scientific method is not equivalent to hypothesis testing, and (2) hypothesis testing is part of everyday reasoning – that is, science involves a lot more than hypothesis testing and hypothesis testing is part of everyday thinking. Why particular hypotheses are seen as worth pursuing at a particular point in time relates to the background set of beliefs which are held about the world. It is not single hypotheses which are tested but a whole 'world-view' or a paradigm (in the terminology of Kuhn, 1962).

Hypothesis testing is often taken as the essence of scientific method or of empirical thought. Obviously hypotheses are formulated and tested in empirical thinking. Behavioural and cognitive therapy have often been represented as closely related to the academic discipline of psychology and, hence, to the view that (1) the experimental method and (2) mechanistic models of the mind are the most scientific and (therefore) the most productive ways to increase our understanding of human behaviour. Historically this link began with the development of behaviour therapy but has continued with the use of information processing models to explicate thought processes. The promotion of hypothesis testing as the key to scientific method has also been a feature of experimental psychology, and this has carried over into cognitive and behavioural psychotherapy.

Popper's (1976) 'Hypothetico-deductive' model of scientific practice has been particularly influential. The idea here is that if one adopts a particular way of developing and testing theories (setting up hypotheses which make empirically testable predictions and then attempting to refute them), then one will be doing scientific work and will obtain scientific knowledge. It is worth pointing out that this is a *theory* about the nature of scientific thought and was designed to replace the older view that science consisted of the accumulation of a series of generalisations on the basis of systematic observation and inductive reasoning. The view of science as a process of hypothesis generation and attempted refutation was influenced by the overthrow of Newtonian physics by quantum mechanics and the theory of relativity. It was difficult to maintain that science discovered certainties if what had been taken for the central scientific knowledge for 300 years was incorrect. If certainties were not established by empirical reasoning and experiment then hypothesis refutation was the second best. Popper (1976) argued that empirical reasoning worked by setting up a universal hypothesis and then attempting to refute it by experiment. If the experiment disconfirmed the theory the theory was false. If the experiment did not disconfirm the theory then the theory was 'not falsified'. Why a non-falsified theory should be of use (unless we held it to be true) was a difficulty for this theory. Behind these approaches lies the idea that a particular method characterises science and in so doing sets it apart from other, flawed, 'knowledge'. However, it may be that a number of different methods characterise science; detailed and repeated observation, for example, in addition to hypothesis testing and experimentation, so that no one method characterises all science. The study of botany, biology, physics, astronomy and psychology are all very different. There does not need to be one method that they all use for them to all be sciences. It is wrong to assume that because a method is effective in the exact sciences that it will be effective in psychology.

Some have argued that the use of mechanistic hypotheses distinguishes science. The arguments against the position that to be scientific psychology should emulate physics in regard to using mechanistic models have been made on many occasions (e.g., Harré and Secord, 1970; Taylor, 1964). I will not repeat these arguments here as this would take me away from the central theme of this chapter. Instead I will describe some alternative views of the nature of science and the role of hypothesis testing in science. This is relevant to my main task as it puts the importance of hypothesis testing in a different light. Having done this I will consider three different types of hypothesis used in CBT. Finally I want to address the social and psychological factors which are involved in maintaining the use of particular types of hypothesis in our clinical practice.

The idea that the scientific method is different in kind to ordinary common sense can be challenged. Certainly most of the important technological advances have been made through ordinary common sense and inductive reasoning – for example, the discovery of the annual path of the fixed stars for navigation or the development of agriculture or the wheel. The Copernican revolution which must on any account be one of the triumphs of modern science was not achieved by experimental method or by hypothesis generation and testing. (Although the theory was later tested by careful astronomical observation.) No experiments are possible in astronomy. Copernicus reinterpreted the already available data in the light of a different model, and the chief criterion of the truth of the model was its greater simplicity. Surely Copernicus made a scientific discovery before his theory was tested! At the time that he produced his theory it actually conflicted with the observed orbits of the planets (and could be said to have been disconfirmed by this). The definitive test of his theory came over a hundred years later, but we cannot say that Copernicus would not have been a scientist if the test had not been carried out. The chief advantage of his theory was its simplicity. This should make us wary of the claim that a particular method of investigation is neccesary to discover empirical truths. It is as if we are captivated by the success of Newtonian physics and then imagine that because the experimental method is so powerful that this is the only method of arriving at empirical truths. In reality, as the example of Copernicus shows, a diverse variety of methods of systematic observation and reinterpretation in the light of other observations are involved. Hypothesis generation itself is part of ordinary empirical reasoning. We often set up and test hypotheses, and such tests do not involve the use of experimental design or controlled observation. If my car will not start and it is a damp morning I dry the spark plugs and HT leads to test if a damp ignition system is the cause of the starting problem. Although controlled experimental comparisons convey greater confidence in the conclusions that we can draw about our hypotheses, this process in psychology has become something of a fetish. Sometimes it is implied that if we do not have evidence based on experiment then we have no evidence at all. This is not how we act in other areas of our life (e.g., when we want to start our car). It could be argued that science concerns the development of knowledge rather than acting as a guide to practical action and that it is this which distinguishes these two cases. However, in psychotherapy we are usually in the position of wanting a guide to action and I doubt that the distinction between knowledge and action can really be maintained. The theories which we develop in physics are ultimately a guide to action.

Popper (1976) suggested that science is distinguished by progressing through a process of hypothesis generation and testing. However, Quine (1953) has suggested that no statement stands against the facts on its own, but that what meets 'the facts' is the totality of all our beliefs. So the statement that 'neutrinos have no mass' is not a statement which can be tested against the facts on its own without reference to our other beliefs. A whole series of other statements which are part of the theory within which this statement is made support this statement, and it is possible to alter these other statements if we wish to maintain the statement 'neutrinos have no mass' in the face of apparently contradictory evidence. If I believe that ghosts do not exist and I am confronted by a ghostly apparition of a dead friend I can change my belief about ghosts, but I can also claim hallucination or visual illusion if I want to maintain my belief in the non-existence of ghosts. An example from psychoanalytical psychotherapy might be the hypothesis that when during a therapy session a patient talks in an angry way about a friend this is an example of negative transference (and is really a statement about the therapist). Clearly this statement only makes sense, and therefore can only be tested, within a set of beliefs (e.g., in therapy the patient enacts past traumas; discourse during a therapy session reflects the client's feelings about the therapist). 'Transference' is a concept that implies a great deal of theory. This is, I believe, particularly important in psychology, as will become clear in the remainder of this chapter. In summary, hypothesis testing is a part of ordinary experience which we engage in as a routine part of our daily life. Whether we hold statements (hypotheses) to be true or false depends not just on crucial tests or on how particular hypotheses agree with the facts but also on the totality of our other beliefs about the world. An important implication of this is that hypotheses in psychotherapy will not stand alone but will be supported by other hypotheses both about the individual patient and about patients and people in general. The testing of a specific hypothesis takes place within certain models. Testing of hypotheses may also occur in a variety of ways. I will return to some of these general points at the end of the chapter.

I will describe the three major approaches to hypothesis generation in cognitive-behaviour therapy (CBT) and point to some of the difficulties that arise from each approach. Most of this discussion will be about the generation and testing of hypotheses about individual patients. In science theories are usually developed about types of phenomena in general. But it is also possible to generate hypotheses about particular individuals. Hypotheses can be more or less theoretical. The hypothesis that desensitisation works as a procedure is less theoretical than the hypothesis that it works due to counter-conditioning. However, this is a matter of degree (unless one argues that theory about 'unobservables' is not needed at all, and that science should merely establish what observable states are intercorrelated). (Skinner, 1950, takes this position.) We have some theory as to how it works even if it is as vague as 'exposure'. It is worth pointing out that there is a strong tradition in CBT which eschews the use of hypotheses about individuals relying on hypotheses about categories of patients. In this tradition, what I will call 'external hypotheses' are generated and tested. By this I mean external to the individual. Hypotheses are applied to groups of patients and tested using group design experimentally controlled trials. Thus 'phobic anxiety is reduced by prolonged exposure to the phobic stimulus' is tested across individuals. Indeed, this method is regarded by some as the only scientific way of testing hypotheses and the idea of developing hypotheses about particular patients is not considered to be legitimate, as if the only truths were those which can be generated to groups of people.

Controlled experimental trials do, of course, confer a degree of control which other methods of testing hypotheses lack. However, the idea that this is the only valid way to test hypotheses about the effect of treatment or the underlying causal factors is considerably restricting and, I believe, untenable. If one applies this thinking to another area of human behaviour, such as diplomacy, the conclusion would be that the activity was impossible – and yet we continue to practise it. During the Cuban missile crisis Khrushchev sent two letters to Kennedy which were inconsistent. In the first letter he offered to withdraw Soviet missiles from Cuba if the Americans promised that they would not invade Cuba. In the second letter, sent on the following day, he repeated the offer but added the additional condition that the the Americans withdraw their nuclear missiles from Turkey. Robert Kennedy (1969) reports that he suggested that they dealt with this puzzling situation by ignoring the second, more negative, letter and only responding to the first, more positive letter. The hypothesis was that responding to the positive suggestion would produce a positive response (and, although this was not tested, that responding to the negative message would be likely to encourage the Soviets to argue for their new demand and that in doing this they would become more intransigent). This is a psychological hypothesis. And myriad hypotheses of this type are set up and tested every day. The demand that this should only be done using experimental controlled trials is clearly absurd. Often in psychotherapy our situation is more similar to that of a diplomat rather than a physicist.

Group hypotheses treat individual variation as error – what is tested is the difference in the mean response. Furthermore, the hypotheses are not linked to individual histories – this rather assumes that people with similar symptoms but different histories have more in common in regard to what will be effective treatment than people with similar histories and life problems and diverse symptoms. This might be true, but it is not obvious that this is the case.

Lazarus (1991) has argued that a rational approach is to first use treatments which have been established in group designs as effective for particular problems. If this treatment is ineffective, or if there is no established treatment, he suggests one should consider being technically eclectic in a planned way. This, of course, involves the use of individualised hypotheses. So when faced by the Cuban missile crisis it is rational, given no controlled trials, to set up the hypothesis that responding only to the positive communication will increase the chance of a further positive communication. Now this could, of course, be set up as a general hypothesis – it might even be true – but I think it is important to see that this could also be a very specific hypothesis – not true in general but only of these particular people – in these particular circumstances. Not all true hypotheses about patients are generalisable across people or across time.

Internal hypothesis generation

This involves attempting to generate a hypothesis about a particular individual on the basis of their personal history, behaviour in the session, information obtained about the situations in which the symptoms and other problems occur, etc. In almost all cases this will be done by reference to a particular model. It may be possible to develop a model of a patient's problems which is derived entirely from information from them, but usually a model about how certain problems are to be understood in general is used to structure the information coming from the individual patient. I will discuss three models: functional analysis, Beck's cognitive therapy and schema-focused cognitive therapy.

Functional analysis

The first model for developing an internal hypothesis I want to consider is functional analysis. The roots of functional analysis lie in operant conditioning. Skinner (1950) held it unnecessary to postulate 'intervening variables' in science and held science to be the accretion of correlations. He used individual cases to examine the relationship between stimulus and response. The task of the psychologist was to observe the relationship between independent and dependent variables. He believed that theories of learning which postulated an underlying but unobserved mechanism were unscientific. Functional analysis explained how the occurrence of certain behaviours was a function of specific stimuli. Reference to mental states was not good science. Wolpe (1958) turned this functional analysis into a clinical tool. Psychiatric symptoms (primarily anxiety) were to be understood as having been learned by a process of conditioning. If one understood the learning history of a symptom one understood the cause of the symptom and one could cure the symptom by helping the patient to unlearn the association. He emphasised that current situations in which the symptom occurred were of prime importance. Other workers have analysed symptoms merely in terms of current contingencies (with a corresponding shallowness of explanation). The key aim of a functional analysis is to establish the situations in which symptoms or problem behaviours occur, and the apparent consequences of these behaviours. 'Behaviour' is used in a very loose sense and includes autonomic responses which would not normally be described as behaviour. Although Skinner (1950) claimed that this was theory-free it actually seems predicated on the theory that behaviour can be meaningfully understood as a function of learning – of reinforcement contingencies. This is clearly a hypothesis – albeit a false one. That is, Skinner's suggestion that we do not need theories, but that behaviour can be understood in terms of reward and punishment (reinforcement), is an empirical claim. Now if it is acceptable and scientific to make the hypothesis that 'behaviour is a function of reinforcement' it must also be acceptable and scientific to make the hypothesis that this is not the case, and that behaviour can only be explained by reference to unobservable states.

Wolpe (1958) stresses that it is also important to establish the learning history which has led to a particular behaviour. Although couched in terms of behavioural ontology this procedure actually yields very interesting data. The hypotheses used are very close to the data. One great benefit of this as an approach is that it encourages the collection of detailed information on the situations in which a specific problem occurs. This can lead to generalisations about the type of situation which precipitates that behaviour. For example, Wolpe would want to clarify if anxiety that occurred in public places was related to situations with a theme of being vulnerable to illness, or threat from others, or to being looked at. This theme would then be traced to its 'historical roots' by careful questioning. It is worth pointing out that such themes are implicitly cognitive. Situations in which one is 'vulnerable to illness' have in common only that they are so perceived by the particular patient (i.e., the situations which give rise to a particular expectation). If one tries to eliminate the psychological aspect here (that is 'expectation') this cannot be done as the harmful consequences do not exist at the time the patient is anxious. Here there is the assumption that problem behaviours develop through learning. The specific situations and learning history derived from the client are used to fill in this hypothesis. That learning is the basis of these problems is not itself tested.

I want to illustrate this procedure with reference to a patient whom I treated. He is a 50-year-old man who suffers from paranoid schizophrenia. I want to make it clear that I am not implying that paranoid schizophrenia is caused by psychological factors. There is some (presumably biological) factor which we do not fully understand that generates psychotic states of mind. This does not mean that one cannot generate psychological hypotheses about the content of the psychotic state. Dreaming is caused by biological factors but the contents of the dream can often be traced to psychological triggers or reflect underlying psychological concerns. He was diagnosed as suffering from depression and anxiety in his early twenties. His first psychotic breakdown occurred when he was in his early thirties. His breakdown was precipitated by severe stress – he had been involved in criminal activity which led to him being threatened by other criminals. He began having auditory hallucinations, delusions of reference and paranoid delusions. He also experienced thought insertion. His symptoms were not controlled by medication. He had had numerous admissions to hospital. When I saw him he also complained of anxiety, particularly when leaving the house, and, on occasion, depressed mood. He had little contact with his family and little social contact. He had two friends: one who had a serious physical handicap and a young woman with a personality disorder. He believed that there was a conspiracy to kill him, and he was continually subject to auditory hallucinations, which were persecutory and gave him evidence that people were conspiring against him. This made all social interaction very difficult for him. At times he would become challenging and hostile. He could be generous and kind, and I found him pleasant company. He enjoyed coming to therapy sessions. He had been badly physically abused by a violent and unpredictable alcoholic father and had been in and out of children's homes as a child. One strategy which he found effective when his father beat him was to laugh rather than to cry. He said that this made his father stop beating him. One of his sisters had died in a car crash when he was in his teens.

Classically, behaviour therapists (i.e., Wolpe) using functional analysis regarded psychosis as a purely organic matter in which learning accounts had no place. However, if we agree that psychosis involves a biological process which generates qualitatively distinct experiences we can still explore the way in which learning experiences alter the way this psychosis is expressed. He could be conceptualised, using functional analysis in the following way: because of his early experiences of abuse and the lack of an effective protective figure he learnt to associate people with punishment and abuse. This led to anxiety in any relationship with people. One response to this anxiety (denying his feelings) was effective, but set up a response of denying reality which may have influenced his later psychosis. The content of his psychotic experiences reflects these associations between people and abuse and punishment, much as dreams might. The anxiety response to people colours the content of the experience rather than causing the psychotic experiences. In addition to reflecting themes of danger, however, the hallucinations and paranoid delusions become additional sources of anxiety and reinforce the link between people and punishment and abuse. Feeling persecuted by hostile voices confirms the belief that others are hostile. The belief that others are hostile is the basis of the persecutory auditory hallucinations. Because these experiences are taken for reality by the patient this vicious circle is much more pernicious than in a patient with neurotic symptoms. So the association between anxiety and people has become self-reinforcing. Occasionally he attacks people he believes are trying to harm him. This produces genuinely negative social responses. His attempts at forming more positive relationships are likely to fail because of his paranoid interpretations and requests for reassurance. When he leaves the house he becomes more anxious. He therefore avoids leaving the house or when out escapes to home as soon as possible, reinforcing the association between people and anxiety. In many ways he can be seen as having a psychotic type of agoraphobia. Treatment would focus on graded exposure to anxiety-producing situations and possibly strategies to help him feel less anxious in the company of people (social skills training).

This method of generating hypotheses leads to very testable hypotheses (given the underlying model is not in itself tested). Specific situations (in my patient these included being with people, being with strangers, being away from home or a safe place, auditory hallucinations, paranoid interpretations of an event) either do or do not produce anxiety for example. (The method can also be used to generate cognitive hypotheses – as discussed below.) The major problem with this model is that as an account of human motivation it is false. Man is capable of acting on complicated interpretations of what happens to him and does not respond to 'stimuli' but to 'stimuli as interpreted'. If I believe a noise indicates an intruder I react with fear. The belief, not the intruder, is the essential ingredient – if there is no intruder I am still fearful if I believe that there is an intruder. My suggestion that my patient responds with anxiety to paranoid interpretations of events can only be construed in associationist terms if one pushes the definitions in an unnatural way. An interpretation is not a stimulus. But this part of the explanation of my patient's difficulties is really crucial to any comprehensive account. Also there is an implication that behaviour is produced by situations. This fits well with an autonomic response such as anxiety – but many human problems result from actions. Agency cannot be explained as a response to particular circumstances – if action is explained as a passive response then it ceases to be action. So with my patient an associative account could explain the occurrence of anxiety in certain situations, but to explain why he chose partners who rejected him, for example, cannot be explained simply by associations. (One could suggest that his anxious expectation provided the motivation – he expected to be hurt so felt ambivalent about involvement and therefore chose partners he believed would not require him to commit himself. But the associative part of this explanation is clearly only a small part of the explanation.) None of this is to do with my patient having a psychotic illness.

Beck's cognitive therapy

Traditional cognitive therapy – as developed by Beck – develops hypotheses about patients based on identifying interpretations of the world which generate emotional distress. These interpretations are linked to beliefs about the self, the world and the future. These beliefs are referred to as 'silent assumptions' – the person is not aware that they hold these beliefs but they are not dynamically repressed (they are tacit or implicit beliefs). We all have beliefs we are unaware of in this way – for example, 'I have never been far from the Earth's surface' is a belief we will not have been aware of, although almost all of us hold this belief. It is clearly not dynamically repressed. In the case of the patient I described above a cognitive formulation of his problems might be that because of his early experiences of abuse and lack of an effective protective caring figure, and because of the general chaos that this gave rise to in his early life, he developed the belief that he was vulnerable and that others were either weak or dangerous. He also came to believe that events were essentially unpredictable. Again the content is reflected in his psychotic experiences. In many ways this formulation is similar to that given above as derived from functional analysis. However, the cognitive explanation is simpler and does not involve having to redescribe interpretations as stimuli. Another difference is that is seems natural to explore the belief with the client to see if it seems correct to him. It is also possible to set up tests on a cognitive level. One would predict that if he did have these underlying beliefs this would be reflected in his thoughts and interpretations. One can test if such a belief is held by looking at interpretations that are made. Treatment would focus on trying to build up insight into the role of his past experiences in conditioning his current psychotic experiences.

Schema-focused cognitive therapy

Over the last ten years a more complicated model has been used to generate internal hypotheses in cognitive therapy. This involves the use of ideas from Jeffery Young's (1994) schema-focused cognitive therapy. Essentially this incorporates some quasi-psychoanalytic ideas into Beck's cognitive model. The central problem in emotional disorders is still a series of beliefs – but these are called 'early maladaptive schemas' to emphasise the influence on information processing and the supposed origins in early childhood. They are distinguished from Beck's 'assumptions' in being associated with a high level of affect and in being centrally associated with the person's sense of who they are. In this model the patient actively fights to maintain these dysfunctional sets of beliefs, and it is this which distinguishes Young's from Beck's model. Also the schema-focused theory attributes a quasi-autonomous character to the different schemas: the schema is talked of as 'fighting to survive'; this involves a model which incorporates the splitting of the self as a central part of the theory of mind. In other words, rather than the person being represented as having one set of motives, two (or more) parts of the self are postulated – the schema and the part of the patient which is collaborating with the therapist to fight the schema. This is a radical departure from Beck's model. These beliefs are held to be associated with emotional pain and because of this they are actively avoided. This is very reminiscent of 'defence mechanisms' in psychoanalytic theory. Young describes three 'schema processes':

1   Schema maintenance.
2   Schema avoidance.
3   Schema compensation.

These three factors are the additions to the cognitive model; they are the refinements of the hypotheses used. Schema maintenance refers to processes which the patient engages in which confirm the dysfunctional belief. This includes ways of behaving which produce results which seem to confirm the belief, and also includes biased information processing. So in the case of my patient the paranoid ideation was an example of faulty information processing which maintained his underlying schemas. His avoidance of real people also prevented disconfirmation of his belief in the hostility of others (schema avoidance). Schema compensation involves dysfunctional ways of behaving, apparently to negate the belief (e.g., a person who feels inferior acts in a superior manner with others with predictably negative effects). My patient would behave in kind and generous ways towards people. Unfortunately this sometimes laid him open to exploitation and he got involved in relationships which predictably ended in rejection, confirming his underlying beliefs. Schema avoidance indicates ways in which the person avoids the underlying belief (e.g., a person who feels vulnerable avoids emotional relationships). My patient did indeed avoid emotional relationships – in fact he avoided people altogether. All these processes imply some 'splitting' of the self – and this is a significant change from Beck's model. This aspect of the theory provides a more comprehensive way of describing my patient. An analysis of my patient using schema-focused cognitive therapy might be that he had schemas relating to abuse mistrust. Because of his childhood experiences of abuse and the lack of an effective protective figure he learnt that other people are dangerous and abusive and that he was vulnerable. These schemas were evident in his early anxiety symptoms and also colour his later psychotic experiences. The schemas become self-maintaining in the manner described above. His psychotic experience can be seen as the playing out of the schemas towards himself. He hears voices saying that they will kill him or voices insulting him. He takes this for reality. One 'part of himself' – the quasi-autonomous schema – behaves in an abusive way to another part of himself. This type of intra-psychic relationship can be depicted in schema theory in a way which cannot be done in traditional cognitive therapy. In non-psychotic patients the schemas are not taken by the client to be autonomous entities, but still function in this way. Testing hypotheses derived from this theory is particularly difficult. It is difficult to see what would count as a definitive test that someone was actively maintaining an abuse schema that went beyond the facts which were responsible for producing that hypothesis. And we cannot resort simply to asking the client if this is what they believe, as we might in standard cognitive therapy, as the patient may be actively resisting being aware of the schema. One is sailing close to a self-perpetuating form of hypothesis generation which has no implications outside of that set of ideas.

Jacqueline Persons (1989) has illustrated a method of generating and testing cognitive hypotheses which explains the patient's difficulties and which can be used to guide treatment. This can be done using the traditional or schema-focused theories. She suggests that we should generate beliefs (or another psychological mechanism) which the patient holds which (a) explain all their current presenting problems, (b) fit with the circumstances which have precipitated the recent problem, (c) fit with the childhood experiences which the patient reports. She suggests the following as tests of the hypothesis developed:

1   The hypothesis should explain all of the problems that a patient presents.
2   The hypothesis should fit with childhood experiences.
3   The hypothesis should fit with the precipitating experiences.
4   The therapist should be able to tell a story about how the belief led to the current difficulties.
5   The patient should accept the hypothesis as true.
6   The effect of treatment can also be used as a test of the hypothesis.

These 'tests' largely involve consistency and simplicity rather than by making predictions. (Why the patient's assent is considered to be a test of the truth of the hypothesis is obscure. It seems clear that this is a test of whether this is a useful theory in therapy – in the sense of a good way to communicate with the patient – but this is a different matter to the truth of the theory.)

Persons suggests that to have an individualised hypothesis of this type is helpful in constructing treatment packages tailored to individual requirements and that it helps to deal with potential difficulties in treatment. She also argues that it can help to redirect treatment when it is not working.

An advantage of both traditional and schema-focused cognitive hypotheses (using beliefs to understand the patient's difficulties) is that it provides a more comprehensive and more human account of the patient's difficulties than the older behavioural account. What I mean by this is that it rationalises the problem and makes it understandable in terms of the client's desires and beliefs. It gives the type of account that we give of ordinary action.

One problem with this type of hypothesis is that, in making reference to 'non-observables' (i.e. beliefs and thoughts), testing the hypothesis is much more difficult. Whether someone believes that, for example, they are a 'special person' is open to dispute. If someone agrees that they do believe this, this does not prove that this is so. Of course a denial that this is the case does not prove that they do not believe it. Often we judge that someone believes this on the basis of behaviour rather than verbal avowal. I am not arguing that we *cannot* know if this is true as a logical positivist or behaviourist might – rather that this is a complex judgement admitting of no simple test.

The schema-focused approach leads to a more flexible system of hypotheses. However, the problems involved in testing such hypotheses are multiplied. Essentially we are now dealing with unconscious processes. What the criteria are for correct interpretations of this type is notoriously obscure. In the *Interpretation of Dreams* Freud mentions a woman who dreamt that all the things she wished for did not happen. Freud (1953) claimed this was not a disconfirmation of his hypothesis that dreams are wish-fulfilment, because she wanted to prove that his theory was false! It is not that this *could* not be true but that we would never know if it were false.

Summarising the advantages and disadvantages of the three models, one can say that an increase in the comprehensiveness of the model is accompanied by a decrease in its testability. Testability is not the sole criterion of a good theory; the elegance or simplicity of a model is also important. This is why Occam's razor appeals to our reason. Popper argued that 'unfalsifiability' (such as occurs in the complex type of hypothesis associated with schema-focused therapy) rendered this type of theory unscientific. However, it does seem to be quite common in scientific thinking to fit awkward facts into well-established theories by pleading special circumstances. So if someone seems to be able to bend spoons in a manner which defies the laws of physics it is reasonable to assume that there is some trick – although we do not know what it is. If we seem to meet someone long dead it is reasonable to claim it was an hallucination – thus denying the evidence of our senses. These factors led Quine (1953) to argue that hypotheses do not meet sensory experience singly, but rather that all our hypotheses (beliefs about the world) meet sensory experience together. We can always choose to hold on to one belief if we change others in our belief system. Kuhn (1962) has argued that such belief systems ('paradigms') are maintained by socio-psychological factors in the behaviour of scientists (see the reference for further details). However, in the case of hypotheses in psychotherapy, we are not in the same position as that of physical scientists. In psychotherapy there are a number of competing models. This makes the probability of any one of these being true very low. It counts against the truth of these models that other psychotherapists believe in contradictory models. We are truly in a pre-Newtonian state. That is, there is no one dominant paradigm which all informed practitioners work within and contribute to. We avoid the dissonance this produces by belonging to professional associations where others confirm our view, by reading specialist journals which conform to our way of thinking and by selective attention to certain information. This allows us to turn a blind eye to the uncomfortable fact that a majority of educated and informed psychotherapists will not agree with us in our hypotheses, because whatever our view more people disagree with it than agree with it.

When our clients succeed we take this as confirmation of our models; when they fail we blame the patient (or his 'pathology') – we don't take it as evidence against our model. Furthermore, our professional identity and our belief that we are performing a constructive activity are also centred on our belief in our particular model. Our income as therapists rests on the validity of the model we work within. To question the legitimacy of the model is to question the need for one's own employment. It is not that we deliberately falsify our beliefs. Rather we work in contexts that allow us to retain certain useful beliefs in comfort. We turn a blind eye to uncomfortable counter-evidence. We function much like a patient within Young's schema-focused model to retain our schema of our own effectiveness. It makes us feel much better to 'know' rather than to sit on the fence. All these social psychological and psychological factors influence us in non-rational ways to believe certain hypotheses. Because we have a lot of personal investment in our own way of working we are attached to our model of psychological problems and are less prepared, for reasons of self-interest, to doubt these ideas. This line of thinking obviously owes much to Foucault (1965), but we do not have to follow him in doubting that 'truth' has any meaning. Because we are working in an area where so little is really known many 'models' can work and no one paradigm has been given universal assent. It is worth recalling that perfectly rational men (possibly including Isaac Newton) also believed in the truth of astrology and magic not so very long ago (Thomas, 1971).

These factors should make us tentative in our degree of belief in our hypotheses. It is not only our hypotheses that stand in need of evidence but also the models on which these hypotheses are based. The models we use to guide us and interpret our patients have not been shown to be true – we only act as if they have.

However, this does not mean that we should abandon the use of internal hypothesis generation and testing. The evidence of what techniques are effective from controlled trials is very limited. Once we move beyond exposure and non-specific factors of therapy we are by and large in uncharted water. We can do nothing if we do not generate internal hypotheses. The problem is our own tendency to move from hypothesis to beliefs. I have pointed to some of the irrational sources of our belief in our hypotheses, and the objective reasons for doubting them, to suggest that we should be more modest in our claim to know and also to present the frame within which 'hypothesis testing' takes place. It is not simply a question of a particular method (hypothesis testing) which makes for good empirical theories. The adequacy of the theory as a whole is fundamentally what is important. This cannot be subjected to any definitive test but depends on the utility of the theory and how it functions in a variety of cases. Theories can become divorced from the evidence. All states of the world are compatible with the theory. If the theory serves other social purposes this can be a self-perpetuating situation. In my view, psychoanalysis is an example of such a theory. It is not, however, that the theory is 'non-falsifiable' but that it is used in a non-empirical way.

I have argued that if we concentrate on specific hypotheses about patients or disorders we can be misled into believing we have established certain facts about the causally generative mechanisms which produce certain problems and the effectiveness of our therapy. This is misleading because it obscures the poverty of our explanatory systems. It is the poverty of our explanatory systems that allows the many different schools of psychotherapy to co-exist. I have also stressed that hypothesis testing is part of everyday reasoning and not to be seen as an esoteric practice. What we do know about patients through clinical experience is also evidence (but with due regard to my previous argument that we function using a confirmatory bias). If I am correct this is not a comfortable position for cognitive psychotherapy, or indeed for psychotherapy or psychology in general. However, as we tell our patients, it is better to acknowledge the limitations of what we truly know than to practise self-deception.

References

Beck, A. (1989) *Cognitive Therapy of the Emotional Disorders.* New York: International Universities Press.

Foucault, M. (1965) *Madness and Civilization.* New York: Random House.

Freud, S. (1953) *The Interpretation of Dreams.* London: Pelican.

Harré, R. and Secord, P. (1970) *The Explanation of Social Behaviour.* Oxford: Basil Blackwell.

Kennedy, R. (1969) *Thirteen Days: The Cuban Missile Crisis, October 1962.*

Kuhn, T. (1962) *The Structure of Scientific Revolutions.* Chicago, Ill.: University of Chicago Press.

Lazarus, A. (1991) 'Does chaos prevail? An exchange on technical eclecticism and assimilative psychotherapy', *Journal of Psychotherapy Integration* 1 (2): 1–6.

Persons, J. (1989) *Cognitive Therapy: A Case Conceptualisation Approach.* New York: W.W. Norton & Company.

Popper, K. (1976) *Conjectures and Refutations.* London: Routledge & Kegan Paul.

Quine, W.O. (1953) *From a Logical Point of View.* Cambridge, Mass.: Harvard University Press.

Skinner, B.F. (1950) 'Are theories of learning really necessary?', *Psychological Review* 57: 193–216.

Taylor, C. (1964) *The Explanation of Behaviour.* London: Routledge & Kegan Paul.

Thomas, K. (1971) *Religion and the Decline of Magic.* London: Penguin Books.

Wolpe, J. (1958) *Psychotherapy by Reciprocal Inhibition.* Stanford, Calif.: Stanford University Press.

Young, J.E. (1994) *Cognitive Therapy for Personality Disorders: A Schema Focused Cognitive Therapy.* Sarasota, Fla.: Professional Resource Exchange Inc.

Chapter 10

Comparing models in cognitive therapy and cognitive analytic therapy

David Allison and Chess Denman

Introduction

The two authors (DA and CD) set out to compare and contrast schema-focused cognitive behaviour therapy (CBT) (Young, 1994; Beck and Freeman, 1990) with cognitive analytic therapy (CAT) (Ryle 1990, 1995, 1997). In order to do so they chose alternately to present and comment on a case treated by DA.

DA writes

All good psychotherapy should be eclectic psychotherapy, by which I mean that the therapist should be flexible enough to ensure that the model fits the patient, not the reverse. A therapist knowledgeable in a range of psychotherapeutic interventions and means of conceptualising difficulties will always have the advantage when it comes to working with complex or particularly challenging patients. Cognitive therapy (arguably the most effective form of short-term psychotherapy) is rapidly establishing itself as a marvellously eclectic system of psychotherapy, unashamedly 'borrowing' from a huge range of diverse approaches to psychological treatment.

The last 30 years have seen cognitive therapy become both an elegant and sophisticated model of psychotherapy that has proven popular with patients and purchasers of healthcare alike. Contrary to common misconception, cognitive therapy has demonstrated itself to be concerned with much the same issues as those that concern the dynamically oriented therapists. Issues such as whether quantum change in personality disorder is possible are being explored by cognitive therapists who have developed specific models for the treatment of these groups. We are sensitive to the fact that affect is at least as important as cognition in treatment, and draw upon the work of experiential theorists in instigating treatment plans with patients specifically to mobilise affect. Even transference is no longer sacred to dynamic psychotherapy as the new breed of cognitive therapists attempt to construct cognitive models for incorporating this elusive concept within a coherent case conceptualisation.

Currently, psychotherapists are under increasing pressure to prove themselves as scientific in the way in which interventions are selected. Good scientists never deal in certainties, only in testable hypothesis. I hope that the following case study will demonstrate not only the flexibility of cognitive therapy but also its 'scientist practitioner' philosophy of hypothesising possible cognitive structures relating to problems and the subsequent testing and redefining of the same.

CD writes

Cognitive analytical therapy has since its inception tended to arouse sceptical interest in cognitive therapists. There are, in general, two major groups of responses. Some people who hear accounts of CAT comment that they can see little difference between what they are doing and cognitive therapy. Others tend to see CAT as watered-down psychodynamic psychotherapy with all its many faults (from a cognitive perspective). CAT is neither of these. Instead it brings a distinctive theoretical perspective on human behaviour which partly draws on psychodynamic ideas, cognitive psychology and social constructivist perspectives. Theorists of CAT have mainly been concerned to elaborate its internal theoretical structure, but CAT, via its chief protagonist A. Ryle, has also engaged with psychoanalytic thinking. There has, heretofore been less engagement with cognitive therapy. This chapter is intended as a contribution to that engagement.

We wanted to explore the clinical effects of these two therapeutic modalities on the evidence-gathering, case-formulating and intervention-planning activities of the therapist. We try to illustrate here the different views taken by cognitive and cognitive analytic therapists of the material presented during a CT treatment.

DA writes

The name of the patient discussed in the following case history, together with some geographical information, has been changed in order to preserve patient confidentiality. We are grateful to 'Andrew' for giving us permission to discuss his case. Andrew is a 22-year-old trainee building surveyor referred for cognitive therapy by the psychiatric department. His presentation was characterised by multiple anxiety features. He suffered from a moderately severe panic disorder, social phobia, claustrophobia and a fear of heights.

The initial consultation involved creating a cognitive conceptualisation of his anxiety and socialising him into the model of treatment. As panic attacks appeared to be the most debilitating of his difficulties, it was agreed that these would be our initial focus of treatment. A straightforward symptomatic model of panic was construed, with him highlighting the role of catastrophic interpretations of innocuous symptoms of anxiety in maintaining the panic cycle. For Andrew these interpretations were concerned with the belief that panic would inevitably result in 'loss of control' unless the symptoms could be avoided. When we further explored this by discussing the meaning of control within this context, Andrew was able to describe vivid catastrophic images in which he saw himself as acting 'crazy' during a panic attack; screaming for help, collapsing on the floor surrounded by a crowd of unsympathetic onlookers.

In the majority of cases patients suffering from panic make a full recovery using the basic cognitive interventions of recognising the misinterpretations they make about their anxiety symptoms, learning to challenge the validity of these interpretations through a process cognitive therapists call guided discovery and, finally, by testing out more benign explanations of their symptoms while actually experiencing full-blown panic attacks. This latter is often achieved by provoking symptoms of panic in the therapist's office.

Andrew and I agreed to instigate a fairly aggressive approach to his panic. That meant that from the first treatment session we were provoking panic symptomatology in the office and testing the validity of his predictions. Standard homework involved the monitoring of his anxiety and the deliberate provocation of symptoms in feared situations.

CD writes

CAT shares with cognitive therapy the initial aim of conceptualising the patient's condition and of socialising the patient into treatment. Socialising the patient is particularly important in a non-psychologically minded and non-psychotherapeutically oriented patient group. In the initial sessions a CAT therapist would aim to:

Session 1
- Make a bond with the patient.
- Explain the nature and timetable of treatment.

- Start to take an extensive history, possibly introducing specialised tool.

Session 2
- Continue taking a history.
- Review results of tests/tools.
- Clarify understanding of the treatment process by the patient.
- Make a list of key problem areas.
- Initiate monitoring of these areas.

Session 3
- Refine list of key problem areas and link these to underlying difficulties.
- Test out and seek for evidence in relation to initial elements of the case formulation (called a reformulation).

Session 4
- Present to and work with the patient on the text of a letter outlining the reformulation of the case to include key problem areas, underlying maladaptive procedural sequences and historical reconstruction of their origin.

CAT differs from cognitive therapy at this stage because there is no focus on symptom relief in the early sessions. For cognitive therapists the initial focus on symptom relief makes the patient feel better immediately, provides the patient with evidence that the cognitive model works, and so helps to build a treatment alliance. In CAT the relief offered in the early sessions is generated by the experience of being understood and listened to by an individual who puts considerable and visible effort into this task. Self-efficacy may also be increased by the various monitoring tasks as in general (but not always) they tend to help cut the problem down to manageable size.

DA writes

Treatment progressed extremely well and within four or five sessions we had begun to look at his social phobia in more detail. It was as we began to discuss this I became aware that the theme of loss of control undermined all of his anxiety problems. With regard to his social anxiety he would not be able to conceal the extent of his anxiety, that he would blush, stammer and make a fool of himself in public. Similarly he felt that his more specific phobic anxiety problems would cause him to again lose control in public, resulting in social humiliation.

As we began to unravel the relationship between his beliefs that anxiety was evidence of loss of control, and that this would result in his being humiliated by others, it was manifestly clear that purely symptomatic models of anxiety were no longer sufficient. For Andrew was describing much more deeply held beliefs about the importance of appearing 'in control' to others at all times that represent what cognitive therapists call schemas.

Schemas are enduring beliefs about the self, others and the rest of the world, often formed in childhood, and through which significant events can be processed. They are rigid and inflexible cognitive structures that may lie dormant for many years and be triggered into a hyperactive state by a trauma that resembles that which originally led to their inception. They are extremely primal, formed without the benefit of a mature thinking style. For example, the child who is shouted at by an irate mother many times is likely to develop beliefs about his or her own responsibility for the outbursts (i.e., 'mum shouts at me because I am bad') rather than to consider rationally all the other alternative reasons that may explain mother's irritability. When activated in childhood the same lack of processing resources is apparent when exploring the patient's negative automatic thoughts.

In attempting to delineate core structures that had resulted in Andrew's desire for complete emotional control and fear of humiliation, we highlighted the links between his various anxieties and his fear of loss of control and began to discuss his desire to be someone who never felt any emotion. We talked about his belief that expression of negative emotions could lead to humiliation and to discover early experiences of this which would account for his developing such beliefs. In essence, as his symptoms were rapidly improving we began to develop a more longitudinal conceptualisation that would explain the onset and development of his difficulties.

CD writes

While a CAT therapist might in extreme circumstances, or if not doing CAT very well, change the formulation produced after the fourth session this would not generally be the case. So in relation to Andrew we would hope to have arrived by Session 4 at an understanding resembling that produced by the cognitive therapy in Sessions 5 and 6, but at the price of not yet having tackled the anxiety symptoms directly. This has advantages and disadvantages. On the plus side, patients can complain that they find cognitive therapy cutting to the chase before they have had a chance to reveal the full extent of their worries. On the minus side, for a highly anxious and sceptical patient CAT can be experienced as woolly and ineffective.

This is a minor difference of emphasis when compared with the differences between CAT and cognitive therapy in relation to the core ideas of schema on the one hand and target problem procedure (TPP) and reciprocal role procedure (RRP) on the other. While cognitive therapy bases its deeper formation on the basis of core beliefs which are enduring and which bias information processing, CAT prefers to use the concept of procedural sequences as its unit of analysis. Procedural sequences are goal-directed sequences of aim formation, environmental appraisal, action and reappraisal which are used to carry out all kinds of behaviour. They tend naturally to endure only if they are adaptive and successful because the reappraisal element acts to eliminate procedures with too many negative effects. Maladaptive procedures (target problem procedures) remain maladaptive for structural reasons which may involve avoidant vitiating of the check step as in phobias (traps) or halting of the procedure before it ever runs owing to an anticipated severe negative outcome (snags). They may also continue to be deployed because they are the best of a bad bunch (dilemmas). In every case, though, while there are traceable adaptive or attemptedly adaptive past origins for all the procedures, however maladaptive they currently are, their persistence is a result of continuing reinforcement and failure of revision.

A special kind of procedure describes interpersonal and intrapersonal relationships. A core template called a reciprocal role (which involves self, other and a binding concern – e.g., mother, child, care giving) informs the formation of procedures designed to meet its aims and which tend either to build up and confirm the role or to dissipate and dissolve it (such reciprocal roles being rarely found in the psyche because they are short lived).

CAT, by emphasising reciprocal roles and procedures, maintains a consistently interactional and interpersonal stance which lies in the psychological tradition of Brunner and Gibson. The emphasis is on the failure to revise maladaptive procedures. Procedures are sequential, aim-directed, and maintained by repeated environmental enactment. Unlike schemas, they are not conceived of, so much as intrinsically enduring, or composed of aggregations of beliefs, memories, feelings and overlearned responses. This theoretical stance is combined with a therapeutic view derived from the work of Vygotsky which emphasises the capacity of higher functions (especially sign mediation of social interaction and language) to intervene in and alter lower order functions. Cognitive therapy too requires recruitment of higher functions, but a CAT therapist would therefore tend to work 'top-down' from a general explicit formulation shared with the patient to specific interventions designed to aid procedural revision. This can be contrasted with the bottom-up approach, in this case where individual symptoms were tackled first.

DA writes

Exploration of themes inherent in Andrew's negative thoughts, and the meanings he ascribed to feeling symptoms of anxiety, had already led me to hypothesise that he held a core belief of himself as weak and helpless. The reasons for this view of himself appeared to have their genesis in the extremely over-protective relationship he had (and to some extent continues to have) with his parents. Andrew had been a somewhat sickly child suffering from severe asthma and his parents displayed what he described as an almost suffocating anxiety for his welfare. His older sister took on the role of a 'body guard', accompanying Andrew wherever he went and interceding on his behalf whenever he had altercations with his peers.

He was often bullied at school and he has traumatic memories of being beaten by the other boys while suffering from asthma attacks. At such times he was obviously utterly unable to defend himself and he remembers his classmates standing over him laughing, while he lay on the floor unable to breath due both to the asthma attack and the beating he had endured.

From such information we hypothesised a core self-schema stated as 'I am weak' and a core schema about others as 'They will always try and kick you when you are down'. His rules and dysfunctional assumptions resulting from these core beliefs were constructed as:

- 'I must never show any signs of weakness'
- 'Anxiety is a sign of weakness'
- 'If I am strong and always in control nobody will be able to hurt me (physically or emotionally)'

These schemas and associated rules and assumptions appear to have remained dormant until Andrew was 16, when, tragically, his best friend was killed in a road traffic accident. At the time Andrew coped well and it was not until two weeks later, in a school assembly in which his friend was being remembered, that he displayed any sign of real grief. In his own words he 'completely broke down'. Sobbing uncontrollably he was led from the assembly by a teacher, who then proceeded to reprimand him for 'showing himself up in public'. There was worse to follow, as Andrew found himself ridiculed by his classmates for his grief; they taunted him, suggesting he was 'queer' for being so upset by the loss of a male friend.

It was during the following six months that Andrew started to develop symptoms of the anxiety that characterised his presentation when he commenced treatment. In the light of the history he described it was apparent that Andrew had developed two major dysfunctional strategies in response to his schemata.

The first of these is schema avoidance. This refers to affective, cognitive and behavioural strategies for maintaining the activity of core schema to a minimum. For Andrew, affective avoidance was essential. He believed that emotional states might result in catastrophic loss of control that would make him vulnerable to harm from others. Therefore he would not allow himself to feel emotion and it was observed several times that when talking around emotion-laden subjects he would dissociate to some extent. Indeed, many of the painful issues we were able to conceptualise in treatment did not come to light until we were in the latter stages of treatment due to a pervasive and painful mixture of affective and cognitive avoidance. For example, many of the incidents of bullying that we discussed were not remembered until well into therapy.

The second strategy was that of schema compensation, a term closely related to that of reaction formation in analytical therapy. I had observed early in treatment that Andrew seemed to use his clothes as a metaphorical suit of armour. Although he earned only a moderate wage, he always dressed with infinite care and usually wore, somewhat ostentatiously, 'labels' such as Armani. He drove an expensive car and his whole outward appearance was somewhat intimidating. Andrew often talked of how he wanted to be 'the man in the suit'. The man in the suit never experienced anxiety, was confident in every situation and was never thwarted in his ambitions. Andrew's goal was to appear flawless. If there was no point on which he was open to criticism then he would remain invulnerable from harm.

As Andrew and I conceptualised his core processes and the roles of schema avoidance and compensation by carefully looking for evidence of their activity both in the past and present, I became painfully aware that I could be in danger of inadvertently shoring up his avoidance strategies. Andrew had for many years been trying to suppress anxiety, and indeed any painful emotion, in the fear that it would overwhelm him. The symptom-oriented phase of treatment might, in effect, enable him to better avoid discomfort without testing the damaging hypothesis that emotion was catastrophic. It seemed possible that Andrew might end treatment still desperately trying to be the 'man in the suit'.

CD writes

By a different route from CAT the cognitive therapist reaches a formulation of the case which is entirely comprehensive and covers so much of the same ground as a CAT therapist would cover that it is possible to recast the cognitive formulation in CAT terms.

From a CAT perspective Andrew has internalised a single powerful reciprocal role template which is slightly complex in having three parts. First, a weak, helpless and humiliated part. This is in relation to a cosseting protective part (originally his family). It is also in relation to a bullying humiliating part. Finally the cosseting part not only constructs the weak and helpless part but also involves a construction of the outside world as bullying and humiliating. This reciprocal role represents the constructions of his original family, which Andrew grew up with and which were amply confirmed by various experiences – particularly being beaten for being asthmatic and humiliated for crying in public. Andrew's fundamental aim is to avoid feeling weak and helpless. The process called schema avoidance would be described in CAT as a response to feeling potentially weak and helpless in relation to a bullying and humiliating other. To avoid this he walls himself off and dissociates, but this means that he never tests his initial appraisal of the situation. Indeed, he may even read his walling off strategy as evidence for, rather than a response to, the hostility of the world, and so the reciprocal role template is built up. The process called schema compensation would issue from the relationship of weak, helpless self and cosseting other. This is internalised by Andrew who now cossets and bodyguards himself as others did for him (self-care often being driven by a reciprocal role template of care received from others). But the self now provides a cosseted space in which the outside world is constructed as fault-finding, wanting to humiliate and bully, but Andrew feels himself invulnerable. Sadly the underlying assumption is never tested, and there are also side effects to this position such as a false look and the expense of maintaining it.

What advantages might the CAT formulation have? First CAT would be able to make two predictions at this point. Reciprocal roles are learned as paired self – other templates, and switching between self and other positions (role reversal) can and does occur. Potentially, therefore, Andrew might be a cosseting and overprotective person – say in relation to his own children constructed as weak and helpless – but he might also be a bullying humiliator constructing someone weaker than himself as weak and helpless. Second, reciprocal role patterns exhibit role induction. In an interpersonal situation someone who powerfully adopts one reciprocal role will tend to exert pressure to reciprocate in the other role to any other individual around. Consequently we might expect Andrew's therapist to be pulled into acting out any of the three parts of Andrew's picture. Being alert for these possibilities in advance could help the therapist plan for likely adverse events and ameliorate their consequences.

It is also possible that a more global view of Andrew's difficulties might have helped him to bring some of his painful issues into the therapy earlier. Although, by the same token, patients can on occasion find the 'in your face' nature of the reformulation more than they can stand and, instead of being helped to stay in therapy, run from the experience in terror. However this is a much rarer occurrence than therapists fear it will be.

DA writes

For Andrew to remain the 'man in the suit' would have been a therapeutic tragedy. The process of therapy had seemed to have unlocked some of Andrew's emotional trauma and this was particularly evinced in the strong therapeutic relationship we had developed. Andrew had once said that his feelings towards me were very similar to those he had previously had towards the friend who died, and we had been able to use this in order to look at some of the unresolved feelings he had about his friend's death.

The comprehensive model we had developed suggested that emotional avoidance was severely curtailing Andrew's life, and that for this to improve the therapeutic task would be for him to test his beliefs about the dangers of emotional expression.

This was discussed openly with Andrew, and I had offered him further sessions in which he might test his hypothesis about emotion. Perhaps not surprisingly, he was more than a little ambivalent about this. However, his main objection to a process that would involve experimental techniques to mobilise affect was that the normal session length would be inadequate for such work. He feared that the session would end with him possibly experiencing high levels of affect that he would have to resolve unsupported. This seemed a reasonable objection and we finally agreed on a time table of ten two-hour sessions which would allow for affect arousal and appropriate containment.

We had agreed to focus on his feelings about the death of his best friend, as he believed that he had been unable to express his grief properly about this. We incorporated both focusing and vivid imagery techniques to good effect during sessions. By the end of the third session Andrew was showing signs of strong arousal, expressing feelings of grief, and to my surprise, a great deal of anger. This had been avoided by attempts to rationalise the senseless nature of the death of Paul (his friend). He had tried to deal with this by developing beliefs that 'everything happens for a reason', and that therefore it was not an empty tragedy. It was when the purpose of these beliefs (rationalisation) was gently challenged that the anger surfaced.

My role during this was much less directive than is normal in cognitive therapy. Once affect had surfaced, function became supportive, encouraging Andrew to facilitate discussion about what had happened and how this either served to confirm or disconfirm his dysfunctional assumptions about emotion.

Tasks were assigned to be completed outside of therapy in which he began to acknowledge feeling anxiety with his friends. He was astounded to find that most people were able to empathise with him, and would admit to having experienced similar sensations at one time or another. While a similar intervention had been deployed earlier in treatment, it was only now that this seemed to result in some cognitive restructuring. During this period of work he began to see that anxiety was part of normal experience and not evidence of an inherent defectiveness. He found that he could 'stand' emotional discomfort and this resulted in him being able to re-evaluate his core belief that he was weak.

He still has some way to go. While he now allows himself to go out looking less than perfect, this still provokes some anxiety. However, he is committed to working on this. He keeps a daily log in which he records evidence suggesting that other people feel it is OK to talk about anxiety, and his belief in his own core processes continues to fall.

CD writes

Andrew's cognitive therapy now moves into an atypical (for cognitive therapy) phase. An advantage which CAT and cognitive therapy share is therapeutic eclecticism backed by theoretical rigour. In CAT the rule is stated as 'you may modify treatment as you will, but you must have a rationale based on the reformulation and on CAT's theoretical base for doing it', and this is true also of CT. There would, however, have been differences between a CAT approach and a cognitive one at this point. Possibly the increase in session length would have been resisted as tending to build up the idea that Andrew was specially vulnerable, and possibly here there is evidence that the therapist is being pulled into a cosseting role with the patient. Equally CAT's possible insistence on the boundary might well have played into a countertransference identification with the bully–humiliator pole of the reciprocal role procedure. Instead the therapist would have used the anxiety, combined with the mutual reciprocal role induction (transference and countertransference), to try to give Andrew an emotionally relevant understanding of the overall conceptualisation and how it worked. A CAT therapist would also have continued to draw Andrew back to the reformulation, working through the three 'Rs' of CAT: reformulation, recognition and revision. In relation to assigning tasks outside the session, though, CAT would be entirely in agreement with the cognitive therapist's approach. Continuing its stress on written sharing, right at the end of therapy the therapist would have given a goodbye letter summarising progress and areas still to be worked on. The normal schedule for a follow-up visit would be in three months time, but sooner if the patient's progress seemed uncertain.

DA writes

At the end of treatment I wanted evidence of two different kinds to be assured that there had been real and lasting improvement.

Andrew's anxiety levels have sharply declined. He has not had a panic attack for nearly four months, was not avoiding situations that might provoke anxiety, and had even been up in an aeroplane. But this was not enough. In Andrew's case I was also looking for evidence of interpersonal changes that would indicate a shift in his core schemas.

This was to appear at our follow-up session arranged a month after our final regular session. Andrew had just commenced his first intimat relationship with a woman and had been able to overcome his initial surge of anxiety when he realised he was developing strong feelings for her. He had previously never been able to form relationships with women because he had been terrified by the degree of self-exposure involved in developing intimacy.

Andrew's case is particularly interesting because it raised important questions about what constituted an improvement. For many patients subjective reports of experiencing less anxiety or dysphoria are often enough, but the formulation of Andrew's case suggested that, to some extent, resolving his anxiety at the symptomatic level, while making him feel better, may actually have exacerbated his interpersonal difficulties.

The cognitive therapy principles of continuous reassessment, guided discovery and an unfolding case formulation that develops over the entire period of treatment ensured that, as a therapist, I had the flexibility to adapt to changes in the focus of treatment as new material emerged.

CD writes

CAT therapists too want evidence of improvement. Often initial measures are given at the start of treatment, and during therapy a rating sheet of the key maladaptive procedures and progress in revising them is filled in. At follow-up all this data would be reviewed. Change in symptoms is the *sine qua non* of any therapeutic endeavour, but, while necessary, it is not a sufficient condition for therapeutic success. Additionally, a CAT therapist would look for evidence of procedural revision and benign modification of the reciprocal role structure. This can be evaluated by a sensibly structured clinical interview by an interviewer who can be dispassionate about the outcome of therapy.

Conclusion

This presentation has sought to highlight differences of theory and technique between cognitive and cognitive analytic therapy. However, their similarity needs to be drawn out. Both therapies are committed to an evidence-gathering, and hypothesis-testing way of working, which involves drawing the patient in as collaborator. Many other therapeutic brands claim to be doing this too. However, CAT and CT are unique in offering a systematic method for trying to ensure that this happens rather than remaining a pious hope.

References

Beck, A.T. and Freeman, A. (1990) *Cognitive Therapy of Personality Disorders.* New York: Guilford Press.

Ryle, A. (1990) 'Cognitive-analytic therapy: active participation in change: a new integration', in *Brief Psychotherapy.* Chichester: Wiley.

Ryle, A. (1995) *Cognitive Analytic Therapy: Developments in Theory and Practice.* London: John Wiley & Sons.

Ryle, A. (1997) *Cognitive Analytic Therapy and Borderline Personality Disorder: The Model and the Method.* Chichester: Wiley.

Young, J. E. (1994) *Cognitive Therapy for Personality Disorders: A Schema-Focused Approach.* Sarasota, Fla.: Professional Resource Exchange Inc.

Chapter 11

Evidence-based practice and the psychodynamic psychotherapies

Phil Richardson

What is evidence-based practice?

Evidence-based medicine (EBM) has been defined as: 'the conscientious, explicit and judicious use of current best evidence in making decisions about the care of individual patients. The practice of evidence-based medicine means integrating individual, clinical expertise with the best available external clinical evidence from systematic research' (Sackett *et al.*, 1996). Evidence-based practice is a broadening, to healthcare in general, of the principles of EBM.

Fundamental to the evidence-based approach to healthcare is the idea that equitable provision be guided by standards of evidence concerning the effectiveness of treatments. The gold standard of such evidence has widely been viewed as the randomised controlled trial (RCT) which has now become the dominant method for evaluating drugs and many other treatment methods. The collation of information about the findings of such trials has become a growth industry in recent years and various sources of abstracted information are now available, including the Cochrane library (Cochrane Collaboration, 1999).

An evidence-based approach to healthcare stands in contradistinction to conventional methods of medicine in which clinical experience would typically be combined with a knowledge of biological principles to yield a best-practice decision in any particular case. Within this perspective, value is given to the notion of clinical authority or expertise and, if a senior colleague cannot provide an immediate source of such expertise, reference can be made to a respected textbook.

Evidence-based practice (EBP) does not eschew the role of clinical experience but simply argues that it is such experience which will complement and enable the appropriate interpretation of available evidence – so that it is only in the absence of an evidence-based approach that reliance upon clinical experience alone becomes inadvisable. The present chapter examines some of the problems which arise when considering an EBP approach in the psychodynamic psychotherapies.

Standards of evidence

A requirement of EBP is that clinical decision-making be largely informed by good evidence concerning best practice. What constitutes good evidence might at first be thought to be simple; namely, that it is evidence from research carried out with sufficient scientific rigour to be both believable (e.g., internally valid) and applicable (i.e., generalisable – or, roughly speaking, externally valid). On this basis, a series of assumptions are made about what constitutes acceptable evidence, and a hierarchy of value is typically ascribed to different sources of evidence: RCTs are thought to yield stronger evidence than open case series, which yield stronger evidence than clinician consensus, which may yield stronger evidence than patient views about effectiveness, etc. (Department of Health, 1996a; cf. Chapter 1 in this book).

Using such a hierarchy it becomes possible to identify the evidential criteria whereby treatments may justifiably be described as empirically 'validated' or 'supported'. (NB: the latter term is increasingly preferred since it avoids the implication of finality contained within an all-or-none notion of validation.) As evidence accumulates treatments can be seen as increasingly supported from an empirical standpoint – (Chambless and Hollon, 1998.) Lists can then be drawn up of treatments, with a sufficiently solid empirical base for use in routine care (and thus, in the USA, for support by public or private healthcare insurance schemes) and incorporation in clinical guidelines (RCP, 1994) – with the assumption that empirically poorly supported therapies must remain 'experimental' until they accumulate adequate empirical support (APA Task Force, 1995).

Evidence for the benefits of the psychodynamic psychotherapies

Psychodynamic psychotherapies (PDP) are, for the most part, poorly empirically supported – according to the evidential criteria commonly applied in contemporary reviews (Chambless and Hollon, 1998; Dobson and Craig, 1998; Nathan and Gorman, 1998; Roth and Fonagy, 1996). For example, in one of the most comprehensive and accomplished comparative psychotherapy outcome reviews, Roth and Fonagy (1996) found that PDP achieved their minimal criteria for full empirical validation only in the treatment of depression for the elderly, and failed to do so for the treatment of any child or adult disorder. Moreover, their standards of 'partial validation' were also only achieved by PDP in a handful of conditions. These findings have been largely echoed in several more recent reviews and overviews (DeRubeis and Crits-Cristoph, 1998; Dobson and Craig, 1998; Nathan and Gorman, 1998; Fonagy *et al.*, 1999).

On the surface, then, it would appear that for psychodynamic psychotherapy to be practised within an evidence-based framework an important initial task may be that of gathering the relevant evidence concerning its effects. Much will depend, however, on the ways in which evidence is defined, the kinds of evidence which are acceptable within the framework of evidence-based practice, and the special problems which may arise when a set of methodological criteria – developed for the evaluation of research evidence outside the domain of psychotherapy – are applied within that domain. This chapter is largely devoted to exploring these issues.

Which evidential criteria in psychotherapy outcome research?

From the Sackett *et al.* definition (see p. 157) it might be thought that the primary task of the evidence-based approach is that of identifying good-quality evidence. In reality a prior task may be that of determining what constitutes good-quality evidence. The standards of scientific acceptability which apply to evidence in the domain of physical medicine may be relatively clear – and subject to relatively common agreement. Those which might properly apply in the domain of psychotherapy (and especially psychodynamic psychotherapy) are less clear and are certainly far from universally agreed (Elliott, 1998). Whilst there may be certain core principles which apply widely to the evaluation of treatment methods it also seems probable that each field of enquiry will have – to some extent – its own unique evidential standards.

Examples of the way in which differing standards of evaluation may need to apply in different research domains are numerous. For example, at some stage in the evaluation of any new form of pharmacotherapy it would be expected that the treatment be compared with a placebo. This enables its specific pharmacological impact to be identified when its psychological impact has been controlled for (Pocock, 1984). The use of the placebo control condition in psychotherapy research, however, where all treatments have a primarily psychological impact, is now regarded as an inappropriate and blunt way in which to identify the specificity of a treatment's effects (Parloff, 1986). Various forms of process research may enable the identification of the psychological processes whereby a treatment of demonstrated efficacy has its action (Garfield, 1990), but the placebo control condition has largely been abandoned for this purpose.

Similarly, the importance of double-blind methodology in assessing the effects of treatment is axiomatic where pharmacotherapy research is concerned (Pocock, 1984). It is hopelessly impractical – and hence irrelevant – for psychotherapy outcome evaluation. The rationale for using double-blind methodology is to minimise the potential biasing effects on patient and/or therapist which may arise from knowledge about and attitudes towards the treatment concerned. Neither patient nor therapist can remain blind to the fact of receiving or giving psychotherapy, however, and once again, more sophisticated methods are needed to examine the extent to which the patient and therapist's knowledge and attitudes influence therapeutic outcome.

In contrast there may be methodological criteria of special relevance to psychotherapy research – which may be of lesser importance in other kinds of treatment trial. An example might be the extent to which the quality of the therapy, which was delivered in the trial, has been demonstrated or can reasonably be assumed. Variations in pill content and quality are likely to be small in drug trials. Variations in the content and quality of psychotherapy could be considerable. Comparative psychotherapy studies involving psychodynamic approaches have sometimes used expert therapists – an example being the Sloan *et al.* (1975) RCT which found psychoanalytic therapy to be equivalent in effectiveness to behaviour therapy and superior to a waiting list control condition. Others have used non-expert therapists – as in the Bellack *et al.* (1981) study – where the psychodynamic therapy was used as a control for non-specific factors and, not surprisingly, was less effective than social skills training or drug treatment.

The list of criteria for assessing methodological quality in outcome studies in any therapy domain is likely to be long. It will include considerations of adequacy of design, sample, measurement, therapy integrity, follow-up periods, data analysis and reporting, as well as other features. Scoring criteria have frequently been employed to assess methodological adequacy, particularly for use in systematic reviews (e.g., Jadad, 1998; Shapiro *et al.*, 1994), and there is some evidence to suggest that as methodological adequacy drops, so the apparent effects of treatment (i.e., effect sizes) go up (e.g., Shapiro *et al.*, 1994). At the very least this underlines the importance of paying adequate regard to the evaluative methods employed in individual studies.

In view of the inevitably imperfect nature of applied research, reviewers cannot realistically exclude all studies which fail on a single criterion of methodological adequacy. Thus the relative weighting given to different methodological criteria will influence the likelihood that studies appear in reviews and hence contribute, either positively or negatively, to the evidence base relating to particular therapies. The Bellack *et al.* study, using psychodynamic psychotherapy as a placebo, meets many of the criteria of a good-quality study and therefore finds its way into reviews of the efficacy of PDP, albeit as a study that is acknowledged to add little to our understanding of its outcome (Roth and Fonagy, 1996). The Sloan *et al.* study, whilst in some ways providing a far more valid test of (expert) therapy on a (clinically representative) group of mixed neurotic patients, is excluded from some recent reviews for failing to meet the criterion of specificity of patient sample (see p. 160).

The above example reinforces the point that a single set of 'evidence-based' research criteria cannot respond across the board to the needs of reviewers – or of individual clinicians who, in the absence of clear guidelines, are trying to find their way through the maze of research relevant to their particular area of practice. It is a commonplace in scientific circles that two narrative reviews of the same source material may arrive at different conclusions. Clarity is achieved in systematic reviews and meta-analyses through explicit stipulation of the rules, whereby individual studies contribute to conclusions. This clarity should not be confused with certainty about the correctness of the chosen rules.

It is not suggested here that, were a differently organised set of cogent scientific criteria applied to the evaluation of outcome studies on PDP, the present dearth of acceptable evidence would suddenly be transformed into a plethora. It is simply proposed that proper attention be paid to the adoption of psychotherapeutically relevant methods in psychotherapy evaluation research.

The RCT as gold standard

It is not difficult to see why the RCT has been largely adopted as the premier paradigm for treatment evaluation research. Findings from individual case studies, however systematically conducted and however compelling, cannot with confidence be applied to larger populations, and single case study methods typically pose problems for the clear identification of a cause–effect relationship between treatment and outcome (Roth and Fonagy, 1996). Studies based on groups of patients, selected according to clear criteria, may be more convincing where generalisability is concerned. The use of pre- and post-treatment measures may enable documentation of change across such patient groups. When controlled (e.g., by comparing treated patients with others who receive a different or delayed intervention), one may also have greater confidence that the study is not simply tapping the effects of spontaneous symptom fluctuation over time, or an effect of repeated measurement – independently of treatment received.

Without random allocation to the conditions being compared, however, a causal relationship between treatment and outcome cannot be confidently assumed. The two or more groups being compared in a non-randomised trial may always have been different with respect to some (possibly unidentified) variable, and in such a way that their eventual outcomes following treatment appear spuriously to reflect a true treatment effect, but would in any case always have been different. Randomisation to treatment condition – from the same initial sample – eliminates systematic sources of sample bias and, when combined with explicit matching of groups on key variables (as for example in the minimisation technique – Miller *et al.*, 1980), also reduces the likelihood of chance differences in factors which might confound the valid comparison of outcome across groups. In sum, the inherently experimental design of the RCT affords greater confidence than other designs in the inferred causal relationship between the independent variable (treatment) and the dependent variable (outcome).

Problems with RCTs

There are many problems with randomised trials, however, as well as with other aspects of the methodology which commonly accompanies the RCT. These have been well summarised elsewhere (e.g., Jadad, 1998) and will only be selectively sampled here.

Several of the drawbacks of the randomised trial derive from the fact that randomisation as a basis for treatment allocation is highly atypical of the way in which treatments are ordinarily administered in normal clinical practice. This has two implications. First, patients who consent to randomisation (or whose therapists consent to their randomisation) may not be typical of patients in general. Second, the fact of receiving a treatment on the basis of the haphazard choice implied by randomisation may itself influence the psychological impact of the treatment. This may be relatively unimportant where the aim of a trial is to assess the physical impact of a physical treatment but could be critical where psychological treatments are concerned. These factors combine to raise questions about the generalisability of the findings of RCTs to the patient population in general.

It is important to note, however, that a number of the difficulties with RCTs have been addressed elsewhere in treatment evaluation research, and with solutions that may equally apply in the psychotherapy research field. For example, the use of an 'intention to treat' design overcomes some of the problems arising from potentially biased samples (Jadad, 1998), and 'patient preference' designs can examine the impact of randomisation *per se* (Brewin and Bradley, 1989). An example of the latter in psychological treatments research is the comparison of randomised with non-randomised patients treated with CBT in Williams *et al.* (1999). In this study no differences were found in outcome between the two groups, challenging the notion that the use of randomisation inevitably poses a threat to external validity. Nevertheless, the external validity of RCTs cannot be automatically assumed and should arguably be tested in effectiveness studies (see pp. 163–164).

Moreover, for a randomised controlled trial to give meaningful results about the efficacy of a particular form of therapy it is increasingly recognised that it is necessary to describe clearly the patient group on which the treatment was tested in the RCT. This leads to the requirement of a relatively homogeneous patient sample and the necessity to exclude cases in which significant co-morbidity or other confounding variables may be present. For example, if a treatment for depression were shown to be efficacious on a sample of patients who were not only depressed but who, at the same time, suffered from other mental health problems, it might be difficult to know whether the treatment had its effects through a beneficial impact on depression *per se* or on some other aspect of psychopathology. This may further limit the external validity of studies of this kind insofar as patients without co-morbidity may also be atypical of those commonly referred to mental health services.

Efficacy vs effectiveness

These and similar considerations relating to the methodology of formal treatment trials have given rise to the distinction between the concepts of efficacy and effectiveness. Efficacy studies are the formal controlled treatment trials which ask whether a clearly stipulated treatment approach has particular effects on a precisely defined patient population. Effectiveness research is concerned with whether the treatments in question are actually effective in the context of everyday clinical practice with everyday patients and therapists.

Several reviewers have drawn attention to the potentially limited generalisability of the findings from efficacy studies and of the need for effectiveness studies to be carried out before an evidence-based approach can be truly applied.

In addition to the atypical and potentially biasing effects of randomisation and the potentially distorted nature of clinical samples, there are other factors which may enhance the internal and construct validity of efficacy studies yet reduce the generalisability of their findings. Examples include: (a) the extensive and multifaceted approach to outcome assessment and extensive therapy monitoring which are atypical of clinical practice, (b) the fact that treatment methods themselves may be atypical – either through an unnatural but enforced standardisation, or the fact that formal trials typically test therapies over shorter treatment periods than apply in routine practice, or because standards of therapeutic practice may be higher in formal trials, and so on. When added to the fact that efficacy studies very often fail to incorporate a long-term follow-up, one can see why a sceptical eye is warranted when considering their clinical relevance. A growing research literature is now addressing the question of clinical representativeness in outcome studies. For a thorough discussion of many of these issues see, for example, Goldfried and Wolfe (1998), Roth and Fonagy (1996) and Shadish *et al.* (1997).

The balance of disadvantage for PDP

The distinction between efficacy and effectiveness research is important when considering the evidence-base for the psychotherapies. It is well known, for example, that the cognitive-behavioural therapies have a far more solid grounding in efficacy research than is currently the case for the psychodynamic psychotherapies (Department of Health, 1996b). The evidence base provided by such efficacy research may be of direct relevance to only a small proportion of the patients who typically access services, however; namely, closely scrutinised and expertly treated patients who are homogeneously and non-comorbidly depressed – with no associated anxiety or personality disorder, for example – who have agreed to accept treatment by random allocation, etc. With this in mind, the apparent imbalance in the evidence base between cognitive-behavioural and psychodynamic therapies starts to look rather different. This is especially so given that the more 'complex' patients commonly excluded from formal efficacy trials may be the harder ones to help, whose outcomes from the kind of brief therapies for which the evidence base is strongest might be altogether less positive. Moreover, the relative dearth of longer-term follow-up data from most efficacy studies carried out to date reduces still further their value as an exclusive basis for evidence-based practice. Very little clinical effectiveness research has been carried out on any of the psychological treatments, where most therapeutic models are therefore in a similar position as far as empirical support is concerned (Department of Health, 1996b).

It is worth noting perhaps that the efficacy/effectiveness distinction can be overstated (cf. Chambless and Hollon, 1998): although the requirements for establishing different forms of validity (e.g., internal vs external) are very often in conflict they are not necessarily so. RCT methodology is not the exclusive preserve of efficacy studies. For all its problems, it is equally applicable and equally relevant to effectiveness research (cf. pragmatic trials). Likewise efficacy studies can be designed wherever possible with clinical representativeness in mind (Shadish *et al.*, 1997).

Special problems of efficacy research in PDP

It is clear therefore that evidence-based practice is far from straightforward. The difficulties in interpreting evidence in general (e.g., the problems of interpreting efficacy studies), and the distinctive characteristics of psychotherapy research itself (e.g., the problem of weighting quality of therapy in the hierarchy of value ascribed to methodological criteria) combine to suggest that the relevant evidence base for psychotherapy practice will not always be evident. In addition there are a number of problems which become particularly acute when seeking to apply an evidence-based approach to the psychodynamic psychotherapies.

Categorising the relevant evidence

For evidence about treatment effectiveness to be usable by individual clinicians it needs to be collated according to classificatory principles which make it accessible. Predetermined categories of evidence can then be applied to predetermined categories of patient problem/characteristic, identified by diagnostic criteria or some other system of classification. If patient x presents with disorder y for which the treatment of choice is p (i.e., p has been shown to be the most efficacious in a randomised controlled trial), then an evidence-based approach to patient care would support the choice of treatment p.

In keeping with the medical roots of much psychotherapy, and perhaps for lack of a better classificatory principle, reviews of evidence typically organise findings around diagnostically identified patient groups. The reasoning behind this is simple. Without being clear to which group a particular set of findings might apply, it is impossible to know how to interpret or apply those findings (Roth and Fonagy, 1996). Findings on the outcome of psychotherapy for patients with depression may have a different meaning from those on psychotherapy for anxiety. This will be especially so when it is known that the ordinary clinical course of different disorders, without treatment, will vary. Insofar as treatment response can be relativised to a particular patient group, the generalisability of the associated findings is easier to assess. (NB: the otherwise excellent RCT by Sloan *et al.* (1975) – mentioned above – looked at mixed neurotic patients and therefore, as a test of the efficacy of PDP, is limited in what it can tell us owing to its lack of specificity with regard to the treated conditions.)

A fear commonly expressed among psychotherapists is that in its simplest form this approach to evidence-based practice might seem to imply that the complexity of the individual case could be reduced to a single unitary theme or classificatory principle. Thus in depression, say, the assumption would be that what it is that depressives have most in common with each other (i.e., the characteristic features of depression) will be more relevant to treatment choice and outcome than all those features and characteristics that are individual, and thus vary across patients.

A simple approach in which identification of a particular disorder implies choice of a particular treatment presumably works well for those conditions (e.g., infectious diseases) where individual differences may moderate treatment response, but will not strongly affect treatment choice. It may also dovetail better with an approach to psychological treatment that focuses primarily on overt symptoms or problems (e.g., behaviour therapy).

If, on the other hand, individual differences in factors other than illness/problem category were highly predictive of outcome then such an approach might encounter difficulties. Suppose, for example, it were shown that patient preference for particular treatment styles (e.g., for prescriptive as opposed to exploratory therapist behaviour), or some other individual difference variable, was related to psychological treatment outcome in depression, say. This would reduce the applicability of a simple model where diagnosis-*x*-implies-treatment-*y*. (NB: the relevance of aptitude-treatment interaction (ATI) studies to psychotherapy outcome research is increasingly being explored – cf. Shoham and Rohrbaugh, 1995.)

This complicating factor is not problematic for a simple model of evidence-based practice to the extent that the additional evidence (in this case about patient preference) can be built into the algorithm which would tell us, here, that depressed patients with preference 'a' might be treated with treatment 'x', while those with preference 'b' could be treated with approach 'y'. This works fine and can fit comfortably within a formal diagnostic perspective for as long as the superordinate classificatory principle remains that of the disorder being treated – in this case depression. If treatment preference, or some other individual difference variable, were found to be more strongly predictive of outcome than problem category then the problem of organising and consequently accessing the relevant evidence – to enable an evidence-based approach – becomes more complex. It is no longer a disorder that is being treated but a person.

Process and outcome research to date suggests that neither treatment modality nor psychiatric diagnostic status account for more than a very limited proportion of outcome variance (cf. Garfield, 1998). As with other psychological treatments, research on PDP must attempt to identify those individual difference dimensions of greatest relevance to predicting outcome if an evidence-based approach to psychotherapy is to become more than a pale imitation of a medical formulary.

Problems with the use of psychiatric diagnosis

ICD and DSM diagnoses are bio-behavioural in nature and in that sense might be considered to be more facilitatory in the evaluation of outcome research findings for biological or behavioural/cognitive treatments. Psychodynamic approaches to psychotherapy generally use a different set of diagnostic criteria, with the result that a generalised set of claims concerning the effectiveness of that treatment cannot be made specifically in relation to formal diagnoses. The theoretical basis underlying psycho-dynamic approaches to psychotherapy would not lead to the conclusion that they will be effective in every case of depression, say. Indeed, from a psychodynamic standpoint the lack of specificity of psychiatric diagnostic categories renders them largely uninformative. A diagnosis of anxiety may be no more meaningful to a psychodynamic psychotherapist than a diagnosis of chest pain to a respiratory physician or stomach pain to a gastroenterologist. These would not be regarded as diagnostic categories, so much as symptoms of any number of possible underlying disorders. This might imply that an alternative set of classificatory principles would be expected to be more predictive of the outcome of psychodynamic psychotherapy. Whether this is so or not remains, for the time being, an unanswered empirical question. Future studies could usefully address the relative predictive power of formal diagnoses and psychodynamic formulations in the prediction of psychodynamic psychotherapy outcome.

This leads us on to a further consideration that is specific to the evaluation of psychodynamic psychotherapies; namely, the significance of the dynamic unconscious. As has been noted elsewhere (e.g., Roth and Fonagy, 1996), formal ICD and DSM diagnoses take no account of unconscious processes in evaluating patients and cannot therefore be seen as highly consistent with an approach to treatment based heavily upon such factors. Similarly excluded by formal diagnostic categories is the developmental perspective. Formal psychiatric diagnoses say little or nothing about aetiology and yet from a psychodynamic standpoint, aetiological considerations may have great importance for choice of treatment approach. For example, in cases of childhood sexual abuse, resultant mental health problems could later take the form of anxiety, depression or some other psychopathology. To speak of the treatment of anxiety or the treatment of depression in such cases would be meaningless, when in fact the therapeutic work would be affected predominantly by considerations of the sexual abuse itself.

For these reasons, an evidence-based approach built around the collation of evidence, which is structured by formal diagnoses, may be of limited relevance to the evaluation of treatment trials related to psychodynamic psychotherapy.

Limitations of the drug metaphor

If the use of formal diagnoses, as a framework for collating evidence about psychotherapy outcomes, highlights difficulties with a simplistic illness model for psychological problems, then consideration of the nature of psychotherapy itself may underline the limitations of the 'drug metaphor' (Stiles and Shapiro, 1989). EBM implies application of a treatment to a disorder. In the same way that the disorder is satisfactorily summarised by a particular diagnostic description, so the treatment is seen as a distinctive entity to be 'applied', almost as one might apply a poultice or an antibiotic. This ignores the evolutionary and potentially self-correcting nature of therapy and, within that, the central role of the therapeutic relationship in creating (i.e., not just mediating) the therapeutic process. Stiles and Shapiro (1989) provide numerous examples of the limitations of conventional process–outcome research founded on the principle that identifiable treatment ingredients will have a simple and unidirectional impact on treatment outcome. Moreover Shapiro *et al.* (1994) have demonstrated the very limited mileage to be obtained from process–outcome research based on such premises. These considerations are likely to be especially problematic in the therapies, like PDP, for which the therapeutic relationship is viewed as central, rather than simply facilitative – as in CBT.

Evaluation of long-term therapies

Special problems arise in the accumulation of an evidence base concerning long-term therapies – some relating to study design, others to cost-effectiveness. Examples will be given of each.

Where design is concerned, it is a requirement of a randomised trial to have a comparison condition assessed at the same end-points on relevant outcome measures as the treated group (Jadad, 1998). The comparison condition typically involves either minimal or no treatment on the one hand or a treatment of known effectiveness on the other hand. Comparison of long-term psychodynamic psychotherapy with no treatment poses particular design problems if the psychodynamic psychotherapy is likely to be so long term that it is unrealistic (and unethical) to expect a no treatment control group to go without treatment for the entire period of the trial. Yet unless treated and untreated patients can be compared at equivalent end-points this contaminates the comparison between therapy and its absence.

This problem can sometimes be overcome by the use of a minimal treatment control condition which may or may not be given to both groups of patients (i.e., those who also receive the treatment being evaluated and those who do not). In this case the evaluation of the formal treatment takes the form of assessing its incremental benefits relative to the minimal treatment.

In areas where brief treatments may have only very limited effectiveness it may be argued that more efficacious longer-term treatment may also be more cost-effective. Where cost-effectiveness is concerned, however, Maynard (1997) has pointed out that factors affecting treatment choice within an evidence-based framework may be quite different when seen from the perspective of population health (e.g., by commissioners of services) than those which might be applied on an individual basis by a clinician considering the needs of his/her individual patient.

Take, for example, a conventional treatment costing £1,000 and extending survival time in a terminal disease by one year. A new treatment costing £4,000 might be found to increase life expectancy by two years. The clinician, adopting an evidence-based approach, will choose treatment B over treatment A since it offers the best prospect for the individual patient. Health economists, however, would recommend the use of treatment A because, for a given sum of money, a greater number of life years can be purchased for the population as a whole. In this case, for £8,000, eight life years can be purchased by the conventional treatment where only four life years can be purchased by the newer treatment. Thus, where healthcare resources will always be limited, economic considerations will always temper the extent to which longer-term therapies may be recommended – a consideration of potential importance to the psychodynamic therapies.

Concluding comments

There are few who would question the fundamental laudability of evidence-based practice as a guiding principle in medicine and as a healthy corrective to maverick individualism. At the same time, we have seen enough in the present chapter to appreciate that the adoption of an evidence-based approach in psychotherapy may generate significant problems of both conceptual and practical varieties. Conceptual problems include the facts that neither people nor treatments can be described simply. Practical ones include the dilemma that while the RCT may be the only convincing method currently available to investigate causality in the relation between treatment and outcome, nevertheless the recognition of this fact should not lead us to forget that it is also, in many ways, lamentably inadequate to the task.

In its selective overview, the present chapter has failed to address numerous aspects of outcome research methodology which may have significance for the evaluation of pychodynamic psychotherapy. These include problems associated with appropriate choice of outcome measures and, in particular, the use of dynamic criteria in assessing patient progress; the benefits and demerits of single case and other (e.g., qualitative) research methodologies in evaluating PDP; problems associated with standardisation, and in particular manualisation, of therapeutic methods; measurement reactivity problems which may arise when investigating therapy adherence and other approaches to assessing treatment integrity. And then, of course, we should not forget that, in psychoanalytic circles, there is a substantial body of opinion which would question the fundamental epistemology underlying modern empirical approaches to the evaluation of therapeutic activity (e.g., Perron, 1999).

There are indications, however, that psychodynamic psychotherapy researchers are rising at last to the challenges posed by formal outcome research. In a recent hotly contested initiative to promote psychoanalytic research, the International Psychoanalytical Association received more applications to fund outcome research than for any other category of investigation (Wallerstein and Fonagy, 1999). Moreover, a recently published open-door review of outcome studies in psychoanalysis and psychoanalytic psychotherapy testifies to the wealth of high-quality ongoing studies in this domain (Fonagy *et al.*, 1999). These should bear fruit in the coming decade. Better late than never!

References

APA Task Force (1995) *Template for Developing Guidelines: Interventions for Mental Disorders and Psychological Aspects of Physical Disorders.* Washington, DC: American Psychological Association.

Bellack, A.S., Hersen, M. and Himmelhoch, J.M. (1981) 'Social skills training compared with pharmacotherapy and psychotherapy for depression', *American Journal of Psychiatry* 138: 1562–1567.

Brewin, C.R. and Bradley, C. (1989) 'Patient preferences and randomised clinical trials', *British Medical Journal* 299: 313–315.

Chambless, D.L. and Hollon, S.D. (1998) 'Defining empirically supported therapies', *Journal of Consulting and Clinical Psychology* 66: 7–18.

Cochrane Collaboration (1999) The Cochrane Library. Oxford: Update Software [available via the Internet or on CD-ROM].

DeRubeis, R.J. and Crits-Cristoph, P. (1998) 'Empirically supported group and individual treatments for adult psychological disorders', *Journal of Consulting and Clinical Psychology* 66: 37–52.

Department of Health (1996a) *Promoting Clinical Effectiveness: A Framework for Action in and Through the NHS.* London: NHS Executive.

Department of Health (1996b) *Psychotherapy Services in England: Review of Strategic Policy.* London: NHS Executive.

Dobson, K.S. and Craig, K.D. (eds) (1998) *Empirically Supported Therapies: Best Practice in Professional Psychology.* Thousand Oaks, Calif.: Sage Publications.

Elliott, R. (1998) 'A guide to the empirically supported treatments controversy', *Psychotherapy Research* 8: 115–125.

Fonagy, P., Kaechele, H., Krause, R., Jones, E. and Perron, R. (1999) *An Open Door Review of Outcome Studies in Psychoanalysis.* London: UCL Psychoanalysis Unit (also available at http://www.ipa.org.uk/R-outcome. htm).

Garfield, S. (1990) 'Issues and methods in psychotherapy process research', *Journal of Consulting and Clinical Psychology* 58 (3): 273–280.

Garfield, S. (1998) 'Some comments on empirically supported treatments', *Journal of Consulting and Clinical Psychology* 66: 121–125.

Goldfried, M.R. and Wolfe, B.E. (1998) 'Towards a more clinically valid approach to therapy research', *Journal of Consulting and Clinical Psychology* 66: 143–150.

Jadad, A. (1998) *Randomised Controlled Trials*. London: BMJ Books.

Maynard, A. (1997) 'Evidence-based medicine: an incomplete method for informing treatment choices', *Lancet* 349 (9045): 126–128.

Miller, R.G., Efron, B. and Brown, B.W. *et al.* (1980) *BioStatistics Casebook*. New York: Wiley.

Nathan, P.E. and Gorman, J.M. (1998) *A Guide to Treatments that Work*. New York: Oxford University Press.

Parloff, M.B. (1986) 'Placebo controls in psychotherapy research: a sine qua non or a placebo for research problems?', *Journal of Consulting and Clinical Psychology* (Special Issue: Psychotherapy research) 54 (1): 79–87.

Perron, R. (1999) 'Reflections on psychoanalytic research problems – the French-speaking view', in Fonagy, P. *et al.*, *An Open Door Review of Outcome Studies in Psychoanalysis*. London: UCL Psychoanalysis Unit.

Pocock, S.J. (1984) *Clinical Trials: A Practical Approach*. Chichester: Wiley.

RCP (1994) *Clinical Practice Guidelines and their Development*. Council Report CR34. London: Royal College of Psychiatrists.

Roth, A. and Fonagy, P. (1996) *What Works for Whom? A Critical Review of Psychotherapy Research*. New York: Guilford.

Sackett, D.L. *et al.* (1996) 'Evidence-based medicine: what is it and what it isn't', *British Medical Journal* 312 (7023): 71–72.

Shadish, W.R., Matt, G.E., Navarro, A.M., Siegle, G. *et al.* (1997) 'Evidence that treatment works in clinically representative conditions', *Journal of Consulting and Clinical Psychology* 65 (3): 355–365.

Shapiro, D.A., Harper, H., Startup, M., Reynolds, S., Bird, D. and Suokas, A. (1994) 'The high water mark of the drug metaphor: a meta-analytic critique of process–outcome research', in Russell, R.L. (ed.) *Reassessing Psychotherapy Research*. New York: Guilford, pp. 1–35.

Shoham, V. and Rohrbaugh, M. (1995) 'Aptitude × treatment interaction (ATI) research', in Aveline, M. and Shapiro, D.A. *Research Foundations for Psychotherapy Practice*. Chichester: Wiley, pp. 73–96.

Sloan, R.B., Staples, F.R., Cristol, A.H., Yorkston, N.J. and Whipple, K. (1975) *Psychotherapy Versus Behaviour Therapy*. Cambridge, Mass.: Harvard University Press.

Stiles, W.B. and Shapiro, D.A. (1989) 'Abuse of the drug metaphor in psychotherapy process–outcome research', *Clinical Psychology Review* 9: 521–543.

Wallerstein, R. and Fonagy, P. (1999) 'Psychoanalytic research and the IPA: history, present status and future potential', *International Journal of Psychoanalysis* 80: 91–109.

Williams, A.C. de C., Nicholas, M.K., Richardson, P.H. *et al.* (1999). 'Generalizing from a controlled trial: the effects of patient preference versus randomization on the outcome of inpatient versus outpatient chronic pain management', *Pain* 83: 57–65.

Chapter 12

Practice-based evidence in psychotherapy

Frank Margison

Fundamental questions

An evidence-based approach to the practice of psychotherapy requires that some basic questions about the nature of therapy be addressed. Evidence-based practice can only be as good as the research on which decisions are to be made. The difficulty in providing an adequate evidence base for at least some of the modes of psychotherapy has been discussed extensively elsewhere (Roth and Fonagy, 1996; Aveline and Shapiro, 1995; Parry and Watts, 1996; Bergin and Garfield, 1994). Within this volume there are several commentaries about the nature of evidence itself (see Chapters 1 to 6).

For the purposes of this contribution the discussion is focused more narrowly on the need to use the best available evidence around which psychotherapy services can be designed (Parry and Richardson, 1996) and treatment delivered (Sackett *et al.*, 1996). The very definition of psychotherapy is highly problematic and the terms 'psychotherapy' and 'psychological treatment' will be used interchangeably.

The conventional term 'evidence-based practice' is increasingly complemented by the term 'practice-based evidence' (e.g., Barkham and Mellor-Clark, 2000; Margison *et al.*, 2000). Practice-based evidence is the natural companion of evidence-based practice, drawing particularly on evidence of effectiveness in naturalistic, unselected clinical samples from which to draw inferences. Practice-based evidence draws heavily on the use of practice-research networks (PRNs), which link empirical research with the development of evidence drawn from large, routine, clinical samples.

The limits of evidence-based practice

Evidence-based medicine is based on a moral claim, some would say an idealisation. The care of each patient should be based on 'conscientious, explicit, and judicious use of current best evidence' (Sackett *et al.*, 1996: 71–72). Even if the logistics of evidence gathering and appraisal allowed a review of this evidence to be used for every patient uniquely, there would still be competing views about what should be considered as 'best evidence'. The conventional hierarchy of evidence used in evidence-based medicine with RCTs as the 'gold standard' may have limitations (Margison and Shapiro, 1996), but a more serious problem arises when we do not know even in which domain of knowledge to search.

Take a clinical problem with a depressed young woman of 26 years with a baby of six months. She subjects herself to frequent self harm, overdoses, chaotic relationships, drug abuse, and alternate starving and vomiting, and has a chaotic/ambivalent relationship to her son. It is difficult to know what question we should pose. We could ask a well-formed question about the evidence of effective treatments for repeated self harm, depression or eating disorder and get useful views about treatments likely to be effective.

A good clinician, however, might use Occam's razor and avoid multiplying entities beyond necessity. This would lead to an alternative formulation of the case as one of borderline personality, leading to a quite *different* literature. Another clinician, taking note of the way she stormed out of the room and then begged for forgiveness might formulate a quite different question about interventions likely to maintain an optimal therapeutic alliance and search the literature on 'alliance ruptures' to therapeutic advantage.

A clinician taking a perspective wider than just the mother could ask about the evidence for and against removing her child because of the adverse consequences which might follow from the child remaining with this mother.

All of these can be viewed as legitimate and potentially useful approaches within the paradigm of evidence-based practice, even though there are, of course, limitations to the extent of the literature for each of these questions. As Kerridge and colleagues point out (Kerridge *et al.*, 1998: 1151), all such questions are based on 'consequentialism', where the worth of an action is based upon its consequences. But this approach is problematic when competing outcomes are being sought, some of which are very difficult to measure or define, and where it is unclear whose interests should be considered in deciding about outcomes.

In dealing with some of the fundamental problems of an evidence-based approach to psychotherapy, we should not neglect the ethical issues arising from the way evidence is gathered and appraised. Some of the ethical concerns are by no means unique to psychotherapy: the need for informed consent of participants, for example, is widely accepted as a prerequisite for any treatment research. Some issues are particularly salient to psychotherapy because of the nature of the treatment. The effects of observation on most clinical practice could be measured in principle, but it is widely assumed that any effects are likely to be small and in any case beneficial. In a drug study, simply adopting a research protocol may improve standards of care. Interesting evidence to support this view came from the 'NIMH Treatment of Depression Collaborative Research Program' (Elkin, 1994: 120–122) where the 'no active treatment' condition had surprisingly positive effects (although still less than all three active treatments). It is possible that the careful observation and standardisation of the 'treatment as usual' condition led to the sizeable 'placebo effects'.

In psychotherapy the effects of observation are much less understood. On the positive side there are suggestions that therapists are able to maintain a clinical focus in well-supervised therapies guided by a flexible manual. On the negative side, therapists in some modes of therapy comment that the presence of a tape-recorder, or even the idea of ratings being completed after the session, has subtle but important effects on the therapeutic relationship. Being a therapist in a treatment trial of psychotherapy can be an uncomfortable experience if the therapist is distracted by thoughts of the therapy being 'dissected' by a third party later. Insufficient work has been carried out on these observer effects on therapists to know what influences can be attributed to observation.

Outcomes which cannot be measured may have worth

Radical empiricists may argue that only that which can be measured is worthy of attention. As will be discussed later, there have been important developments in the measurement of change in psychotherapy. However, it is wrong to think that this issue can be reduced to the technical issues inherent in measurement of reliability and validity. There are important moral choices being made about the values underlying change.

Some outcomes may be valued by both therapist and patient but still be difficult to summarise in words, let alone measure accurately (Holmes and Lindley, 1991: 35). Cynics may argue that such effects must be of trivial importance if they cannot be subjected to accurate measurement. It would be wrong to assume, though, that these experiences are not open to empirical research methods. The methods are likely to be derived from a narrative or meaning framework or a method that gives salience to subjective experience. Such experiences can be incorporated into, say, a 'purpose of life' measure (Crumbaugh and Maholick, 1964, cited in Roberts, 1997: 264), but in so doing a particular world-view is being privileged over others: that the repeatable and measurable is of greater value than 'a poetics of experience' (Mair, 1989). Williams (1972) points out that

> [a]gain and again defenders of such values are faced with the dilemma of either refusing to quantify the value in question, in which case it disappears from the equation altogether, or else of trying to attach some quantity to it, in which case they misrepresent what they are about, and also usually lose the argument, since the quantified value is not enough to tip the scale.
>
> (Williams, 1972, cited in Kerridge *et al.*, 1998: 1152)

Deciding between competing claims

Kerridge and colleagues (1998) have also argued that evidence-based medicine may be unable to help in discriminating between competing claims of stakeholders.

> Evidence based medicine claims to reject the power of expert opinion but it is still mostly doctors who determine research objectives, who interpret research data, and who implement research findings. A number of commentators have called for greater involvement by consumer groups in setting research agendas, but how conflicts between the agendas of the different stakeholders are to be resolved remains unclear.
>
> (Kerridge *et al.*, 1998: 1152)

The ethics of the trials considered in systematic reviews

There are standards by which the technical efficiency of a systematic review may be judged (Dickersin *et al.*, 1994), but there may be difficulties in knowing how information from ethically unsound trials can be incorporated into the corpus of knowledge. The ethical dilemmas vary from the profoundly unethical, as in the case of captive subjects forced to endure experiments, through to trials where the procedures for informed consent were suspect.

The nature of evidence: RCTs

The merits and problems of RCTs have been extensively discussed, but from an ethical viewpoint the dilemma is to gain benefit for the public (the 'common good') by being able to reject worthless treatments with greater confidence, whilst trying to provide the best available care for each patient being entered into the trial. These conflicts would be irreconcilable were it not for the principle of 'equipoise'. This metaphor is derived from knowledge being 'balanced' in such a way that the clinician can genuinely say to the potential subject that it is not possible to know which of two treatments is more effective, or whether the treatment is more effective than placebo. When there is such real doubt the allocation of treatment to a patient by randomisation may be sound ethically. But, there are difficulties in knowing when trials should be terminated because the result is 'known', and 'equipoise' no longer holds. Commonly the clinicians conducting a trial may be inclined to feel that the results are clear before a sufficient degree of statistical power is reached.

Defining psychotherapy: a broad brush?

The term 'psychotherapy' is itself ambiguous and the next section considers whether psychotherapy refers to specialist models of practice or the application of psychological treatment principles across the field of mental health

The recent review of NHS Psychotherapy Services in England (Parry and Richardson, 1996) suggested that psychotherapy can be divided pragmatically into three types:

1　Type A refers to psychotherapy that is an integral part of a complex care plan involving several professionals, often incorporating non-psychological approaches such as medication.
2　Type B refers to a type of therapy undertaken by a single professional but drawing in a planned way on several underlying theoretical models.
3　Type C refers to a therapy again delivered by a single professional drawing on one specific model.

The nature of the evidence we have currently available mainly involves Type C therapies that have been subjected to formal evaluations of efficacy (Roth and Fonagy, 1996). To an increasing extent, the addition of a psychological treatment in the care of a patient with severe enduring mental illness has been shown to be effective (Type A) (for example, the cost reductions shown after adding a family management component in the treatent of patients with schizophrenia; see Gabbard *et al.*, 1997). By its nature Type B therapy has been evaluated in much less detail, because each therapy is designed for an individual drawing uniquely on the combination of approaches which is thought to be most beneficial for the particular range of problems faced by that individual.

It can be argued that consideration of a psychological approach should be part of the assessment for every patient or client being seen as part of specialist mental health service. Given the high prevalence and low detection rates of psychological disorder in primary care, a psychological treatment deserves at least consideration in every primary care consultation.

The context for this chapter is, therefore, the general applicability of psychotherapeutic methods across mental health and primary care services. It is known that services are not distributed according to need and that there are wide variations in the availability of psychotherapy and psychological treatments across the country (Parry and Richardson, 1996).

Are resources being used carefully?

For resources to be used most effectively detailed information from health economics would assist in improving practice. Knapp reviewed the evidence for health economic analysis of psychotherapy for the *Psychotherapy Review* cited above (Parry and Richardson, 1996). Unfortunately the number and quality of studies did not allow for any robust conclusions. However, some broad principles can be applied to the appraisal of evidence. First, a psychological intervention can have additional benefits beyond problem relief which can be 'offset' against the cost of treatment. These benefits are often in the form of reduced costs associated with alternative and expensive treatments such as admission (so called 'cost offset' effects). These supposed benefits have been reviewed by Gabbard *et al.* (1997) and are relevant to any appraisal of the evidence base for psychotherapeutic treatments.

How do we assure quality?

The quality of a service is usually considered to be a topic more closely linked to audit. Conventionally, audit deals with the details of inputs, activities and outputs, asking questions about the standards desired and the potential steps that might lead to change. The whole process forms an iterative loop, with the standards against which the service is to be assessed being themselves continually revised.

Questions about quality have dealt with:

- How comprehensive is a service intended to be?
- How relevant is the intervention?
- How acceptable is the intervention?
- How accessible and equitable is the service?
- How efficiently is the treatment delivered?

Audit and evaluation of quality have been viewed with suspicion by clinicians. They may have concerns about confidentiality, freedom of clinical choice, untoward effects of the audit on the therapist–patient relationship; an excessive concern with costs, medico-legal fears and a lack of trust in how the information might be used (Margison *et al.*, 1998: 79).

Is there a strategy for linking delivery of care with assessment of need?

Our limited ability to predict outcome at the point of assessment, except in the most general terms, surprises many clinicians who feel intuitively that they 'know' how a person will respond to therapy as a result of an often detailed assessment. After several decades of research, however, the only robust predictor of outcome is the therapeutic alliance early in the therapy. Even this conclusion needs to be treated with some caution, as it could be argued that the initial alliance is not independent of outcome but an early measure of joint progress towards common goals, and is hence a self-fulfilling prophecy.

It may be that the apparent difficulty in predicting outcome is an artefact of the homogeneous samples recruited to formal studies of efficacy. In clinical practice several audits have confirmed that a prior history of abuse is associated with worse outcomes or difficulty with engagement (Margison *et al.*, 1998: 84; Feldman and Pugh, 1998: 71). Also, the clinical relevance of the previous level of disturbance has been shown in work on risk assessment. It seems plausible that in psychotherapy, as in most areas of life, predictions of future behaviour based on past behaviour are better than random guesses.

We can argue that assessment of need at the level of the individual is paradoxical. Most psychotherapy research has been done on patients with less severe or episodic disorders (depression, anxiety, panic). It is now accepted that 'co-morbidity' with substance abuse or personality disorder attenuates the effectiveness of psychological treatments. However, the likelihood of the disorder being self-limiting is also linked to these same factors. So, we are left with the paradoxical result that there will be more change per session in those patients who arguably have least need for treatment to prevent chronicity, secondary handicap and other long-term deterioration. The patient who is selectively least likely to respond may be at a critical point where a small change (falling far short of 'cure') might lead to a disproportionate benefit because it has been possible to stabilise an otherwise chaotic situation (at work, or in childcare, for example). This concept of the 'critical benefit' is not easily amenable to our dominant research paradigm (the group design, randomised controlled trial).

What is the expert-model for psychotherapy?

Nosology, the science of diagnosis and classification of disease, is based on two complementary approaches: logical analysis and the ability to detect meaningful patterns. Traditionally, one of the main claims to expertise of the physician has been in distilling the many ways that a disease may present into certain 'essential forms' which were seen as diagnostic entities. Diseases came to be defined according to the extent that they followed particular regularities of symptomatic presentation, signs elicited on examination, and course. These defined the 'syndrome' level of diagnosis. If the syndrome could then be linked to an underlying cause, as represented by pathological changes, then a disease had been identified.

This classical model has been criticised for its poor applicability in many areas of practice; so much so in psychiatry that it was recommended that the syndrome level be retained until a much better understanding of aetiology was gained (APA, 1994).

The whole basis for assuming that there are underlying entities waiting to be discovered is itself highly problematical. With the growth of relativism it is much easier to assume that we describe patterns for a particular purpose; for example, to identify typical response to treatment, or to predict the course of an illness. However, this opened the gate to competing classifications based on different priorities. A classification based on the type of psychological defences used would be different to one based on genetic similarity, and different again from one based on response to different classes of medication.

In psychiatry, the criticisms of the use of diagnostic classification have focused on the lack of predictive power, the enormous overlap between syndromes, the tendency to use diagnoses as pejorative labels, and the spurious certainty conveyed by very tenuous labels (Kendell, 1983: 206).

In the last two decades, the *International Classification of Diseases* and the *Diagnostic and Statistical Manual* have passed through several revisions leading to a fair degree of consensus that multi-axial classifications should be used, and that it is preferable to make diagnoses based on observed behaviour rather than imputed causes. This has led to a common language, but, also, systems which are based on extensive compromise.

Among the weakest areas in the classifications are those most salient to the practice of psychotherapy. The classification of personality disorder has been heavily criticised for low reliability, multiple classification, and heterogeneous *types* of disorders being bundled together. Disorders of sexual function (for example, erectile dysfunction) have been mixed with labels referring to sexual preference (for example, fetishism), and to problems with identity (for example, transsexualism) (Margison, 1997). There have been several attempts to classify depression and anxiety according to models that have some predictive and explanatory power, but currently the diagnostic system is a mixed bag of aetiological concepts, treatment responses, and what were previously considered to be traits.

Pattern-matching?

The first approach to classification was the ability to detect regularities or patterns across many presentations. In psychotherapy, we frequently write as though this is the preferred mode of classification. For example, there are many recent papers based on the countertransference patterns recognised in the therapist. This is a potentially helpful approach from a clinical perspective, but it has little in common with the rest of medicine, where the ultimate goal is to produce a classification based on underlying cause or pathology.

Clinicians acting as supervisors use this recognition mode extensively, drawing on their own clinical experience to help the supervisee to see that their puzzling experience fits into a pattern, with at least some possibility of knowing how events will unfold. This clinical utility needs to be acknowledged, but recognition of similarities leads to a simple, and at times crude classification.

Probabilistic?

The pattern-recognition approach can be contrasted with the systematic use of probability theory. In designing classification systems, modern nosologists rely extensively on powerful statistical techniques (such as logistic regression and discriminant function analysis) to generate and validate diagnostic schemata.

The advantages of such techniques are that they can deal with large amounts of data in a systematic way, and detect regularities that could not be perceived unaided. In generating algorithms for the diagnosis of abdominal pain, they outperform all but the most experienced clinicians, and at the very least act as checks for the clinician so that less obvious possibilities are considered, and, hence, reduce unnecessary investigation.

Technique-oriented?

The classification system has been turned on its head in recent years as techniques or treatment-response have been used first to validate and then to extend the classification. For example, in psychiatry the concept of the 'Lithium-responsive psychosis' was used as shorthand for 'illnesses genetically and biochemically related to Bipolar Disorder'.

In psychotherapy, developing a diagnostic classification has not been the principal target for clinicians, but most of the research evidence on efficacy is based on groups of disorders (Roth and Fonagy, 1996). There has, however, been a recent tendency to group difficulties according to the preferred mode or length of therapy.

Oriented to meaning?

Finally, the approach that has been most valuable for psychotherapists has relied on the underlying meaning structures behind particular presentations. At a simple level this might be to cluster 'responses to loss' or 'responses to trauma' on the assumption that there is something in common, regardless of the symptomatic presentation. This approach has been integrated with other theoretical models to generate new clusters – for example, those generated from attachment theory (Mace and Margison, 1997).

It can be argued that these are just alternative theories around which a classificatory model is devised. Returning to the history of medicine, there is a deeper level to this search for meaning. Clustering the various features of diabetes mellitus or syphilis was an attempt to use the principle of

Occam's razor: not multiplying entities beyond necessity. A simplistic approach to diagnosis might suggest five or more diagnoses (eating disorder, depression, anxiety, alcohol addiction and orgasmic dysfunction, for example), when a clinician might see these all as manifestations of a single disorder of development. Calling this constellation Borderline Personality Disorder might lead to its own problems, but conceptually the clinician is attempting to synthesise various facets of one underlying difficulty which can then be considered aetiologically (for example, as different manifestations of particular reciprocal role procedures (Ryle, 1990: 97)).

Problem formulation vs diagnosis

These have often been seen as alternative approaches. Diagnosis can be seen as reducing phenomena to a core condition, whereas formulation is seen as based on narrative. However, the two approaches are fundamentally linked. A full formulation gathers evidence, crystallises the essential problem, then considers aetiological treatment and prognostic factors. Commonly, though, the essential problem is not a single entity but an underlying pattern that has manifestations in relationships to self and others.

Several research groups have tried to test the reliability of formulation methods. For example, Luborsky and colleagues (1990) have shown that the essential components of their style of formulation (the Core Conflictual Relationship Theme (CCRT)) can be measured reliably. Other elements of a formulation, such as attachment style or defence style, can also be measured reliably. However, the psychotherapy outcome research literature is very heavily reliant on diagnostic categories (Roth and Fonagy, 1996), which may be less reliable than standardised formulations. Roth and Fonagy argue that there is little alternative to using diagnostic categories to appraise evidence, given the way the literature is composed. However, they acknowledge that generalisability based simply on diagnostic category is poor.

First, there is considerable 'co-morbidity' and combined diagnoses do not interrelate predictably, although in general the effects of treatment interventions are attenuated by the presence of a co-morbid disorder.

Second, the criteria for diagnosis are not consistent across studies. Often a low diagnostic threshold (such as the criterion for major depressive disorder in DSM III) has been combined with an arbitrary level on a rating scale such as the Beck Depression Inventory to define the subjects to be included in a study, say, of the treatment of depression. Subsequently, when carrying out a critical review to compare rates of improvement, there are substantial differences in the populations considered to be 'depressed' because of variability in selection criteria.

Third, the main diagnostic systems pay inconsistent attention to *course* of illness. An attempt to rationalise this has been made in ICD 10 where dysthymia has replaced depressive personality to refer to one form of 'chronic' depression.

However other disorders such as avoidant personality, which are equally disabling and which may, similarly, be based on genetic pre-disposition, are considered to be problems of personality functioning and remain within Axis II.

How do we recognise a 'good' service?

Quality is defined in different ways according to the context. We do not use the same methods to evaluate the consistency of components like screws or bolts as we do the usefulness of such a component as part of a complex product like a car. The quality assurance underlying the manufacture is quite different from the sense in which we use the word 'quality' when we drive a car in comfort.

To deal with these different senses of the word 'quality' it is usual to distinguish several overlapping concepts:

- *Service evaluation* is a broad approach that uses concepts and methods from social science research to assess the conceptualisation and implementation of an intervention.
- *Operational research* aims to improve cost-effectiveness by mathematical and logical modelling of a service as a system.
- *Service audit* describes and measures service processes and outcomes.
- *Quality assurance* monitors processes by which care is delivered against predetermined standards.
- *Total quality management* is a management-led commitment to continuous improvement in quality by improvement in processes.
- *Medical audit* is the systematic, critical analysis of medical care, including procedures used for diagnosis and treatment, the use of resources and the resulting outcome and quality of life of the patient.
- *Clinical audit* resembles medical audit, but there is a commitment to a multidisciplinary approach and there is a recognisable cycle of analysing the current situation: setting standards, measuring against standards, reviewing processes in the light of findings, reviewing standards, etc.

Fonagy and Higgitt's (1989) influential paper on service quality suggests a number of questions that can be framed around clinical quality issues for a department. They suggest a range of measures from speed of response to ability to manage crises, with different methods of measurement suggested for each. This framework can be used as a quality assessment tool in its own right, or can be used as a checklist to ensure that audit systems are comprehensive (Margison *et al.*, 1998).

Consistent standard?

From a patient perspective it is important to know that the service that you might receive is based on consistently upheld expectations. Some of these expectations are relatively simple to measure and are concerned with the administration of care. For example, the length of time to wait between a referral being made and actually being seen can be specified, and it is simple to measure the percentage compliance with particular targets.

However, even in such a simple measurement of quality there can be ambiguities. Is the standard comparable between a department that offers therapy from the first appointment and one that offers an initial 'screening' meeting with a subsequent period on a waiting list before the actual treatment is offered?

Clinically, there are substantial problems in ensuring comparability as the 'benchmarks' are much less clearly specified. Some questions are still open to empirical scrutiny. The proportion of patients being accepted for therapy (and the types of therapy offered) can be compared across different ethnic groups to check whether unintended bias is affecting the consistency of the service offered (Margison *et al.*, 1998: 88). The content of assessment letters or reports can be specified and the extent to which clinicians are consistent in their approach can then be measured with reasonable accuracy.

However, neither of these approaches gets 'inside' the therapeutic process. One attempt to look at clinician decision-making used clinical vignettes and the respondents were asked to comment on how therapy might be allocated (Margison *et al.*, 1998: 82). This study showed that therapists were reasonably consistent in allocating types of therapy, but that there were still considerable biases in terms of the extent to which resource availability altered decisions, and in terms of the therapist's experience. One interesting finding from this preliminary study was that raters thought that the suitability of long-term individual psychoanalytic therapy was broadly comparable to that for brief dynamic therapy. This suggests that there was a strong tendency to measure the 'patient's' suitability against some ideal notion of psychological-mindedness that could be applied equally in long- and short-term work.

In the formulation of problems, there is another concept of consistency to be considered. As mentioned earlier, Luborsky and colleagues (1990) have shown that clinicians trained in a similar approach can produce broadly comparable case formulations. Hobson *et al.* (1998) have shown that clinicians are capable of discriminating between the personal attributes thought to belong to either the depressive or the paranoid-schizoid position.

A level of consistency which is even more difficult to conceptualise is the model of 'therapeutic competencies'. In the past, *competence* has been assumed to follow from exposure to a defined training programme. Even with the development of clearer educational objectives it has been difficult to measure consistent performance in ordinary clinical practice. There have been attempts to look at specific conditions to assess therapeutic competence; for example, the ability to work with and resolve 'alliance ruptures' (Bennett and Parry, 1998). However, this has not dealt with the fundamental problem that our clinical practice is not necessarily built on consistent 'models of task performance'.

Flexibility of response in clinicians is valued, but this makes it difficult to set minimum standards of clinical performance. The research approach to this dilemma has been to specify the operational aspects of a clinical model, typically by developing a 'manual', and to elide the two concepts of 'adherence' and 'competence'. For some elements of practice this is reasonable. Adhering to observable standards of responsiveness to defined cues and picking up suggestions of suicidal risk are examples of areas where adherence is synonymous with competence. There are other areas where the level of intensity of a particular therapeutic manoeuvre is demonstrably not a measure of competence. Paradoxically, high levels of 'interpretation' are associated with poorer outcomes (Piper *et al.*, 1991).

There are plausible explanations to account for this counter-intuitive finding, reviewed by the same research group in subsequent research (Joyce and Piper, 1993). For example, it has been argued that therapists may increase their interpretations in an attempt to 'hold' patients in therapy when the alliance is already failing. Whether or not this is an appropriate response (and there are suggestions that it may not be a good response) the competence of the therapist cannot be measured at the simplistic level of adhering to a specified level of 'competently delivered' interventions. In their later analyses, Joyce and Piper (1993: 508) concluded that transference interpretations 'can have a potent impact on the short term therapy process if employed judiciously and based on a careful formulation of the psychodynamics of the patient's presenting complaint'.

Clearly, consistency is important to those who use psychotherapy services, but the level at which such consistency is conceptualised will vary from administrative predictability against defined standards through to consistency of case formulation, and subsequent allocation to treatment.

Expert resource for previous non-responders?

A quite different model for a quality service may be the extent to which the service is used as an expert resource by other clinicians who are struggling with a difficult clinical problem. This is not, of course, confined to psychotherapy. In clinical services for cancer, for example, it is recognised that crude mortality rates would not be a good measure of clinical quality and the stage of the illness and other complicating and co-morbid factors (age, chest complications, etc.) have to be weighed in the balance.

If a local service is set up with good referral guidelines it is reasonable for patients with uncomplicated anxiety and depression, or adjustment problems, to be treated in primary care, perhaps with some input on site from secondary care providers to supervise treatments. Even highly effective treatments such as antidepressants for depression and exposure treatment for simple phobias have a failure rate, and such cases are often referred through several 'pathways' before seeing a specialist psychotherapist. Other patients may be recognised as having some of the features that will make treatment more difficult or attenuate treatment effects. Examples include co-morbid personality disorder and early sexual abuse.

There is a sustainable argument that specialist services should be dealing with the high-risk cases and those who have not responded to earlier treatment, but this has implications for the measurement of quality. It would not be reasonable to expect success rates equivalent to those in primary care if the very index of 'quality' is that a service is recognised as having sufficient expertise to warrant referral of 'difficult cases'.

Self-reflexive practice?

A quite different concept of quality for a service is that it can demonstrate that the whole service and the individual members of the team have a capacity to reflect critically on their own practice. The ability to reflect on one's own contribution, particularly where treatments are failing, is one of the hallmarks of skilful practice. In psychodynamic models this may be understood within the frameworks of countertransference and projective identification. In cognitive-behavioural and cognitive-analytic models similar issues may be understood within a framework of re-enactment, and perpetuation of dysfunctional belief systems. In systemic therapy, self-reflexive practice includes the idea that the therapists themselves are part of the broader system, and models of concurrent ('live') supervision are practical manifestations of the commitment to self-reflexive practice.

Psychotherapy is vulnerable to crass interpretation of complex data

Following from the discussion about the complexity of case formulation and the difficulty of defining cost-effectiveness in a life-long disorder, it is worth reviewing briefly some of the ways in which clinicians feel attacked by simplistic interpretation of complex data.

Bias in assessing 'outputs' in terms of what is easily measured

There have been many attempts to develop measures that are not restricted just to symptoms, but the technical issues of measurement methodology have tended to focus discussion of outcome onto symptom-oriented measures. It could be argued that the conceptualisation of 'illness' has been closely allied to the development of measures. The concept of depression, for example, is very strongly linked to measurable symptom clusters, and clusters of symptoms that can be reliably measured have replaced older concepts such as 'accidie'.

This has helped clinicians to produce well-focused treatment approaches (for example, in cognitive therapy for depression), but there are difficulties in applying this approach to less well-defined conditions, particularly where the problem is at the unassimilated end of the Assimilation spectrum (Stiles et al., 1990).

Dose-response models

Howard and colleagues (1995: 11) have developed a model of change in psychotherapy which distinguishes well-being ('remoralisation') from symptom-relief ('remediation') from long-term improvements in inter-personal adjustment ('rehabilitation'). These three domains tend to change at markedly different rates. Improved morale tends to change relatively quickly whereas symptom-relief tends to occur on a slower scale and rehabilitation on a yet-slower scale. Each of the domains, however, shows a similar relationship between number of sessions and the rate of improvement. All show a negatively accelerated curve (in lay language a 'law of diminishing returns'). The gradient of such a curve varies with the type of problem considered. Hence, remoralisation tends to show a quicker response with symptoms changing more slowly and interpersonal functioning changing slower still. In the latter group, the domains can be further subdivided into issues related to 'control', being 'detached' and being 'self-effacing'. The gradients of change for each of these varying in order with the first being most responsive to change (Howard *et al.*, 1995: 28).

The model of a dose-response curve is very helpful in clinical practice. First, it can help to plan the approximate level of resources needed for different types of problem. Second, plotting a curve for individuals can help to identify cases that need more detailed scrutiny. The so-called 'report card method, which has now been developed in North Western University (Howard *et al.*, 1995: 30–32) and Stuttgart (Kordy, 1997), uses case tracking methods to identify where the intrinsic variability of cases has been exceeded and when a case should be identified as 'in trouble' and hence requiring further analysis in clinical supervision.

These advantages need to be weighed against unsophisticated data interpretation leading to incorrect conclusions. The first error is that those responsible for commissioning services extrapolate the results from many cases to the level of the individual. The aggregated data might suggest, for example, that more than 50 per cent of cases show a clinically reliable and significant improvement (Evans *et al.*, 1998) after, say, ten sessions. It would not follow from this that cases all improve within this timescale, and it cannot be concluded that case duration can be *limited* to ten sessions in all cases. Unfortunately, some commissioners have used the data inappropriately to limit case duration on quite spurious grounds. Maximum cost-effectiveness should not be misinterpreted as meaning a short duration for all patients, as the benefits of therapy accrue at different rates for different domains of difficulty, and across individual subjects.

The main benefits of 'case tracking' are in having a general framework within which individual patient progress can be monitored and atypical trajectories recognised. The application of the model to individual patients needs more careful analysis.

Misunderstanding the nature of the 'inputs'

Part of the difficulties experienced by commissioners of psychotherapy services is that they oversimplify the nature of the 'inputs'. It is unwise to aggregate outcomes in terms of simple variables such as time expended. Two more sophisticated models draw on a 'four-factor' approach and a conceptualisation of 'therapeutic effort' (Newman and Howard, 1986).

The four-factor model

The four-factor model suggests that analysis of change should take into account at least four different variables: clinical condition, goals, resources and availability.

CLINICAL CONDITION

In general, this overlaps with diagnosis, range of symptoms and problems, and disruption to life function. Whilst each of these can be measured independently, it makes little sense to see any of these domains in isolation. Ideally there would be a single measure combining information on all of the domains. Recent developments in national audit and benchmarking have produced systems that can provide a comprehensive view of the patient. For example, the CORE system has been developed to provide comprehensive benchmarking and service comparisons, as well as clinically useful information at the level of the individual patient (CORE System Group, 1998).

GOALS

As well as describing the clinical problem it is necessary to specify the goals of treatment. This brings in ethical dilemmas. For example, if a service commissioner is only concerned with a limited range of outcomes (for example re-offending rates or ability to work in paid employment) there may be a lack of congruence with the goals expressed by the patient. Similarly, advocates of particular therapeutic models may be drawn to seeing outcomes preferentially in terms of the model rather than the goals specified by the patient. For example, a cognitive therapist may focus on the change of negative self-attributions whereas a psychodynamically oriented therapist may focus on personal insight or pattern of relationships. Ideally, there would be congruence across therapeutic modalities about what was important to change. This seems unlikely because different models of therapy come from different values systems and inevitably pay greatest attention to change reflecting the core values of that particular model.

RESOURCES

It is relatively straightforward to measure resources in purely cost terms (although even then the assumptions about costing need to be explicit). However, resources need to be thought of in a broader framework of availability of premises, the personal resources of the therapist (in order to avoid 'burn out') and resources that are difficult to measure accurately (such as the opportunity cost of applying therapeutic effort here as opposed to elsewhere).

AVAILABILITY

One component of the cost is not the literal cost but the value enhancement through the resource being scarce. This economic model is not used in the health service because treatment is free at the point of need, although relative costs of different professionals might be taken into account in health economic studies. In less constrained conditions market forces would increase the price of desirable models of therapy at the expense of those that are less desirable. Availability will vary from area to area, with, for example, psychoanalytic therapy or cognitive therapy being more or less available in different geographical areas for historical and geographical reasons. In modelling psychotherapy, little attention has been paid to scarcity of resources and the popularity of different approaches with users of services.

The concept of 'therapeutic effort'

Newman and Howard (1986) developed these ideas by introducing the concept of 'therapeutic effort' expended on a particular problem. The 'effort' was seen as comprising three distinct components: 'dosage', restrictiveness and cost of resources.

'DOSAGE' IN SESSIONS/WEEK

The concept of 'dose' is taken directly from the parallel of medication: therapy frequency in sessions per week is equated crudely with the dose regime of medication.

RESTRICTIVENESS (HOSPITAL ETC.)

As well as hospital treatment being expensive, Newman suggests that the effort is also pulling the patient in a negative direction by imposing restrictions and hence opposing the goal of autonomy. Therefore, less restrictive alternatives are not only literally less expensive, they also should have a score according to the level of restrictiveness.

COST OF RESOURCES (TIME, SUPERVISION, MATERIAL RESOURCES)

Newman also suggests that the full cost of psychological treatment is often not taken into account, and he suggests that time in total needs to allow for supervision, thinking, note-taking and listening to audio-recordings, all of which are crucial aspects of quality services. There are also material costs to be considered in terms of the cost of heating, lighting and security that in the past were not properly considered. It may be that these factors are now built into the cost equation in the United Kingdom after the resource management initiative, but the wide variations in cost assumptions suggest that this is being done in an idiosyncratic way.

Problems in translating research into everyday practice

Ideally, the clinical research carried out under the heading of 'efficacy research' would translate seamlessly into the domain of routine clinical practice ('clinical effectiveness'). In practice, this has not been the case and there has been notable difficulty in affecting clinical practice through the dissemination of research findings. There are some legitimate reasons for this. For example, the cases studied in many formal trials are based on artificially restricted samples that represent a 'purity' of problem with correspondingly less variation between subjects. The difficulty then is that clinicians do not 'recognise' the patients in the clinical trials as being at all similar to the patients in their own practice.

Models do not fit practice

The two ways in which models tend not to fit day-to-day practice are:

1   Co-morbidity. Patients excluded from formal trials because of the unpredictability from co-morbid conditions are actually very typical

of routine practice. In secondary care, for example, it is relatively unusual to see cases of simple phobias or uncomplicated episodes of depression because these have been treated in the primary care setting before referral on to the more specialised services. Where co-morbidity has been taken into account there have been very definite reductions in the relative effectiveness of standard interventions.

2   *Case complexity.* A related concept is that of case complexity. This is akin to the notion of 'case-mix' in other medical specialities. It might sometimes include co-morbid conditions such as alcohol addiction or personality disorder, but also includes other more subtle reasons why outcomes may be less good, such as previous treatment failure or difficulty in engaging.

Problems in translating practice questions into research

A more general problem in the gap preventing research influencing practice concerns the abstractness of the questions asked in formal research. It is difficult to ask standard evidence-based questions in psychotherapy because often the research data is simply not available. For example, it might be reasonable to know what additional difficulties might ensue from a patient with depression also having been sexually abused and failing to engage with cognitive therapy previously. It would be extremely helpful to a clinician to have answers to questions such as the typical extra demand for sessions to reach a criterion improvement when these co-morbid factors are present.

Bridging the gap

Salkovskis (1995) has suggested the model of an 'hourglass':

*   initial hunches from clinical practice are refined through simple research methods like single case studies,
*   followed by a narrow neck of the process (using mainly randomised controlled designs as the only way to randomly distribute potentially confounding variables),
*   and, finally, the wide lower part of the hourglass allows modifications in suitability criteria to allow broader applicability in clinical settings.

This model is helpful in suggesting that different research strategies are applicable at different points and that a complementary approach is needed. However, the 'hourglass' is unlikely on its own to bridge the current profound gap between clinicians and researchers.

One way of bridging the gap between practitioner and researcher has been advocated by Parry (1996: 443). She suggests that clinicians should be seen as at least stakeholders in research effort, and preferably should be directly involved. More recently this concept has been developed into the idea of practice-research networks (PRNs) to harness the clinical knowledge of practitioners with the methodological expertise of researchers to formulate researchable and clinically relevant questions. As mentioned above, the CORE System Group (1998) has drawn on the expertise of a PRN in the North of England (a branch of the Society for Psychotherapy Research UK) to refine the assessment tool (CORE-A), whilst using many stakeholders to refine the items in the CORE outcome measure, and a wide range of clinical sites to calibrate the measure.

The involvement of clinicians has allowed a clearer formulation of standardised measures which might ultimately be used nationally to aid comparability. The assessment tools have benefited at the same time from the input of expert researchers who can identify pitfalls that might otherwise make the measurements invalid, or at least cumbersome to collate.

Conclusions

Requirements for evidence-based practice and practice-based evidence

A system to support both of these complementary approaches depends on three interlinked requirements:

1 The first requirement is for the *critical questions* posed to be clinically and methodologically meaningful (Sackett *et al.*, 1996). These questions traditionally have been at the level of the individual case, but it is useful to pose similar questions about the organisation of care.

2 The second requirement is to have a *system to measure change* during and following therapy that is clinically appropriate and also fulfils fundamental criteria for replicability, validity, reliability and fidelity (Barkham *et al.*, 1998; CORE System Group, 1998).

3 Finally, psychotherapy needs a good *infrastructure* (Sperry *et al.*, 1996; CORE System Group, 1998). This includes facilities and support to carry out focused literature reviews and critical appraisal. Also, clinicians need an infrastructure for collating and analysing outcome reports in a systematic way.

References

American Psychiatric Association (1994) *Diagnostic and Statistical Manual of Mental Disorders* (4th edn) (DSM-IV). Washington, DC: APA.

Aveline, M. and Shapiro, D.A. (eds) (1995) *Research Foundations for Psychotherapy Practice*. Chichester: John Wiley.

Barkham, M. and Mellor-Clark, J. (2000) 'Rigour and relevance: the role of practice-based evidence in the psychological therapies', in N. Rowland and S. Gross (eds) *Evidence-based Healthcare in Psychological Therapies*. London: Routledge.

Barkham, M., Evans, C., Margison, F. *et al.* (1998) 'The rationale for developing and implementing core outcome batteries for routine use in service settings and psychotherapy outcome research', *Journal of Mental Health* 7: 35–47.

Bennett, D. and Parry, G. (1998) 'The accuracy of reformulation in Cognitive Analytic Therapy', *Psychotherapy Research* 8 (1): 84–103.

Bergin, A.E. and Garfield, S. (1994) *Handbook of Psychotherapy and Behavior Change* (4th edn). New York: John Wiley.

CORE System Group (1998) *CORE System (Information Management) Handbook*. Leeds: Core System Group.

Crumbaugh, J.C. and Maholick, L.T. (1964) 'An experimental study in existentialism: the psychometric approach to Frankl's concept of noogenic neurosis', *Journal of Clinical Psychology* 20: 200–207.

Dickersin, K., Sherer, R. and Lefebvre, C. (1994) 'Identifying relevant studies for systematic reviews', *British Medical Journal* 309: 1286–1291.

Elkin, I. (1994) 'The NIMH Treatment of Depression Collaborative Research Program: where we began and where we are', in Bergin, A.E. and Garfield, S. *Handbook of Psychotherapy and Behavior Change* (4th edn). New York: John Wiley.

Evans, C., Margison, F. and Barkham, M. (1998) 'The contribution of reliable and clinically significant change methods to evidence-based mental health', *Evidence Based Mental Health* 1 (3): 2–5.

Feldman, M. and Pugh, K. (1998) 'Kaizen and the process of audit within an NHS psychotherapy unit', in Davenhill, R. and Patrick, M. (eds) *Rethinking Clinical Audit: The Case of Psychotherapy Services in the NHS*. London: Routledge.

Fonagy, P. and Higgitt, A. (1989) 'Evaluating the performance of departments of psychotherapy', *Psychoanalytic Psychotherapy* 4: 121–153.

Gabbard, G.O., Lazar, S.G., Hornberger, J. *et al.* (1997) 'The economic impact of psychotherapy: a review', *American Journal of Psychiatry* 154: 147–155.

Hobson, R.P., Patrick, M.P.H. and Valentine, J.D. (1998) 'Objectivity on psychoanalytic judgement', *British Journal of Psychiatry* 173: 172–177.

Holmes, J. and Lindley, R.L. (1991) *The Values of Psychotherapy*. Oxford: Oxford University Press.

Howard, K.I., Orlinsky, D.E. and Lueger, R.J. (1995) 'The design of clinically relevant outcome research: some considerations and an example', in

Aveline, M. and Shapiro, D.A. (eds) *Research Foundations for Psychotherapy Practice*. Chichester: Wiley.

Joyce, A.S. and Piper, W.E. (1993) 'The immediate impact of transference interpretation in short-term individual psychotherapy', *American Journal of Psychotherapy* 47: 508–526.

Kendell, R.E. (1983) 'Diagnosis and classification', in Kendell, R.E. and Zeally, A.K. (eds) *Companion to Psychiatric Studies*. London: Churchill Livingstone.

Kerridge, I., Lowe, M. and Henry, D. (1998) 'Ethics and evidence based medicine', *British Medical Journal* 316: 1151–1153.

Kordy, H. (1997) 'Patterns of change: systematic treatment planning in real world complexity'. Presentation at Society for Psychotherapy Research, Geilo, Norway, 27 June 1997.

Luborsky, L. and Crits-Cristoph, P. (eds) (1990) *Understanding Transference: The CCRT Method*. New York: Basic Books.

Mace, C. and Margison, F. (1997) 'Attachment and psychotherapy: an overview', *British Journal of Medical Psychology* 70: 209–215.

Mair, M. (1989) *Between Psychology and Psychotherapy: A Poetics of Experience*. London: Routledge.

Margison, F. (1997) 'Abnormalities of sexual function and interest: origins and interventions', *Current Opinions in Psychiatry* 10: 121–131.

Margison, F. and Shapiro, D.A. (1996) 'Psychological treatments for depression' [letter], *British Journal of Psychiatry* 168 (1): 127.

Margison F.R., Loebl, R. and McGrath, G. (1998) 'The Manchester experience: audit and psychotherapy services in north-west England', in Davenhill, R. and Patrick, M. (eds) *Rethinking Clinical Audit: The Case of Psychotherapy Services in the NHS*. London: Routledge.

Margison, F.R., Barkham, M., Evans, C. *et al.* (2000) 'Measurement and Psychotherapy. Evidence-based practice and practice-based evidence', *British Journal of Psychiatry* 177: 123–130.

Newman, F.L. and Howard, K.I. (1986) 'Therapeutic effort, treatment outcome, and national health policy', *American Psychologist* 41: 181–187.

Parry, G. (1996) 'Service evaluation and audit methods', in Parry, G. and Watts, F.N. (eds) *Behavioural and Mental Health Research: A Handbook of Skills and Methods* (2nd edn). Hove, UK: Psychology Press.

Parry, G. and Richardson, A. (1996) *NHS Psychotherapy Services in England: Review of Strategic Policy*. London: HMSO.

Parry, G. and Watts, F. (1996) *Behavioural and Mental Health Research: A Handbook of Skills And Methods* (2nd edn). Hove, UK: Psychology Press.

Piper, W.E., Azim, H.F.A., Joyce, A.S. and McCallum, M. (1991) 'Transference interpretation, therapeutic alliance and outcome in short-term individual psychotherapy', *Archives of General Psychiatry* 48: 946–953.

Roberts, G. (1997) 'Meaning and madness', in Mace, C. and Margison, F. (eds) *Psychotherapy of Psychosis*. London: Gaskell.

Roth, A. and Fonagy, P. (1996) *What Works for Whom? A Critical Review of Psychotherapy Research*. New York: Guilford.

Ryle, A. (1990) *Cognitive-analytic Therapy: Active Participation in Change. A New Integration in Psychotherapy*. Chichester: Wiley.

Sackett, D.L., Rosenberg, W.M.C., Gray, J.A.M., Harnes, R.B. and Richardson, W.S. (1996) 'Evidence based medicine: what it is and what it isn't', *British Medical Journal* 312: 71–72.

Salkovskis, P. (1995) 'Demonstrating specific effects in cognitive and behavioural therapy', in Aveline, M. and Shapiro, D.A. (eds) *Research Foundations for Psychotherapy Practice*. Chichester: John Wiley.

Sperry, L., Brill, P.L., Howard, K.I. and Grissom, G.R. (1996) 'From clinical trials outcomes research to clinically relevant research on patient progress', in Sperry, L. *et al.*, *Treatment Outcomes in Psychotherapy and Psychiatric Interventions*. New York: Brunner Mazell.

Stiles, W., Elliott, R., Llewelyn, S., Firth-Cozens, J., Margison, F.R., Shapiro, D.A. and Hardy, G. (1990) 'Assimilation of problematic experiences by clients in psychotherapy', *Psychotherapy* 27 (3): 411–420.

Williams, B. (1972) *Morality*. Cambridge: Cambridge University Press.

Chapter 13

Making a success of your psychotherapy service

The contribution of clinical audit

Mark Aveline and James Watson

Introduction

In clinical audit, it is all too easy to confuse activity with progress. Too many audits are decided upon because they are easy to do; they risk being at best worthy and, at worst, dull confirmations of what is already known. Audits can be exciting and challenging. They can identify and review deficiencies in healthcare so that these may be remedied. They can push forward standards of good practice in which we can take pride.

This chapter is based on two workshops led by us during the conference from which the rest of this book was drawn. The purpose of the workshops was to focus on aspects of psychotherapy service that are critical to its success. We report on them directly, as the issues raised in their discussions occur frequently in other settings.

Format

Each workshop was attended by between 20 and 30 participants. In the first half of the workshop, theory and audit practice issues were presented and discussed. We drew heavily upon Crombie *et al.*'s excellent text *The Audit Handbook* (1993). First, we considered:

- key concepts;
- the setting of quality standards;
- how to identify a worthwhile audit project.

Then the workshop divided into four or five small groups and brainstormed performance factors that are not merely interesting but judged to be crucial to the success of the psychotherapy service. Factors were subsequently refined into audit topics. The results were presented to the total group and are now presented to the reader as a source of ideas.

Key concepts

Audit

'Audit is the process of reviewing the delivery of healthcare to identify deficiencies so that they may be remedied' (Crombie *et al.*, 1993). This definition emphasises two important aspects of audit: review and remedy. The one looks back at what has been done and the other forward to an improved future.

Research

Sometimes audit is confused with research. There is clearly a close relationship between the two but 'research is concerned with discovering the right thing to do; audit with ensuring that it is done right' (Smith, 1992).

Quality standards

What gives edge to audit is measuring performance against standards. Setting *quality standards* is an essential part of defining the clinical ambitions of the service. They make explicit the professionally set standards that are responsible and reasonably achievable; both adjectives are important qualifiers. A quality standard has three elements: criterion, target and allowable exceptions. The *criterion* identifies the clinical measure or observation on which quality of care will be assessed; it should be clinically relevant, clearly defined and easily measured. It is important to bear in mind that what makes a good service may be very different for clinicians, managers and service users. Outcomes may be clinical, social, administrative or user-oriented in type. Since correlation between outcome types is often low, multiple criteria are frequently required. The *target* is the expected proportion to meet the criterion (e.g., 95 per cent of referrals being responded to within two weeks of receipt). *Allowable exceptions* are get-outs, allowing some cases to be excluded for special reasons such as inapplicability. For example, in examining the response time from referral to entry into therapy, only the time to first offer of therapy might be considered, thereby excluding those patients who have had two or more offers and still not entered therapy.

Audit cycle

The audit cycle sets out the familiar sequence of observation, standard setting, audit and change implementation. One audit leads into the next

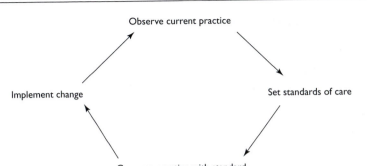

Figure 13.1 The audit cycle.

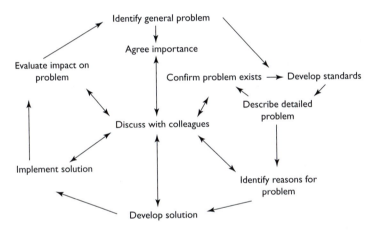

Figure 13.2 The full audit cycle.

(see Figure 13.1). The full audit cycle fleshes out the detail (see Figure 13.2). It emphasises the incessant importance of discussion among involved colleagues and adds an inner circle of confirming that the problem exists, developing standards, quantifying the problem and, crucially, identifying the reasons for it.

Criteria for choosing an audit topic

Life is short. Wasting time with an insignificant audit is a waste of everyone's time. In choosing a project, clinical concern, financial importance, and, we would suggest, political importance are all factors to consider.

Additionally, practical considerations and the degree of individual and group support for the project have to be taken into account.

Is there known to be wide variation in clinical practice? Have major changes in practice been made recently? Are the practices high in risk and, thus, life-conserving if they can be got right? Similarly, conditions requiring rapid diagnosis or treatment would be prime targets for audit. Some conditions may have priority for audit, as they are financially important, either because of their high volume or high cost. Previous audit or literature searches may have indicated levels of achievable benefits, which are not being fulfilled. Finally, the management of complex or difficult conditions is correspondingly difficult to maintain at a good level. Audit may lead to efficiencies in service delivery by, first, identifying problems in co-ordination or sequence and, second, prompting clinicians to devise and implement solutions.

The evaluation of any treatment requires understanding of the social, political and institutional context in which it takes place; this is often forgotton. For instance, what can be properly done with patients with borderline personality differs markedly in private practice, secure forensic units, and out-patient clinics with and without access to acute in-patient beds. Noting only therapist and patient variables can be seriously misleading.

In addition to the scientific and economic criteria detailed above, political importance can be an equally compelling factor in the focus of audit effort. An obvious example is the government imperative on maximum waiting times for hospital assessment and treatment. As the first author recently found in Nottingham, our out-patient response times have been the focus of close scrutiny by the Trust and, behind them, the Health Authority as purchasers. Colleagues in other collaborating mental health services often need information on referral patterns, response times and outcomes in order to manage their service or be informed about the progress of service agreements. Their priority may become the priority of the Psychotherapy Service.

Is the proposed audit achievable? Practical considerations loom large at this stage. Is the identified problem a real problem; does the problem occur sufficiently frequently and is it important? Can the activity be measured? In this instance, can standards be set? Is an adequate sample available? If deficiencies in service are identified through the audit, can change can be effected or is the situation immutable? These questions all point to the superordinate question: will the work be worth the effort?

Discussing the proposed audit in the clinical team will elicit the degree of individual and group support for the project. Ideally, all should be enthusiastic about it – not seeing the project as potentially disruptive or persecuting, or threatening unwarranted managerial (or academic!) interference. Furthermore, in this ideal state the project will be underpinned by the necessary expertise, and the effort required would be acceptable to all those involved in doing the audit.

Refining an audit topic

Once a topic has been chosen, further refinement of the patient group may be necessary. Do subjects need to be selected by age, sex, diagnosis, duration and/or severity of disorder and referral source, or any combination of these defining elements?

Is the location of care or type of psychotherapy important? Are such factors as duration of therapy or therapist characteristics of consequence in the standards being audited? What is being aimed for in terms of outcome – symptom relief, improved self-esteem, conflict resolution, personal maturation, increased mastery and effectiveness or support of best function – over what time period?

Other features of good audit

The primary aim of clinical audit is to improve healthcare. To achieve this, the detailed findings need to be confidential. The audit should be conducted in the spirit of education, not judgement. In scope, it should be parsimonious, focused on significant topics and seeking underlying causes of divergence from agreed or anticipated standards of performance. It almost certainly requires collaboration and, frequently, resource. The standards to be audited need to be attainable and explicit. Any consequent change has to be handled tactfully. There will be knock-on effects and, maybe, a need for more resource. In a good world, audit results may be the lever that delivers better resource. Finally, audits should be repeated to see if the desired effects have been achieved or maintained.

Results from the workshops

Performance factors crucial to the success of the psychotherapy service

We asked the small groups to identify performance factors that are not merely interesting but judged to be crucial to the success of the psychotherapy service. As most of the participants worked in or had close links with specialist NHS psychotherapy services, the identified topics reflected that context. They are, also, reflecting the anxieties of services that often felt criticised and under threat of closure or reform. Generating ideas forced participants to begin to be explicit about the assumptions that underpin the shape of their service and question their validity. This section of the workshop is reported predominantly in the form of questions as there are few categorically correct answers in psychotherapy. Points enclosed in [ ] brackets are post-workshop additions by us. Questions would need to be refined into standards, backed wherever possible by evidence, before they could be audited.

Workshop 1

1   Information to GP/referrer in order to help clinical management
Different standards might apply for different forms of treatment: short- and long-term individual therapy, CBT and psychodynamic, the complexity of the case and the need for co-management with services external to the psychotherapy service. What is the optimum frequency of written communications?; is it the same for short- and long-term therapy?; would the patient see the letter? How useful is the information?; should it serve an educational purpose? How is confidentiality to be managed?; does what is written depend on the nature of the patient's problems, the complexity and/or the required degree of co-management? What does the GP want?; would the GP want something different if the practitioner was aware of different models of communication? [Audit cannot guide whether or not a particular mode of therapy should be offered in a service. Clinical judgement, guided by empirical evidence, should guide decisions of that sort.]

2   Evaluation of population need, demand and adequacy of resource
It is not easy to define services and populations. It was recognised that there is an increasing focus on primary healthcare. Demand and need are not synonymous. Demand is likely to be greater than need. In this age, is 'demand management' the name of the game? Is there under-consideration of psychological therapy in psychiatric practice? Audit to see if psychological therapy is considered at each CPA review in community mental health teams. [With the growth of conversation-based psychological interventions in primary healthcare, much more research is needed, going beyond the currently fashionable evaluation of 'specific interventions' for 'specific disorders'. We favour examination of the importance of non-specific factors and the solving of urgent problems by help-seekers.]

3   How well are therapists matched to patients at assessment/therapy? Does this happen at all? What amount of resource is needed to make this feasible and valid? All the services of the participants routinely give information at assessment on the availability of types of service. Do clinicians routinely ask at assessment for patient preference, is the answer recorded, is it acted upon, how do you decide that the preference is appropriate and/or compelling? To what degree do patients have a right to have particular therapies? [Should services record the offered therapy and the optimum therapy that would be provided in an ideal service with a view to arguing for more resources?] [What patients get out of and/or want from therapy varies over time and phase of treatment (e.g., symptom relief, self-reflection, interpersonal change, life purpose and meaning). Not everyone wants all these elements but matching should take account of changing preference and the potential effect of different therapies.] [Research offers little guidance on the circumstances in which patients would be better treated as couples or families – or in groups. The emphasis on individuals in health service administration makes it easy to forget that we are social beings, belonging to groups, being defined by them and experiencing problems in living in them.]

4   Are therapists getting the right clinical supervision? Quantity and focus, individual and/or group supervision are among the parameters in this area. The supervision of trainees is for the most part well-catered for as this is a core function of a psychotherapy service, but what of the staff clinicians? How often should they have supervision? Should it be individual or group supervision? Should the supervision be with peer(s) or a more experienced colleague? Does the supervisor have to be proficient in the modality being practised by the supervisee? Are there positive advantages in having a different perspective? [This topic would lend itself to research in order to quantify the benefit of supervision and define its better forms.]

Workshop 2

1   Referral pathways
The chief interest was in what happens once a referral is received rather than how and why a referral is initiated. How many assessments are done? What is the drop-out rate? What factors contribute to it? How can 'parcel passing' between services and/or approach be minimised and the objective of a single assessment be achieved? How

to have an accelerated path for patients with more severe/complex/ devastating problems? What or who decides who assesses particular patients? Should the assessor retain responsibility for the patient while they wait for a therapy place?

2   Diagnosis at referral/assessment
Three concerns were interwoven: communication with the larger psychiatric world, meeting patient and referrer needs, and survival, personally and as a service. Diagnosis was not seen particularly as meeting the needs of the patient or referrer but more as a way of testing whether or not the service is seeing the right (agreed) population and hence would have its contract renewed. The balance of type of referral is important; too many of one type (e.g., borderline personality) could lead to therapist burn-out. [How could this be monitored?] When ICD-10 (WHO, 1992) diagnoses are required, is there a 100 per cent entry in the notes and reports? Participants favoured the use of a profiling system such as DSM-IV (APA, 1995). Using diagnosis accurately would require training; the adequacy of the arrangements should be audited. There was a call for the development of a simple measure for health utilisation as so many of the costs incurred by psychotherapy patients fall on non-psychiatric and non-NHS budgets. [Clear, active structural links between specialist psychotherapy services and generic mental health services are of increasing importance.]

3   Result of assessment
What criteria are used and should be used in a good assessment? Agreement with the patient is highly desirable, even essential, but legitimate patient choice has to be balanced against the assessor's professional responsibility to recommend what is best. Certainly the choice needs to be discussed with the patient. Allocation to treatment should respect gender and ethnic aspects when these are relevant, but this depends on the availability of resource; intention and feasibility could be audited. Other assessment factors include the personal history, and biological and social factors, treatability and the pointers from the formulation.

4   Baseline measures and change
Participants wished to link practice to outcome in a more thoroughgoing way than is usual. Sensitive measures of intra-psychic and interpersonal patterns were wanted. The value of target setting and review was recognised. Follow-up with feedback to the assessor and therapist is highly desirable; does it happen? What percentage

attending for follow-up is to be aimed for? Should there be a group review and/or follow-up for patients in group therapy?

We mentioned a new promising standardised measure, Core Outcomes in Routine Evaluation (CORE), a short 34-item instrument for baseline and change measurement, developed with funding from the Mental Health Foundation (CORE System Group, 1998). As well as providing a global score, this public domain measure has four subscales: well-being, problems, functioning and risk. It is designed to be a general measure for benchmarking and evaluation in psychotherapy services.

5   Accuracy of prediction of outcome
This could be on referral, at assessment or on entry into therapy; accurate predictions have major implications for resource utilisation. The participants concentrated on referral. What is the time-frame between referral, assessment and therapy? [What time-frames are acceptable – to patients, referrers, therapists, employers, purchasers, the government?] How can referrals be screened in ways that identify appropriateness and urgency? What is offered pre-assessment (e.g., psychotherapy questionnaires)? To what benefit or disadvantage? Should there be a family assessment as well as an individual assessment? If so, who should be written to?

Audit topics from the workshops

We reformed the small groups and asked each to abstract a few audit topics from the ideas in the brainstorming.

For the purposes of discussion, we grouped the topics that were generated into three categories: structure, process and outcome. *Structure* refers to the availability of the building blocks of the service: where do referrals come from, how many and of what types, what resource (staff, skills and fabric) is available to do the job? *Process* relates to how things are done: are policies, procedures and standards being met, how are complex situations being tackled, why is what was intended not being achieved in practice? *Outcome* is what it is all about: what is the outcome, is it as good as expected, is it comparable to that in companion services, what can be done to improve outcome and service? Having a classification like this helps target audit projects.

In the total group discussion, participants voted on the priority of the topic. The score is given for each item; the greater the score, the more the item met the group's approval.

Workshop 1

STRUCTURE

1   Audit resources available to conduct audits (2)
2   What information is given to referrers/GPs? Could this help management of referrals and serve an educational purpose? (7)
3   A general concern about the quality of referrals (3)
4   Profiling the demand and need of the whole population served and the adequacy of the therapy resource available (8)

PROCESS

1   DNAs – numbers and significance. Can the DNA rate be reduced (2)
2   Matching therapy to patient at assessment. Can it be done, how valid/useful is such matching? (7)
3   Clinical supervision. What is it, how much is necessary and provided, what good is it? (8)
4   The political impact of doing audits (0)

OUTCOME

1   Intake profile (0)
2   Patient satisfaction (5)
3   Referrer satisfaction (4)
4   Questionnaires: focused on symptom and/or functioning. Standardised measures (0)

Workshop 2

STRUCTURE

1   Referral pathways (9)
2   Diagnosis at referral (11)
3   ECR income – billed and received (0)
4   Ethnicity – profile, address, congruence of patient and therapist (7)
5   Does service allow for patient preference? (4)

PROCESS

1   Assessment decisions (11)
2   Hand shaking. To do or not to do? Impact with different patients (4)

3   Threshold for referral. Are referrals being received from the target
    population and in the right number? (0)
4   The gap between expectations of patient and referrers and actual
    practice (3)
5   Ethnicity and satisfaction with service. Drop-out rates (5)

OUTCOME

1   Baseline measures and change over therapy – individual and
    standardised (9)
2   Did the patient receive the therapy recommended at assessment? (1)

Conclusion

This was a workshop in a hurry. The time available for identifying aspects
of psychotherapy service that are critical to its success and their audit was
short, hardly more than enough for a rapid tour of key concepts and their
briefest try-out in practice. Not surprisingly, the factors identified as crucial
were more interesting than the audit topics themselves. They should not
be regarded as a definitive list, rather as a first essay. They point to the
importance of extended discussion in evolving focused interesting audits;
audits that will be critical in their centrality and force. Audit cannot
tell you as a clinician what to do in a particular case. It can tell you if best
practice, based on clinical judgement informed by empirical evidence, is
being achieved and, if not, why not.

Fonagy and Higgitt have many interesting ideas for audit (Fonagy and
Higgitt, 1989). Apart from now conventional audits such as the speed of
dealing with referrals, type and length of treatment, and availability of a
range of therapeutic approaches, they list some intriguing ones. Examples
are the handling of untreated cases, unnecessary disruptions to patients'
treatments, management of handovers from one therapist to another, and
the management of crises.

Other sources of ideas for audit are the concepts of 'critical incidents'
and 'success factors'. Let us first consider critical incidents. The question
is: what in the clinical service has to be got right? I, as first author, suggest
four critical incidents. First, patients must not get lost in the administrative
system. Second, the system needs to be sufficiently flexible that clinical
priority and changing priority can be responded to effectively. Third,
sexual or other exploitative breaches of boundary need to be guarded
against and handled expeditiously and effectively. Fourth, suicide risk and
risk of harm to others needs to be assessed, monitored and judiciously

handled. By judiciously, I do not mean zealously. In my view, psychotherapy and, for that matter, psychiatry, is properly about therapeutic risk-taking. A too-safe life is a constrained life, a reassuring life for bureaucrats but with little potential for development and change. The concept of success factors is another dimension in appraising a clinical service. It is not one for clinicians alone to consider. The voice of patients and relatives should also be heard. One fairly low-level external criterion is the delivery of therapy by trained, well-supervised therapists in the form that meets the best agreed contemporary practice. A much more demanding criterion is to demonstrate that, through therapy, patients are less prone to react to their personally difficult interpersonal situations with habitual maladaptive patterns. Surely this is the goal that we as clinicians should set ourselves. How to do this reliably and validly is a challenge yet to be overcome.

Planning an audit has a value in itself. It forces clinicians to be explicit about the assumptions that underpin the shape of their service and question or affirm their validity. Conducting the audit overlays ambition with reality. It is one element in making the clinical service a success.

Acknowledgement

We are grateful to John Wiley & Sons for permission to reproduce Figures 13.1 and 13.2 after Crombie *et al.* (1993).

References

APA (1995) *Diagnostic and Statistical Manual of Mental Disorders* (4th edn, international version). Washington, DC: American Psychological Association.

CORE System Group (1998) *CORE System (Information Management) Handbook*. Leeds: Core System Group.

Crombie, I.K., Davies, H.T.O. *et al.* (1993) *The Audit Handbook*. Chichester: John Wiley & Sons.

Fonagy, P. and Higgitt, A. (1989) 'Evaluating the performance of Departments of Psychotherapy', *Psychoanalytic Psychotherapy* 4: 121–153.

Smith, R. (1992) 'Audit and research (editorial)', *British Medical Journal* 305: 905–906.

WHO (1992) *ICD-10 Classification of Mental and Behavioural Disorders*. Geneva: WHO.

Index